AF703881

Meaning Systems and Mental Health Culture

Meaning Systems and Mental Health Culture

Critical Perspectives on Contemporary Counseling and Psychotherapy

James T. Hansen

LEXINGTON BOOKS
Lanham • Boulder • New York • London

Published by Lexington Books
An imprint of The Rowman & Littlefield Publishing Group, Inc.
4501 Forbes Boulevard, Suite 200, Lanham, Maryland 20706
www.rowman.com

Unit A, Whitacre Mews, 26-34 Stannary Street, London SE11 4AB

Copyright © 2016 by Lexington Books

All rights reserved. No part of this book may be reproduced in any form or by any electronic or mechanical means, including information storage and retrieval systems, without written permission from the publisher, except by a reviewer who may quote passages in a review.

British Library Cataloguing in Publication Information Available

Library of Congress Cataloging-in-Publication Data
The hardback edition of this book was previously catalogued by the Library of Congress as follows:

Names: Hansen, James T., author.
Title: Meaning systems and mental health culture : critical perspectives on contemporary counseling and psychotherapy / James T. Hansen.
Description: Lanham : Lexington Books, 2016. | Includes bibliographical references and index.
Identifiers: LCCN 2015043467 (print) | LCCN 2015045397 (ebook)
Subjects: LCSH: Psychotherapy–Philsophy. | Counseling–Philosophy. | Mental health.
Classification: LCC RC437.5 .H366 2016 (print) | LCC RC437.5 (ebook) | DDC 616.89/14–dc23
LC record available at http://lccn.loc.gov/2015043467

ISBN 9781498516303 (cloth)
ISBN 9781498516327 (pbk.)
ISBN 9781498516310 (electronic)

To my parents, Bill and Gail, my wonderful wife Mary,
and my two extraordinary sons, Hayden and Hunter.
Thank you for all of your love and support.

Contents

Preface

This book was born out of my experiences as a practitioner and a scholar over the past quarter century. As a practitioner, I was trained in psychodynamic psychotherapy, an orientation that taught me to appreciate internal conflict, unconscious motivation, and the nuances of subjective life. After working at a psychiatric hospital for a few years, I took a job as a professor in a department of counseling where (as is typical of many counseling programs) a humanistic perspective prevailed. Although there are a variety of important differences between psychoanalytic and humanistic orientations to talk therapy, the idealization of individual experience is a strong common denominator. This phenomenological focus helped me to feel at home in my new job as a counselor educator, even though the theoretical details of humanism were somewhat at odds with my previous training.

As I developed, both as a practitioner and a scholar, my appreciation for human experience began to extend beyond individuals to groups and cultures, which, like individuals, also construct meanings. Ironically, during the 1990s and 2000s while I was increasingly acquiring an appreciation for various levels of human meaning making, mental health culture was gradually adopting ideals that severely devalued meaning systems. The rise of biological psychiatry, symptom-based diagnostics, and the medical model for talk therapists has created an objectifying culture, which generally regards the clients of counselors and psychotherapists as broken objects rather than as potentially understandable people who have problems of living. Furthermore, as I investigated this cultural shift, I learned that an appreciation for meaning systems was not merely my theoretical preference. Empirical, multicultural, and philosophical evidence all converge on the conclusion that an appreciation for meaning systems and relationships should be at the heart of the helping encounter.

Along the way, my struggles with the theoretical integration of psychoanalysis and humanism blossomed into a full-fledged interest in particular philosophical issue related to the helping professions, which are elaborated in my previous book, *Philosophical Issues in Counseling and Psychotherapy: Encounters with Four Questions about Knowing, Effectiveness, and Truth* (2014a). When I wrote that book, I regarded my two primary interests, philosophical issues and mental health culture, as fairly distinct domains of inquiry. I do not see it that way anymore. Philosophical and cultural issues in mental health care are both about the ways that people make sense of the world. This book, then, unifies my interests. It is about the meaning systems people create, the way these meanings have been suppressed by mental health culture, and the impact of this suppression on contemporary counseling and psychotherapy.

The above account of the history of my interests is merely descriptive, however, and does not do justice to the strong feelings I have about the rise of ideologies of objectification in mental health culture. It frustrates and saddens me when clients attribute their anger to "my bipolar disorder"; when children who have understandable emotional problems are raised to think of themselves as being biologically defective; when problems of living are reduced to disorders or chemical imbalances; and when counselors and psychotherapists adopt a medicalized model of helping, which inhumanely reduces clients to constellations of symptoms. When I attended case conferences twenty years ago, the subjective life of clients was usually the primary focus of attention. Nowadays, the conversation is frequently dominated by discussions about symptoms, DSM diagnostics, treatment plans, and medications. Not only has this transition felt like a personal loss, but I believe the evidence clearly shows that it is a severe loss for the talk therapy professions.

Because I am a professor and a practitioner, I have had the luxury of taking a participant-observer perspective on mental health culture, practicing within it but also observing it from the critical vantage point of academia. This dual role has kept me from being swept away by waves of objectification, which have increasingly taken hold of the culture over the past three decades. After working for a few hours as a practitioner, I have had the benefit of examining my experience for a few more hours as a scholar. This cycle has repeated itself throughout my career. Therefore, I have had the opportunity to stand outside of the culture, look at it from a critical distance, and weigh the evidence for the various values that currently dominate mental health care. My strong conclusion is that the objectifying forces in mental health culture have generally caused counselors and psychotherapists to severely devalue the factors that should be foundational to their work.

I feel a strong sense of responsibility to share this conclusion, particularly with those who are immersed in the culture and do not have the opportunity to critically examine it. Indeed, if I had simply continued my original career trajectory and remained a practitioner, I would have probably reflexively and uncritically acquiesced to the objectifying trends that have taken over mental health care. When one is immersed in the values of a culture, it is often difficult to conceive of alternatives. To cultural participants, the values of the culture they operate within can be like gravity: invisible, taken-for-granted, seldom thought about, reflexively acted upon, pervasive forces that strongly influence everything. Awareness can only occur if these forces are identified, brought to light, critically examined, and screened for logical contradictions; critical reflection on one's own experience and consideration of empirical evidence are also important elements of consciousness raising. Sometimes cultural common sense is actually harmful nonsense; the mass devaluation of meaning systems by counselors and psychotherapists is a case in point.

In order to communicate this message in the form of a book, my passion for pointing out what I view as the absurdities inherent in contemporary mental health culture had to be tamed by the standards of academic discourse. If you have ever wanted to urgently communicate a vital message to someone, shake them out of their current, maladaptive perspective, and strike them with the intense emotional force of your strongly felt convictions, but you knew that the optimal way to persuade the person required you to tame your message, present it in a less heated, factual way, which curtailed your expression of passion, then you probably have a sense for the way that I felt while writing this book. I believe I have respected the standards of academic writing by making sure that my assertions are backed by logic and evidence. However, when my passionate side gained steam, I also conveyed my points in alternate ways, such as anecdotes, humor, sarcasm, experiential thought experiments, and personal reflections. I hope that these methods of communication provide the reader with a sense of the experiences that gave rise to my perspectives and add to the entertainment value of the book. Indeed, because this book is about meaning systems, it arguably would have been hypocritical of me to conceal the quirky, passionate, conflicted, subjective stew in which my ideas had marinated.

Through scholarly and rhetorical means, then, this book is designed to promote awareness of the objectifying values of contemporary mental health culture and the need to revalue meaning systems in counseling and psychotherapy. The introductory chapter is designed to impress the reader with the vital importance of meaning systems. In chapter 1, I delve deeper into the relationship between meaning systems and psychological suffering. Various ways of conceptualizing human meaning making is the primary topic of chapter 2. The next chapter provides a historical overview of mental health culture, with particular reference to the ways in which meaning systems have been regarded during different eras. In chapter 4, I further elaborate objectifying trends in contemporary mental health culture. Using the conclusions drawn in the previous chapters, I discuss the training of talk therapists in chapter 5. In the final chapter, I summarize the key points and provide some further reflections. Throughout the book I use the terms counselor, psychotherapist, talk therapist, and therapist fairly interchangeably to refer to professional talk therapists. This usage is reflective of my consistent observation that there are generally minimal differences between various professions with regard to the practice of talk therapy.

I certainly do not expect everyone to agree with my conclusions. Indeed, I hope that you find yourself having a combination of reactions while reading, including agreeing with, laughing about, becoming excited by, and actively disagreeing with the positions I have taken. In short, I hope that you find the book engaging. My goal, then, is not to win you over to my side, although I certainly would not mind if you end up agreeing with my central points. Rather, my goals are to promote awareness and to facilitate the emergence of a vital conversation.

Acknowledgments

I have many people to thank for the ideas that appear in this book. My perspectives about meaning systems and mental health culture were forged in a rich, dynamic, intellectually stimulating professional milieu, which was populated by colleagues, students, clients, and supervisees. I am very grateful for these relationships, but, due to the sheer number of interactions I have had over the years, it is sometimes difficult to be precise about whom to acknowledge. To complicate matters further, some of my influences are characterized by long-term, steady, growth-enhancing support. Other, more fleeting, relationships, however, have often been tremendously influential to me. Clients, for example, have occasionally made offhand remarks that have stuck with me for years, have had incredible implications for my work, and have suddenly lit up new intellectual realms that were formerly too dark for me to see. With these complexities in mind, I am responsible for the positions I put forth in this book, but I am grateful to the many people who helped me arrive at them.

Students, supervisees, and clients have been an incredible source of inspiration and ideas. One of the most joyful ironies of my professional life has been that my attempts to teach, train, and help others have consistently resulted in me being taught, trained, and helped. My experiences with students, supervisees, and clients animate these pages, and I am grateful for their influence.

I am fortunate to work in a supportive academic environment that encourages autonomy and scholarship. I am thankful to Lisa Hawley, my departmental chair, who has worked hard to maintain this environment and has been consistently supportive of my endeavors. I appreciate my friend and colleague, Todd Leibert, for reviewing some of these chapters and providing helpful feedback. I am grateful to Bob Fink, Phil O'Dwyer, and Luellen

Ramey for their friendship and support. They have all contributed to my intellectual growth and the ideas that appear in this book.

Outside of my department, my primary professional affiliation is with the Association for Humanistic Counseling. The members of this organization are some of the brightest and most welcoming people I have encountered in my professional life. I greatly value the friendships, support, and exchange of ideas that have resulted from my involvement with this exceptional group.

I have had a wonderful experience working with the people at Lexington Books. Amy King, in particular, supported my idea for this book from the beginning and has been instrumental to seeing it through. Her assistant Francinia Williams has been timely, kind, and encouraging throughout the process. I thank them both.

I am most thankful for my family. My parents, Bill and Gail Hansen, have supported me in innumerable ways throughout my life. My wonderful wife, Mary, and my extraordinary sons, Hayden and Hunter, were encouraging and patient while I was writing this book. I am very grateful for their love and support.

Introduction

Pause and try to recall the last ten minutes of your inner experience. Depending on whether you were alone, speaking with someone, or engaged in an activity, you will probably have varying degrees of success accessing the numerous emotionally-tinged background thoughts you inevitably had during this time frame. Regardless of how many details you can recall, this ten minute span was surely constituted by a rich, nuanced series of experiences that are entirely unique to you.

If you had been eating, for instance, a particular food, taste, or scent may have lit up a series of experiential flashes related to your childhood, a recent dining experience, health concerns about the nutritional content of your food, specific memories about someone with whom you associate the cuisine, or an entirely surprising set of experiences that seem manifestly unrelated to the activity in which you were engaged. Furthermore, each singular experience is associatively connected to other memories, thoughts, feelings, and fantasies in a seemingly endless, multi-layered web of personal meanings.

Even if you do not attend to your background experiences, they are undoubtedly present. Indeed, there seems to be virtually no escape from the unrelenting phenomenological flow of internal meanings. In this regard, the ability to meditate is a hard won skill precisely because it is notoriously difficult to disengage from the barrage of thoughts that threaten to contaminate the peace of mind that meditation is designed to achieve. Even our sleep is filled with dreams containing fantasies, thoughts, feelings, and images that are uniquely our own.

In addition to the personal meanings that continually flood our psyches, cultures, groups, and social enclaves are also constituted by unique structures of meaning. As a professor, for instance, I regularly engage in a series of socially mandated relational structures and rituals, such as grading papers, providing guidance to persons who play the student role, and offering my writing to distant strangers for anonymous review. Each of these interactions is governed by norms that define certain actions as acceptable and others as violations. Consider the various roles you play and the rules that govern your interactions in different settings. If you are a member of a sports team, aggression toward opponents may be considered praiseworthy. However, this same quality is likely a severe violation of the norms of your workplace. These social norms, of course, were not found pristine in nature; they were invented, and are maintained, by relational participants.

Human experience, then, is thoroughly imbued with personal and relational meaning systems. A simple phrase, such as *the stars in the sky*, has an entirely different meaning to a society of poets than it does to members of an astronomy club, because these groups have different rules, norms, and interpretive guidelines for meaning assignment. In addition to these communal meanings, each member of these groups will inevitably have unique associations, memories, and various idiosyncratic structures of meaning connected with this phrase. Every object of thought or perception is saturated with meaning systems. It is seemingly impossible not to bring meaning to the realities we encounter.

Because they are an omnipresent shaping force of life, meaning systems should arguably be a primary consideration when attempting to alleviate psychological suffering. There are a potentially infinite number of cultural and personal meanings to consider when someone complains of sadness, for example. Perhaps the sadness is connected to a recent loss, childhood trauma, severe guilt, a painful life transition, or a longstanding sense of inner emptiness. Depending on cultural factors, the person may be experiencing distress over failing to adhere to a religious doctrine, shaming their family, or wanting to pursue a life path that their parents would never approve. It is no coincidence, then, that traditional systems of counseling and psychotherapy emphasize careful listening as integral to helping. Attentive, nonjudgmental listening is the surest route to understanding the meanings that give life to psychological suffering.

Given the vital role that meaning systems obviously play in problems of living, it is extraordinarily ironic that the prominent ideologies of contemporary mental health culture are arguably all aimed at the obliteration of meaning. In this regard, the primary structuring force in mental health care is undoubtedly the Diagnostic and Statistical Manual (DSM; American Psychiatric Association 2013), a book that categorizes varieties of human suffering exclusively according to lists of symptoms. A DSM formulation of the hypothetical client with sadness noted above would purposely eschew personal meanings and, instead, categorize the person according to a supposedly objective list of symptoms, such as suicidal ideation, changes in patterns of sleep, and anhedonia. The rise of brain-based reductionism is another example of a strong, contemporary trend that obliterates meaning systems (e.g., McHenry, Sikorski, and McHenry 2013). Neuroscience has no room for the nuances of subjectivity; it is ideologically steered by the flashing lights of magnetic resonance imaging machines, not the personal meanings that brightly illuminate the course of our lives.

Ideologies that strip away the deeply personal factors involved in psychological suffering have arguably resulted in certain advances, such as medications that provide relief from distress. Perhaps the general paradigm of regarding emotional problems as resulting from objective, observable defects will, in the future, generate novel treatments that help make a better life for people who are desperate to find a way out of their psychic pain. I certainly hope that this will be the case. At its worst, though, objectifying clients recklessly robs them of their sense of agency, converts them into helpless objects, ignores their cries to be understood, teaches them that they are defective, invalidates their cultural meanings, stigmatizes their suffering, and turns them into passive, dependent recipients of whatever mental health interventions happen to be in vogue. Given these obvious risks of objectifying psychological problems, and the fact that it is extraordinarily counterintuitive to turn a blind eye to the ubiquitous meanings that animate every human life, it is remarkable that ideologies of objectification have come to dominate mental health culture.

This book is about the implications of these strong, objectifying forces for the practices of counseling and psychotherapy. The treatment of clients as specimens has a long and disturbing history that regularly alternates with admirable attempts to listen to them. Although you can probably detect my biases by now, cultures of meaning and objectification have each had their share of damaging practices and blind, irrational periods of exuberance, which have usually resulted in far greater harm than good. Because we are currently in a technocratic culture of objectification, however, it is important to raise critical questions about the lack of appreciation for meaning systems in contemporary helping practices. Are the meanings that people construct and live by important for the practices of counseling and psychotherapy? How did the helping professions come to endorse ideologies that are wholly objectifying? What are the various ways that we can understand meaning systems? Are the ambiguities of subjective life worth our focus?

THE IMPORTANCE OF MEANING SYSTEMS

If you have any doubts about the importance of the human tendency to prolifically generate meanings, consider that this characteristic would not be a prominent trait unless it had been crucial for the survival of the species (Dennett 1995). It is not difficult to imagine reasons that the ability to make sense of the world was a highly adaptive trait. On an individual level, our evolutionary forerunners who were capable of developing narratives that strung seemingly disparate events together into coherent, semi-predictable storylines would clearly have had a survival advantage over those who lacked this skill. The ability to psychologically link sunset with the time when a vicious predatory animal ordinarily makes an appearance, for example, would have undoubtedly been an important adaptive skill. Human survival also depended upon the ability of people to cooperate with each other in groups. Establishing social norms, defining acceptable behavior, and specifying criteria for banishment helped to ensure levels of cooperation, safety, and reciprocity that promoted the survival of the species.

Indeed, nature has bequeathed us an interesting, anatomical clue that unequivocally affirms the importance of human meaning making. Specifically, the number of neurons devoted to internal processing in the brain far exceeds the number that mediates sensations from the external world (Harris 2005). This evolutionarily determined proportion suggests that the meaning we make of sensory input has significantly greater implications for our survival than the sensations themselves. Rukeyser (1968) succinctly and poetically captured this truism by noting that "the universe is made of stories, not of atoms" (111).

Raw survival aside, there is also ample evidence that meaning making is vital for personal well-being. Theorists, particularly those from the existential (e.g., May 1979; May, Angel, and Ellenberger 1958; Yalom 1980) and humanistic camps (e.g., Maslow 1968; Rogers 1980), have elevated meaning making to the highest psychological priority. In his aptly titled book *Man's Search for Meaning*, Frankl (1963) described his hellish experiences in a concentration camp. He noted that his fellow inmates who were able to make meaning out of their experiences and envision a hopeful future fared far better than the inmates who were unable to do so. All inmates witnessed and experienced horrifyingly cruel, sadistic treatment from the guards and officers; this variable was a tragic constant for everyone. What, then, Frankl wondered, might account for the hopeful attitude and the ability to psychologically sustain these conditions that he noted in certain inmates? Imagining that their suffering had meaning, Frankl hypothesized, was the quality that separated the hopelessly forlorn from those who had greater longevity and a sense of purpose. Frankl used this insight to develop logotherapy, a form of psychotherapy that highlights the essential human need to find meaning in life.

Frankl's close theoretical cousins, the humanists, also emphasized the importance of finding meaning and purpose in life. Psychological humanism draws from the existentialist insight that meaning making is a key psychological variable that determines well-being (DeCarvalho 1990; Hansen, Speciale, and Lemberger 2014). However, humanists added their own conceptual spins to this insight. For instance, according to Maslow (1968), one of the most important and influential psychological humanists, people have an inherent drive toward psychological growth and self-actualization. Fully becoming oneself not only requires one to discover their vast, internal fountains of meaning, but baser needs, such as food and shelter, must be satisfied before self-actualization can occur. Rogers developed a system of psychotherapy from humanistic principles (Rogers 1951). By centering his approach on clients, not on the expertise of therapists, Rogers' approach to counseling allowed the meaning systems of clients to emerge naturally, unimpeded by therapeutic authority. This client-centered therapy approach essentially prescribed certain relational conditions, such as unconditional positive regard, for therapists to implement that were designed to facilitate the emergence of client growth toward a more actualized state (Rogers 1957).

The insights of the existentialists and humanists are arguably critical to understanding human happiness, suffering, and fulfillment. However, one need not be a brilliant theorist or spend time in Auschwitz to come to similar conclusions. The importance of finding meaning can easily be detected in everyday life. When young adults enroll in college they are challenged to select a major that will eventually guide their careers. Finding meaning in academia and work is an important developmental task for young adults. Correspondingly, when all of the children have left a household the parents often have to develop new purposes to structure their lives. Every stage of life arguably entails a reinvention of self that is guided by the lights of ever-changing systems of meaning.

Individual meaning systems, for better and worse, have had a monumental impact on the world. Gandhi and Martin Luther King, for instance, were dedicated to the ideal of nonviolent resistance as a means for overcoming oppression. This ideal, like all meaning systems, was a human invention, not something found pristine in nature. These civil rights leaders became strongly committed to peaceful ways of resolving conflict, and we are all the better for it. Alternatively, Hitler also formulated a way of making sense of the problems of his nation that centered on the Aryan race and the destruction of Jews. Hitler's meaning system caused untold misery and destruction. Meaning systems, then, are not intrinsically good or bad. They are simply ways of making sense of the world that can have either desirable or undesirable consequences. Occasionally, certain meaning systems spread rapidly and are adopted by large groups of people. Again, sometimes this contagion can be a benefit to humanity and other times it can be a plague on our existence.

As a case study in the power of meaning systems, consider the Heaven's Gate cult, which began to recruit members in the 1970s (Perkins and Jackson 1997). The founders of this cult formulated a supernatural system of meaning that involved alien beings and the goal of cult members evolving into a higher state of existence, which would have no need for the pleasures that mortal bodies crave. Eventually, their beliefs led cult members to kill themselves in mass, over the course of several days, as a means to leave their earthly bodies behind, board a spacecraft, and join the higher plane that they knew was awaiting them. Upon examination of the bodies, it was discovered that numerous members had castrated themselves in an effort to ensure that they would not be tempted by sexual pleasures. Perhaps the most surreal and bizarre records that have been left about the cult are videotaped interviews of cult members just prior to the mass suicide. The members appear to be the quintessence of serenity in these interviews. They are positively brimming with peace, ecstasy, and barely contained giddiness about their upcoming cosmic adventure. These interviews are a strong testament to the power of meaning systems.

Consider, then, that life is simply a series of events. There is no meaning that is intrinsic to the events themselves. Every meaning that is formulated can be considered a human superimposition onto the indifferent happenings of day-to-day existence. If someone was abused as a child, for instance, there are potentially infinite ways that the person could make sense out of their experience: it was deserved because of their inherent wickedness; it made them the good person that they are today; or Satan had possessed the abuser who was otherwise a loving person. Meaning systems create the realities we inhabit. They can compel people to kill or die for a cause or endure unimaginable suffering for the promise of some greater narrative ending. The meanings that humans superimpose onto events of living can also elevate humankind to higher levels of happiness, fulfillment, and peaceful co-existence.

It would be the height of absurdity, then, to insist that meaning systems should be ignored or that they do not matter. In fact, despite the experience-removed, technocratic, superficialities that dominate contemporary culture, the mental health professions must surely recognize the importance of meaning systems. After all, professions that are devoted to human change could not possibly trivialize or ignore the obvious power of beliefs to maintain or alter behavior. If any ingredient is a change agent, it is the meanings by which lives are guided. One would think that psychotherapy and counseling practitioners would be virtually defined by their deep appreciation for the nuances of human meaning, despite the emphasis on superficialities endorsed by the larger culture. Strangely, just the opposite is the case.

Over the past four decades, the helping professions have increasingly adopted ideologies of objectification (Elkins 2009; Hansen 2009). Granted, these ideologies are meaning systems in and of themselves. However, these objectifying systems of thought begin with the assumption that the meanings humans generate are entirely irrelevant to bringing about change. Identifying disorders, implementing treatment plans for particular clusters of symptoms, and executing carefully planned therapeutic techniques to combat psychological illnesses are all visions of the helping process that emanate from the current ideologies of objectivity (Hansen 2003; 2009). Taking an external view, which regards clients as disturbed objects, rather than an internal perspective, which honors, validates, and considers the meanings that clients live by, has been the fashionable way to structure the helping encounter for decades (Elkins 2009; Hansen 2009).

Perhaps there is some justification for the now completely medicalized profession of psychiatry to adopt a purely descriptive, objectifying explanatory model of psychological suffering. Although wildly over-prescribed, medications, which are virtually the singular treatment tool of contemporary psychiatrists, can be effective in reducing symptomatic complaints. There are numerous problems with the objectifying, pill-based approach that contemporary psychiatry has taken to the diagnosis and treatment of mental health problems, including rampant diagnostic inflation, diagnostic faddism, unnecessary stigmatization, the use of medications to treat problems that could be effectively treated with far less intrusive and harmful measures, the self-serving invention of new disorders, the chemical imbalance hypothesis (for which there is no evidence) that is marketed to patients as incontestably true, and the mass drugging of children (Davies 2013; Frances 2013; Greenberg 2010). Again, however, for a minority of those seeking mental health services, certain medications may, indeed, be the best help available. Therefore, it is not entirely unreasonable, at least from a purely ideological point of view, that professionals whose treatment interventions consist exclusively of drugs that are designed to ameliorate particular symptom constellations would adopt an objectifying, symptom-based model as their professional standard.

In contrast to psychiatrists, however, counselors and psychotherapists do not prescribe medications. Talk therapists alleviate psychological suffering by establishing helping relationships. Although practitioners who use pharmaceutical-based interventions arguably have some logical basis for objectifying their patients as drug-responsive constellations of symptoms, relational helping absolutely depends upon a deep appreciation of the idiosyncratic subjective and cultural meaning systems that animate the lives of counseling clientele. To make this point obvious, reflect on your deepest, most intimate relationships. Are they characterized by a value of objectification, or are the participants invested in understanding the inner experiences of one another? If, after she came home from work upset, I told my wife that her distress is probably a sign of an underlying mood problem, and that I had some techniques that might help her, it would not be a shining moment in our relational history. On the other hand, if I attempted to understand her experience, the idiosyncratic, nuanced sets of meanings that animated her troubles, we would be operating on much stronger and intimate relational ground.

Counseling and psychotherapy are thoroughly relational professions. Indeed, decades of outcome research has consistently demonstrated that the quality of the therapeutic relationship is the largest within-treatment contributor to outcome variance (Wampold 2001). There is no evidence to suggest that therapy offices are specialized zones where all of the usual rules that inform the construction and maintenance of optimal relating no longer apply. Of course, counseling is a professional endeavor, so counseling relationships differ, in certain respects, from nonprofessional relationships. Professional or not, however, quality relationships are only established, maintained, and deepened when there is an abiding appreciation for the experiential nuances of subjective life; it is absolutely a mistake to regard therapeutic relationships as qualitatively different from everyday relationships. Therefore, it is the epitome of common sense that meaning systems should be at the heart of relational healing. The odd fact that they are not is due to interesting, but regrettable, historical, economic, and cultural transformations that are discussed in subsequent chapters.

At this point, it is worthwhile to turn to another question that is related to the wholesale endorsement of ideologies of objectification by relational professionals: Why does virtually no one seem to care? One would think that there would be massive protests among counselors and psychotherapists decrying the harm that can be wrought from objectifying clients. There have been rumblings in this direction from certain members of the talk therapy communities (e.g., Elkins 2009; Hansen 2006), but these voices have, at best, been from the outside margins of the helping professions. However, given the facts that objectification is a violation of the most basic and commonsensical tenets of human relating, outcome research has consistently demonstrated that the quality of the therapeutic relationship is the most powerful within-treatment factor in determining counseling outcomes, and practitioners of talk therapies are supposed to be, and often advertise themselves as, relational specialists, it is downright bizarre that the move to objectification is rarely mentioned, or seemingly even noticed, by professional organizations, academic institutions, training centers, researchers, theorists, or even helping professionals themselves. Although the usual culprits of political and economic incentives partially account for this seemingly inexplicable failure to address the obvious, another factor arguably also contributes to the baffling silence of helping professionals in response to this bizarre cultural turn. Specifically, ideologies can become so dominant that people fail to notice them.

IMMERSED IN A DOMINANT NARRATIVE

Most people probably do not give much thought to gravity or air. In a certain sense, this is extraordinarily ironic. Gravity and air are not only necessary for our moment-to-moment survival, but they are some of the most omnipresent features of physical reality. Why, then, is the attention of the average person almost never attuned to the facts that a powerful force continually prevents them from floating away or that their lungs regularly inhale a life-sustaining element, which surrounds them wherever they go? The reason, of course, is because we are so immersed in these physical realities that we usually fail to notice them.

Analogous to physical realities, people can also be blind to the prominent ideologies that constitute their cultural ecosystem. The average person does not suffer negative consequences for lifelong inattentiveness to gravity or air; even if these forces are never considered, life generally goes on. Alternatively, a failure to notice, reflect on, and think critically about the ideologies in which we are immersed can have tremendously harmful results. Slavery, the persecution of Jews in Nazi Germany, and the classification of gays and lesbians as mentally ill are just a few examples of practices that were initiated and sustained by social meaning systems. Harmful practices cannot continue without the ideologies that support them. It is difficult to endorse slavery, for example, without the assumption that the enslaved are less than human; regarding slaves as people who are entitled to the same level of dignity and respect as nonslaves would undermine the entire enterprise. Throughout history, brave, enlightened minorities have often objected to the malignant beliefs that constituted their eras. However, there is good evidence that most people robotically go along with the cultural status quo, without even noticing that the injustices of their time are kept alive by illogical, contradictory, and damaging systems of thought.

Counselors, psychotherapists, and their clients are currently immersed in a culture that has been overtaken by ideologies of objectivity (Hansen 2014a). Like oxygen, these ideologies sustain the ecosystem but go relatively unnoticed by its inhabitants. The wholesale reduction of psychological problems to symptom constellations, the assumption that clients are ill, deficient beings who are incapable of managing their lives, the seating of human suffering in the brain or DNA, and the idea that experience-removed, technical interventions or medications are the proper, most advanced ways to address emotional suffering are all cultural fruits from the tree of objectification, which, by definition, necessitates the suppression of meaning systems. Again, this is an incredibly ironic cultural turn, given the commonsensical necessity of meaning systems to any relational endeavor, including counseling and psychotherapy. However, as noted above, few participants in contemporary mental health culture seem to notice or care.

In this regard, numerous theorists have commented on the strange phenomenon of people being hypnotically entranced by the dictates of their societal milieu. In her book *Monoculture*, for instance, Michaels (2011) described the hidden, but pervasive, capitalist assumptions that have overtaken American culture. This economic storyline is so pervasive that it has lodged itself deep within individual minds, thereby encouraging people to think of themselves as commodities, mere cogs in the capitalist machine. Michaels makes a compelling case that this monocultural storyline has insidiously impacted diverse areas of society and life, including education, health, and creativity. Rorty (1979) analogously argued that philosophers often become beholden to particular metaphors, which determine their philosophical investigations. The metaphor may be so pervasive that no one even notices it, yet the metaphor serves as the completely accepted, unquestioned starting point for all scholarly exploration.

Dawkins (1976), an evolutionary biologist, described the process by which prominent ideas are transmitted. Likening the spread of ideologies to genetic transmission, Dawkins coined the term *meme*, which is an idea or practice that spreads throughout a culture. Analogous to genetic transmission, a meme spreads according to the principles of evolution, such as natural selection and adaptation. Related to Dawkins' concept of memes, Ray (2009) described religious belief systems as viruses, which circulate throughout cultures and infect inhabitants. According to Ray, once infected, religious people are rendered unable to think critically about their belief systems and become vectors, unthinking drones, devoted to infecting others.

Numerous commentators, operating within diverse intellectual traditions, then, have described the ways in which dominant ideas can take over the minds of cultural inhabitants. Beliefs can become so seemingly self-evident and taken for granted that they serve as universal and hidden starting points for discourse and decision making. By coalescing into institutions, ideologies become part of the cultural infrastructure, thereby giving beliefs greater power, force, and, ironically, invisibility. In addition to cultural commentators, theorists, particularly those whose ideas have formed the foundations of counseling and psychotherapy, have noted that individuals often blindly follow the dictates of their personal psychologies. Therefore, the power of meaning systems guides us at both cultural and individual levels. Just like cultural beliefs, personal meanings can be such a pervasive part of one's psychology that they exert their influence without being noticed, even though they may play a strongly determinative role with regard to an individual's thoughts, feelings, and behaviors.

Psychoanalysis, for instance, proceeds from the assumption that a repressed unconscious is the driving force behind human behavior (Gabbard 2010). By definition, people cannot know the contents of their unconscious or the influence it has on their lives. For instance, an adult woman, who experienced her father as cold and abandoning, may have repressed the constellation of thoughts, feelings, and memories about this painful relationship. However, without realizing it, the woman may resurrect this repressed relational template to organize, guide, and make sense of contemporary relationships. This completely hidden, reflexive psychological habit may cause great pain and dissatisfaction in her romantic life. Although the presumption of an unconscious is a central feature of Freudian theories, the idea that one can be entirely unaware of vital, determinative elements of one's psychological life is an assumption that is shared by most traditional theories of counseling and psychotherapy.

Cognitive theorists, for example, presume that irrational or maladaptive patterns of thinking are the cause of psychopathology (Mahoney 1991). People, without knowing it, act upon certain core beliefs that result in their suffering. Cognitive therapists often prescribe homework designed to promote awareness of the hidden thoughts that determine the lives of their clients. Behaviorists, analogously, presume that unidentified stimulus-response contingencies maintain undesirable behaviors (Skinner 1974). Unlike psychoanalysts and cognitivists, who assume that the source of problems resides within individuals, behaviorists believe that factors in the external environment cause and maintain undesirable behaviors. Like their theoretical counterparts, however, behaviorists presume that these environmental contingencies are often hidden, people react automatically to them, and that helping clients involves making them aware of (usually through some sort of formal tracking) the environmental reinforcers and punishers that maintain undesirable behaviors. Therefore, regardless of whether the source of the problem is located within individuals or in the external world, psychoanalysts, cognitivists, and behaviorists share the assumption that people react unknowingly and automatically to the factors that cause their suffering.

There is abundant evidence, then, that individuals can respond reflexively to toxic cultural and personal meaning systems. With their minds set on autopilot, people often plod through an unexamined existence, blindly accepting and following the dictates of their social milieu, regardless of the consequences. The bizarre, nonsensical, and generally unopposed, acceptance of ideologies of objectification by talk therapists is a case in point. These ideologies are part of the cultural infrastructure, hidden in plain sight. It is difficult to battle such an entrenched value system, but there is a strategy that can be effective.

AWARENESS AS THE ANTIDOTE

Following is a brief summary of the essential points I have made in this introductory chapter: a) human beings, by nature, are prolific generators of meaning systems; b) meaning systems have tremendous consequences for human betterment and suffering; also, attentiveness to the nuances of subjective experience is vital for the formation of intimate relationships; c) counselors and psychotherapists, therefore, should be acutely attentive to the subjective and cultural meanings that their clients bring to the helping encounter; d) paradoxically, talk therapists have largely abandoned a focus on meaning systems in favor of the ideologies of objectification that are rampant in contemporary culture; and e) in addition to economic and political reasons, ideologies of objectification have taken over the talk therapy professions because these ideologies are built into the conceptual infrastructure and ideological ecosystem of contemporary mental health culture, thereby, ironically, making them less detectable targets of critical scrutiny than they would be if they were freestanding ideological entities that stood out from the cultural surround.

The essential problem, then, is that talk therapists, generally speaking, have unreflectively subscribed to ideologies of objectification, which, by definition, negate the meaning systems that should be at the center of professional helping. What might be done about this problem? To answer this question, consider the course of action that traditional counselors and psychotherapists, regardless of theoretical orientation, take when clients reflexively engage in maladaptive responses to life situations. In short, talk therapists promote awareness. Psychoanalysts promote awareness of unconscious conflict; increased awareness of irrational thoughts is the standard intervention used by cognitive therapists; behaviorists instruct their clients to carefully attend to stimulus-response contingencies to become aware of factors in the environment that cause and maintain their symptoms. Increased awareness, in various forms, has been the mainstay of psychological treatment for over a century. Multicultural theorists have also noted the importance of people becoming aware of their cultural biases (Hoffman, Cleare-Hoffman, and Jackson 2015). Indeed, awareness is considered a vital multicultural competency because it facilitates an appreciation for alternative worldviews and critical examination of the values of one's own culture (Sue, Arredondo, and McDavis 1992).

In keeping with the talk therapy and multicultural traditions, the purpose of this book is to promote awareness of the relatively unquestioned adoption of objectifying ideologies (and concomitant rejection of meaning systems) by contemporary counselors and psychotherapists. In the subsequent chapters, this ironic cultural turn is considered from historical, philosophical, cultural, and empirical perspectives. Specifically, chapter 1 considers the relevance of meaning systems for psychological suffering and healing; chapter 2 reviews various perspectives, such as constructivism and social constructionism, on the formation and maintenance of the meanings that people create; next, chapter 3 provides a history of mental health culture; chapter 4 examines objectifying trends in contemporary society and mental health culture; chapter 5 discusses the implications of the meaning-objectification dialect for the training of talk therapists; and the conclusion summarizes the primary points of the book and provides further reflections. I certainly hope that these chapters promote increased awareness of a cultural turn that has caused counselors and psychotherapists to abandon the very values that they should be fighting to uphold.

Chapter One

Meaning Systems and Psychological Suffering

Imagine that a representative from a distant planet was assigned to conduct a comprehensive study of earthlings. After an extended period of living with human beings, studying their history, manner of living, physical properties, and belief systems, the alien was to submit a comprehensive report that described earthlings in great detail, their cultures, investigative methods, day-to-day lives, what was important to them, the ironic elements of their pursuits, and all other information that would be useful to understand the inhabitants of that distant orbiting rock, which circled that faraway star.

Upon discreetly landing and donning a disguise to appear as an earthling, this cosmic spy would freely mix with humans and take measures to ensure that no one would discover her true identity. To complete the mission, the alien would naturally spend substantial time at libraries, museums, and universities, where human history is recorded and studied. However, she would also travel widely and purposefully interact with people from various cultures and walks of life. After completing the lengthy mission, and collecting enough information to provide a comprehensive understanding of earthlings to her home planet, she would hop in her spaceship, travel home, and plop down her giant report on the desk of her superiors. Imagine reading that report. What might it contain?

Of course, the content and structure of the report would be determined by the motivations that gave rise to the investigation in the first place. Whether learning about humans was a means to develop an alliance with them, invade their planet, or use them as a food source would have different implications for the type of information that the report contained. Suppose, though, that the aliens were truly, and benignly, simply interested in understanding their cosmic neighbors. Even under these circumstances the contents of the report would at least be partially determined by the manners of earthly life that the aliens found novel in comparison to their own ways of being. Putting all of these considerations aside, though, what do you, the reader, imagine might be the most salient, interesting features of the report? In short, what are the factors that are essential to understanding human beings?

Surely, the report would contain information about the bodies of earthlings, how these bodies had adapted to the conditions of the planet, and other biological information. To understand humans, one has to know about their physical properties. However, if the report simply contained biological information about earthlings, it would be of virtually no help in understanding them, the reasons they behave in certain ways; why they do the things they do; why they engage in certain, seemingly bizarre, repetitive patterns of behavior that superficially appear to have nothing to do with their survival; and the odd ways, individually, culturally, and as a planetary whole, that earthlings regularly sabotage their own well-being, even to the point of endangering the entire species. If the report simply stopped at biological facts, it would be woefully inadequate; the mission would have been deemed a complete failure.

In fact, my guess is that the bulk of the report would contain information about the numerous, complex, fascinating meaning systems that humans create. What other information could possibly explain the diverse, contradictory, self-sabotaging, altruistic, inexplicably bizarre, frequently warring behavior of earth dwellers? On a macro level, the only data that has a chance of accounting for the horrifically tragic, bizarre phenomenon, which has recurred throughout human history, of geographic neighbors spending centuries torturing, killing, and enslaving one another over subtle, inconsequential differences in their doctrines about supernatural entities, for example, is the meanings and beliefs that people construct and endorse as vital, real, true, and worth dying for.

The adoption of meaning systems that determine lives, of course, is not just a cultural phenomenon. Individual seekers of social justice who are imprisoned for decades, give up their lives, or make other great sacrifices for their strongly held ideals, for instance, are representative of a phenomenon that can only be understood in terms of meaning systems. To further illustrate the importance of meaning systems at an individual level, endeavoring to discover the neurobiology of a person who feels compelled to continually guard himself against the government agencies that are trying to read his mind to obtain the secrets of the universe, which have only been revealed to him, is arguably a worthwhile, and perhaps beneficial, pursuit. However, even the most comprehensive biological information will never aid in understanding the reasons that this particular person chose to live his life in certain ways. For this type of understanding, one has to know what is psychologically important to the person.

Returning to the alien report, some might object that I have given insufficient weight to the human scientific discoveries that the report would undoubtedly contain. Certainly, the report would have a substantial section on human discoveries about the natural world and the ways in which human findings compare with alien ones. As significant as this section might be, however, my guess is that it would not be as meaningful and interesting to the aliens as the reasons that humans had chosen to investigate certain areas over others. What people choose to explore is not determined by the natural world itself; it is determined by human interests. To illustrate this point, the aliens might be intrigued and perplexed that significant scientific effort has gone into investigating weight loss methods, developing compounds that put humans in a tranquil state, or uncovering the factors that make people more prone to purchase a particular product. The aliens would probably scratch their heads (or antennae) in wonderment that the resources devoted to the above examples are incomprehensibly larger than the resources devoted to developing cures for diseases that cause great pain, suffering, and even death, but, in the odd judgment of earthlings, occur too infrequently to warrant investigation.

Earthlings, the aliens would learn, have a strange penchant for exploring both the infinitesimally small and the cosmically large, even though neither directly contributes, in any immediate or obvious ways, to human survival or the alleviation of suffering. The particular investigative niches that earthlings had chosen to carve out would surely fascinate the aliens. Again, the state of the natural world can never fully account for the reasons that scientists choose to investigate certain phenomena or develop academic disciplines that are devoted to particular subjects. These types of explanations can only be found in human meaning systems.

The vital contribution of meaning systems to all aspects of life, including the creation and maintenance of human suffering, would have been blatantly obvious to the hypothetical aliens, but is strangely overlooked, or outright dismissed, by mental health professionals during particular eras of mental health care. As I demonstrate in a subsequent chapter, mental health care can be understood as a culture, which has its own rituals, dogmas, and dynamic professional infrastructure (Hansen 2009; 2014a). Over the past two centuries, mental health care has alternated between cultures that idealize meaning systems and those that denigrate them (Porter 2003; Shorter 1997).

Both biological and psychological perspectives are important for helping people who suffer from emotional problems. Mental health culture should arguably be structured by a balanced view, which gives equal weight to mind and body understandings in the treatment of mental health problems. People have undoubtedly been helped by both biological psychiatrists, who intervene on a physical level, and talk therapists, who leverage their understandings of meaning systems to alleviate problems of living. In an ideal world, body- and mind-based professionals would work together in harmony, tailoring treatment to the needs of every client. However, politics, territoriality, economics, professional grandiosity, and sheer greed have prevented this harmonious vision of professional life from becoming a reality, despite cultural lip service to integrated models, such as the biopsychosocial perspective. Instead, particular eras and subcultures within mental health care are variously dominated by either a body or mind orientation to mental suffering. When one of these visions is dominant, the other is suppressed, trivialized, and even actively derided (Hansen 2009; 2014; Porter 2002; Shorter 1997). In this regard, the suppression of meaning systems in contemporary times is clearly a cultural phenomenon, not a sign that talk therapy approaches are unhelpful or that biological perspectives are inherently superior. There are reams of research evidence to confirm that psychotherapeutic interventions provide lasting benefits to people with mental health issues and, in many cases, are superior to biological approaches (Seligman 1995; Wampold 2001).

To be clear, then, the reason I have continually harped on the importance of meaning systems is not because I believe that this perspective is inherently superior to a biological point of view. Both views are helpful and have their place in the alleviation of suffering. Rather, I have emphasized the importance of attending to human experience to raise consciousness about the cultural suppression of meaning systems in contemporary mental health care. The meanings that people create have tremendous implications for understanding their lives and fashioning interventions to help them. However, mental health professionals currently practice in an era that idealizes material (i.e., bodily) interventions. Descriptive psychiatry, pharmaceutical treatment, genetics, and neurobiology rule the day (Greenberg 2013; Hansen 2009). As in past eras, the cultural dominance of biological perspectives has resulted in the suppression, and arguably denigration, of talk therapy approaches, which, traditionally at least, have operated in the realm of the mind. Therefore, I have emphasized meaning systems as a cultural corrective, to sensitize readers to the vital and obvious importance of the individual and social constructions of meaning that are generally neglected, and even trivialized, by contemporary mental health culture. The primary ideological tool of modern day mental health care, which has resulted in the suppression of meaning systems, is the medical model.

MEANING AND THE MEDICAL MODEL

The medical model of treatment is a meta-theory that has traditionally structured and guided biological interventions (Wampold 2001). The medical model dominates contemporary mental health culture (even the talk therapies) and has contributed substantially to the suppression of meaning systems

(Hansen 2009; 2014a). To understand the cultural impact of the medical model, it is necessary to examine the foundational assumptions that support it.

The medical model emphasizes the importance of accurately identifying, or diagnosing, disorders. A disorder (or disease, illness) is a deviation from normative functioning, often caused by a hidden, underlying factor, that interferes with the successful adaptation of the organism. For instance, if someone is having stomach pain, fever, and abdominal swelling, these problems may be symptomatic of an underlying condition known as appendicitis. Accurate diagnosis is vitally important in the medical model because treatment interventions are ideally determined by the identification of the underlying causes of symptoms.

The second part of the medical model is the development of a plan of treatment based on the specific cause of the illness. If an illness is caused by a bacterial infection, then an antibiotic might be the treatment of choice. On the other hand, if the underlying problem is a tumor, surgical removal of the toxic hunk of flesh might be the best solution. In the medical model, an understanding of the cause of the problem ideally determines the prescriptive treatment that will be administered. It is not difficult to appreciate the logic behind this approach, which is that the best way to address an illness is to develop a treatment that is carefully designed to attack the root of the problem. Of course, professionals who offer biological treatments do not always know the underlying cause of a condition. A person, for example, may be prescribed a pain reliever, even if the source of the pain is unknown. However, the general aim of the medical model, both in practice and research, is to determine the causes of illnesses, so that a particular treatment for the specific cause of a condition can be formulated.

It is worth noting that not all medical treatment professionals have embraced the idea of the specific-treatments for discrete-causes model. Osteopathic physicians, at least traditionally, operate from a holistic ideology, which views problems in the context of the entire person (Gevitz 2004). This holistic approach to medicine begins with the assumption that the body operates as a unified system. If bits and pieces of the body are examined and addressed in isolation, then the inevitable systemic consequences of an intervention will not be appreciated. People, in short, are greater than the sum of their parts. Tinkering with one part will have consequences for other parts and the system as a whole. Therefore, according to traditional osteopathic ideology, the whole person, not just artificially isolated biological bits, must be considered when fashioning medical interventions.

I presented the above material on holism to demonstrate that the assumptions behind the traditional medical model, as compelling as they might seem to the Western, analytical mindset, were not found pristine in nature. People constructed the idea that the best way to cure a medical disorder is to isolate the problem from the person and develop a specific treatment that attacks the problem at its source. Of course, this approach to medicine has yielded tremendous benefits to humankind. However, it is not the only ideological point of view about how to help people who are suffering from physical problems.

For various historical, political, and economic reasons, which are reviewed in a subsequent chapter, the medical model has been embraced by contemporary counselors and psychotherapists (Elkins 2009; Hansen 2014a; Wampold 2001). Modern talk therapists diagnose problems and develop treatment plans based on diagnoses. For instance, if a client suffers from depression, the therapist might develop a treatment plan oriented around cognitive-behavioral interventions to reduce the symptoms of depression. In keeping with the medical model, then, modern therapists ordinarily: a) diagnose a problem based on behavioral observation, history, and client report; and b) develop a treatment plan designed to reduce the symptoms of the diagnostic condition. Note that this contemporary model of psychotherapy is structured by the medical model; particular psychotherapeutic treatments are prescribed for specific disorders, just as physicians prescribe certain medications for particular illnesses (Wampold 2001).

On a purely clinical level, there are no compelling reasons that psychotherapy or counseling should be guided by the medical model. Indeed, meta-analysis of psychotherapy outcome studies clearly demonstrates that the medical model is an exceptionally poor fit for the work of talk therapists (Wampold 2001). It is not surprising, then, that surveys have shown that talk therapists are generally dissatisfied with many aspects of the DSM-5 (American Psychiatric Association 2013), the manual that embodies the medical model in contemporary mental health care (Raskin and Gayle 2015). Again, reasons for the adoption of the medical model by counselors and psychotherapists involve historical, economic, and cultural factors that are reviewed in a subsequent chapter. For now, however, it is worthwhile to examine the dominant medical model and its relationship to meaning systems, which clearly play a vital role in psychological suffering as well as every other facet of existence.

Note that there is little room in the formal medical model for a consideration of meaning systems. Of course, individual practitioners who use the medical model often take a client's feelings, sensitivities, and worldview in mind when they are engaged in a helping interaction. However, the formal medical model encourages counselors and psychotherapists to use the meaning systems that shape, and are integral to creating, psychological suffering and healing, merely as a means to the end of selecting specific interventions for particular, isolated problems. With the medical model, the end goal is for discrete disorders to be treated with prescriptive interventions. To support this approach to practice, medical model research involves determining which problems are most responsive to which treatments. As a result, the medical model cordons off problems and interventions from the rich psychological and cultural contexts that give them life.

Of course, talk therapists who are guided by the medical model gather histories and other information about the lives of their clients. In the case of an anxious client, for instance, conscientious counselors would certainly learn about the history of the anxiety, the impact it had on the client's life, the situations in which it arises, and other contextual information before formulating a plan to intervene. However, within the medical model, this information gathering process is a means to the end of determining the nature of the problem so that a precise treatment can be established. If the anxiety is chronic, for instance, the treatment might be different than if the anxiety is acute and situational.

Similar to physicians, then, medical model therapists control the information gathering process in the helping encounter. Medical model counselors and psychotherapists are presumed experts, who ask certain questions, and pursue particular psychological avenues, in order to reveal the diagnostic information they seek. Clients, under this vision of the helping process, are large, babbling containers of disorders. In order to ascertain the true nature of a client problem, medical model therapists must use their expertise to get beyond the meaningless distractions of irrelevant, sputtering meaning systems so that the discrete problem, and appropriate treatment technique, can become apparent. In contrast, alternative, particularly traditional, models of psychotherapy place great value on meaning systems. Humanistically oriented practitioners, for instance, deliberately cultivate meaning systems to understand the problem from the client's perspective, facilitate the emergence of a helping relationship, and foster the growth of the whole person, not just the elimination of discrete, artificially decontextualized disorders.

Although I have been quite critical of the application of the medical model to counseling and psychotherapy (primarily because it eschews the meanings that are so obviously important to the task of psychological helping), it is important to note that I am not arguing that the medical model is inherently defective, misguided, or harmful. Ideological models are tools. Certain tools are appropriate for particular tasks and inappropriate or harmful for others. Therefore, it is always a mistake to broad brush an ideology as altogether good or bad. As a tool, conclusions about an ideology can only be made in a particular use context. In short, we can never simply ask whether an ideology is inherently worth endorsing; we have to inquire about the particular uses for which it might be suitable (Hansen 2014; Rorty 1999). As an analogy, it would be absurd to make a determination about the intrinsic value of hammers. Hammers are indispensably valuable for carpenters, but useless for violinists, physicists, and mathematicians. Ideologies, paradigms, and models are tools, akin to hammers. The periodic table of elements, for instance, does not have any intrinsic value. It is completely worthless to architects, but chemists cannot start their professional days without it.

The medical model has proven to be a useful ideological tool for medical professionals. When I consult my physician with a medical complaint, I certainly hope that he gathers the necessary information to determine the precise nature of the problem and an effective treatment. However, when I visit my therapist, I absolutely do not want her to regard me as a medical object to be fixed. The medical model is arguably a very good and effective tool for medical professionals, but terribly unsuited for the work of talk therapists, akin to a violinist using a hammer instead of a bow to play her instrument. I am not making this strong assertion about the medical model on philosophical, commonsensical, and intuitive grounds alone. Meta-analyses of psychotherapy outcome studies, over decades of research, have consistently found that specific techniques account for less than 1 percent of the variance in psychotherapy outcomes (Wampold 2001). The medical model, of course, strongly promotes the use of specific techniques for particular disorders, a paradigm that has proven effectiveness for the medical professions, but, according to vast empirical evidence, is decidedly ineffective, and arguably outright harmful, for conceptualizing and planning the course of talk therapy treatment.

To be fair, there are instances when the use of the medical model would be appropriate and useful for psychological problems. Generally speaking, when problems are highly delimited, specific, and isolated, the medical model is often a helpful way to conceptualize them (Beutler and Harwood 2000; Groth-Marnat 2009). For instance, if the life of a client is grand except for the debilitating anxiety she experiences upon encountering snakes, it would almost certainly be a mistake to engage this client in a long-term, exploratory psychotherapy. This discrete snake phobia would likely best be helped by the specific treatment known as systematic desensitization (Wolpe 1958). That is, the technique of gradual exposure to snakes, with concomitant relaxation exercises, would likely be more effective for this hypothetical client than engaging in open-ended therapeutic conversations about her personal meaning systems. That being said, after over twenty-five years of working in numerous mental health settings, I have yet to encounter this prototypical client who has no psychological baggage, and for whom life is thoroughly fulfilling, except for a single, isolated, situationally circumscribed symptom. This type of client is a good candidate to become a participant in a psychotherapy outcome research study when the investigators are looking to confirm the effectiveness of a specific technique. However, research that makes use of subjects with these characteristics has little applicability to the real world of clinical practice, where complex, multi-faceted, developmentally based problems are the norm.

The medical model, then, is arguably useful for medical professionals but mostly unhelpful for talk therapists. It is interesting to speculate about the reasons that this model is not equally suitable for both professional realms. Indeed, at a superficial level, the goals and activities of medical professionals and talk therapists appear very similar. These parallels make it tempting to draw the conclusion that the same paradigm (i.e., medical model) should be used to guide the work of physicians and talk therapists. For instance, both medical professionals and psychotherapists attempt to help people who have complaints about their well-being. Patients who experience problems in the physical realm consult medical professionals. The clients of talk therapists seek help for emotional suffering. Note that, in both cases, people who come for professional help desire relief for some kind of deviation from normative functioning that has interfered with their ability to adapt to life optimally. Furthermore, the medical professions have had tremendous success by using prescriptive treatments for discrete patient complaints. Therefore, the use of the medical model may seem like an obvious paradigm for psychotherapists and counselors to adopt, not only because of the apparent similarities in the work of body and mind helpers, but also because the use of the medical model has generally yielded great benefits for medical professionals and their patients. Of course, just because a model is useful in one field, it does not necessarily mean that it will be useful in another, even if the general work paradigm of the fields appears similar. In this regard, beneath the surface similarities, there are vast differences in the work of medical and talk therapy professionals.

As an example of a key difference between these professional groups, medical practitioners treat bodily conditions that represent deviations from normality. If a patient's bone is broken, this is unequivocally a condition that requires medical attention because bones are normally intact. Likewise, cholesterol levels require treatment if they are significantly above the normative range. In the medical model, a phenomenon is defined as abnormal if it deviates significantly from an established baseline of normalcy; a determination that something is abnormal can only be made if a definition of normal functioning has been established. Porting this medical, diagnostic model over to the mental health realm, then, requires the existence of firmly established definitions of psychological normality, so that mental disorders (which can only be defined as deviations from normative psychological functioning) can be established.

The problem with definitions of psychological normality, of course, is that, unlike objective, semi-stable medical definitions, whatever is defined as normal in the mental health realm shifts and changes according to culture, geographic region, and period of human history, among other factors (Hansen 2003; Szasz 1961). At particular points in mental health history diagnostic labels were used to describe numerous, supposed pathological conditions, such as slaves who ran away from their masters, women who wanted to work outside of the home, and people who had same-sex attractions (Rimke and Hunt 2002; Shorter 1997; Whitaker 2002). Without a firm, enduring definition of psychological normality, definitions of mental illness change according to cultural values. "Dependent Personality Disorder" (American Psychiatric Association 2013, 675), for instance, is a diagnosable, characterological problem in a culture that values individuality and independence. In contrast, collectivist cultures would probably view moving away from one's family and only contacting them once a month (a laudable sign of independence and mental health in the United States) as behavior indicative of a high degree of psychopathology. Indeed, to further illustrate this point, the Diagnostic and Statistical Manual (DSM; American Psychiatric Association 2013) does not contain an *independent personality disorder* for those who show too much independence from others (Fancher 1995); independence is apparently never a problem, at least for those who reside in the culture where DSM definitions of psychopathology were invented.

In short, one problem of porting the medical model to the talk therapy realm, despite superficial similarities in the work paradigms of the medical and therapy professions, is that normality, and concomitantly psychopathology, can never be objectively defined in the mental health realm (Hansen 2003; Szasz 1961). In medicine, numerous diagnostic deviations from normal functioning have been identified. A broken arm is a pathological condition, regardless of culture or time in human history, because bones are normally intact. Whatever problems are defined as mental health disorders, alternatively, change according to shifting cultural values. Perhaps there will come a day when firm bio-markers, which represent a deviation from normative biological functioning, are identified as causing particular mental health disorders. Notably, no chemical imbalances have been discovered to date, despite the propagandistic marketing of the psychiatric profession (Davies 2013; Greenberg 2010). However, if these discoveries are made in the future, mental health disorders would cease to be mental; they would simply be physical disorders like any other medical condition. A pure mental health disorder, with no biological origin, then, is always, by definition, a societal construction.

It is not unreasonable, of course, to suppose that biological factors will be discovered to account for severe, stereotypic conditions, such as schizophrenia, intractable forms of chronic depression, and mania. Perhaps describing these disorders as mental is simply a way of bookmarking them until their biological origins are discovered and they can be rightfully reclassified as medical conditions. However, even if biomarkers are eventually discovered for certain psychological conditions, professionals would still be challenged to determine what constitutes a disorder; this issue of defining disorders versus normalcy will not simply disappear when biological correlates for certain conditions are discovered. In this regard, Martin Luther King, Jr. and Jesus Christ had some of the worst cases of "Oppositional Defiant Disorder" (American Psychiatric Association 2013, 462) on record. There is no doubt that many people living in their times considered them severely disordered individuals and would have welcomed biological evidence to support this conclusion. Indeed, heroes of social change, who are often derided by the majority during their lifetimes, may very well have biomarkers that play a causal role in their behavior. During his day, many people, perhaps a majority, would have welcomed the opportunity to cure Martin Luther King, Jr. of his pathological behavior. In short, even if biomarkers for certain ways of being are discovered, we are still left with the problem of how to define which psychological states should be considered disordered. This seemingly apparent fact is quite obviously lost on many of the promoters of biological understandings of mental health conditions, who oddly seem to believe that their investigative pursuits will result in the discovery of some sort of biological holy grail, which, when found, will render deeper questions about context, culture, and meaning systems irrelevant.

That being said, do not mistake my argument for a romanticization of mental health conditions as noble social protests or as a representing a belief that afflicted individuals may have achieved some form of enlightenment that the rest of us cannot comprehend. Certain philosophers and theorists have taken this position about severe, debilitating conditions, such as schizophrenia (e.g., Laing 1969). I do not share their views. Having worked with people afflicted with schizophrenia for many years, it is difficult for me to view their condition as anything more than instances of needless psychological suffering and wasted human potential. I certainly hope that lasting help, in whatever form, arrives for these individuals in the coming years. However, the theoretical point I am highlighting is that the medical model, with its ideological focus on the root causes of disorders, can never help us define what constitutes a disorder of mental functioning in the first place.

Notably, though, the clients of psychotherapists and counselors typically do not have severe, stereotypic conditions; they have problems of living. By medicalizing problems of living (e.g., adjustment disorder) as if they were discrete psychopathological entities, talk therapists have become indoctrinated into a medical model ideology, which strips away the meanings that give life to problems, and, instead, encourages a conceptualization of the helping process as consisting of the application of specific techniques to symptoms or disorders (Elkins 2009). This medicalization of problems of living fosters the illusion that psychological difficulties are discrete entities that can be objectively judged as pathological. To illustrate one of the problems with this approach to psychological suffering, suppose, for example, that a client is anxious, has crying jags, and other symptoms that meet the criteria for a depressive disorder. A therapist who operates within the medical model would be ideologically primed to select techniques aimed at lessening the severity of these symptoms. However, what if the symptoms were a response to chronic job dissatisfaction, for example? Would reducing the symptoms of depression be a good plan of treatment for this client? If the psychotherapist implements techniques to reduce the depression, the client may plod through his job in a psychologically anesthetized state, no longer suffering from depression, but continuing the same, poor fit of a job for years to come. Perhaps the depression should be cultivated and examined, not eradicated, so that the suffering might serve as the impetus for meaningful vocational change. Sometimes suffering is trying to tell us something; it may be better to listen to the message than to silence it with techniques (Davies 2012).

Indeed, sometimes individual suffering is trying to tell us something about larger social issues (Hansen 2010a; Hillman and Ventura 1992). For instance, imagine that a transgender client comes to see a counselor with symptoms that the DSM would characterize as a depressive disorder. Combating the discrete symptoms with specific techniques, as the medical model would encourage counselors to do, automatically frames the problem as residing within the client. That is, the client is displaying symptoms, so the counselor should, according to the medical model, formulate an individualized plan to reduce them. However, perhaps the source of the problem is not the client but a society that refuses to accept transgendered individuals. It is completely natural for someone who lives in a society that regards her as a sick, immoral freak to experience depression. Instead of taking a myopic, individualized, medical focus, perhaps the counselor should validate the client and support social justice initiatives aimed at empowering the transgendered community. By individualizing problems, the medical model risks ignoring, or even actively colluding with, larger, systemic pathologies.

The talk therapy application of the medical model, then, individualizes problems and absurdly reduces the complexities of psychological helping to lessening or getting rid of symptoms. When using the medical model, counselors and psychotherapists automatically don ideological blinders, which encourage them to completely ignore the rich meaning systems that contextualize client problems. Note that above I used the phrase "talk therapy application of the medical model." This is because counselors and psychotherapists actually use a bastardized version of the medical model, which is not true to the model used by medical professionals. To illustrate this point, suppose a patient reports to a medical doctor with chest pain. Imagine the course of events that would follow. Tests would be conducted to determine the source of the pain, whether, for example, it was due to superficial muscular strain, indigestion, or a heart problem. As part of the assessment, the physician would likely inquire about the patient's level of stress, family history, and dietary habits. The symptom of chest pain would be considered a surface manifestation, a sign that something might be medically amiss at a deeper level. It would be an instance of severe medical malpractice if the patient were just prescribed a pain reliever, with the exclusive criterion for treatment success being remission of the chest pain. In contrast, talk therapists, when using their version of the medical model, devise treatment plans to reduce symptoms, analogous to a physician simply prescribing a pain reliever for a complaint of chest pain. In the psychotherapy application of the medical model, the symptoms are equivalent to the disorder. Thus, symptom reduction becomes the ultimate goal of treatment.

The reason that symptoms are equivalent to disorders in the mental health domain is because the diagnostic manual used by psychotherapists and counselors consists exclusively of symptom constellations (Decker 2013; Greenberg 2013). Take a moment to flip through the DSM. Note that every disorder is simply a list of symptoms; disorders are defined as groups of symptoms. When operating under this strange, completely counter-intuitive vision of human problems, curing disorders means abolishing symptoms, period. Again, this is completely unlike the formal medical model wherein symptoms are signs of an underlying problem; the symptoms themselves are usually not considered equivalent to the problem. Granted, medical professionals may treat symptoms without being able to determine the underlying problem that the symptoms represent. However, under the formal medical model, this is an ideologically regrettable situation. In the medical model as applied to psychotherapy and counseling, the exclusive treatment of symptoms is laudable, standard practice.

It is extraordinarily ironic that this model of treating symptoms has become ascendant in contemporary psychotherapy and counseling, particularly because, as mentioned above, consistent evidence from meta-analyses of psychotherapy outcome studies has demonstrated that techniques account for less than 1 percent of the variance in outcomes (Wampold 2001). However, despite all of the rational and empirical arguments, perhaps the most persuasive evidence against the use of the medical model by talk therapists can be found in the realm of personal experience. With this in mind, I invite you, the reader, to participate in an experiential exercise. Begin this exercise by recalling a time when you felt burdened, talked to someone about your troubles, and left the conversation feeling a sense of relief. Do not limit your example to instances with professional helpers but feel free to draw from experiences with anyone who has been helpful to you, such as your spouse, minister, friend, a stranger on a bus, or a colleague. Pause and take a few moments to recall the details of the interaction. Try your best to remember what occurred. After you have recalled the conversation to the best of your ability, answer the following question: What did the other person do to help restore your peace of mind?

I have asked this question to students and trainees for over a decade. Invariably, people report that the helper listened nonjudgmentally, did not try to fix the problem, validated what the person was experiencing, listened intently, and tried to understand the problem from the person's point of view. Not every person lists all of these factors, but these are the primary, and virtually exclusive, set of responses I have consistently received in my informal, at least decade-long study, using hundreds of subjects. Notably, no one has ever said that the helper reduced the problem to a set of symptoms and devised a plan to get rid of them. In fact, to further illustrate my point, suppose that a co-worker came to you angry about a work situation. Instead of making empathic attempts to understand what the situation meant to her, you tell her that she might have a diagnosable anger problem, which can be helped by the implementation of certain techniques. What do you imagine her reaction would be? Do you think she would experience this intervention as helpful?

The essence of psychotherapy and counseling should clearly be a deep appreciation for the meaning systems that contextualize client problems. The medical model (at least the bastardized version of it that has been adopted by talk therapists) reduces problems to symptoms, thereby stripping away the meanings that animate psychological suffering. Rational, empirical, and experiential evidence, along with basic common sense, all point to the conclusion that meaning systems should be at the heart of the talk therapy endeavor. Indeed, as I demonstrate in the following section, individual, social, and cultural meaning systems are integral to understanding the sometimes strange, paradoxical phenomenon of psychological suffering.

MEANING SYSTEMS AND PSYCHOLOGICAL SUFFERING

Why do people experience psychological suffering? Perhaps part of the answer can be gleaned from the observation that lower animals are not stricken with the same potential for mental anguish as humans. For instance, my dog might suffer from a certain modicum of distress over a relational loss. If I were to suddenly disappear from his life, my guess (and hope) is that he would notice and perhaps be despondent about it. However, it is not my impression that he spends much time regretting the past, feeling guilty, worrying about the future, or fretting about the things he might have done with his life had he not been so preoccupied with fetching balls and sleeping. Sometimes I envy him and try to learn from his example. My human nature eventually gets the better of me, though, and I psychologically return to my tornadic pit of spiraling meaning systems, which endlessly collide, violently spark, and distract me from the ongoing moments to which I should be attending. Such is the ironic fate of human animals, whose large brains helped them to survive but also cursed them with the ability to contemplate the past, the future, and the meaning of their existence.

Meaning systems, then, are a primary source of psychological suffering. The way people make sense out of the ongoing challenges of life has a lot to do with their experience of living. However, meaning systems are not only a source of suffering but can also be bright, healing oases from which peace, hope, tolerance, and love are drawn. Recognizing the power of the mind and the meanings it constructs, traditional psychological theorists have proposed psychotherapeutic orientations that highlight the individual, psychological processes that create and maintain perceptions of the world. Investigators have also explored meaning making as a social and cultural process. Because meanings are inextricably tied to both suffering and healing, it is important to review the meaning making process from individual, social, and cultural perspectives.

Individual Meaning Making

Consistent with a Western emphasis on individualism, traditional psychological theorists located the meaning creation process in individual minds. Early psychoanalytic theory, for instance, posited a psychosexual stage model, through which all people must pass, which has a determinative role in creating character style and symptoms (Freud 1905/1953b). According to this early Freudian model, the body, with its inherent lusts and anatomical givens, forms the basis for the mind and the meanings it creates. As a result of this vision of meaning making, castration anxiety, for example, is an inevitable struggle for boys, as the condition of having a penis naturally leads one to worry about losing it. Because people (particularly as they are socialized) come to regard many of the meanings spawned by their biological state as repugnant and shameful, certain anxiety-arousing constellations of thoughts, feelings, and fantasies are psychologically sentenced to dwell in an inaccessible realm of the mind known as the unconscious. The frightening meanings that inhabit the unconscious, however, glow hot with libidinal investment, a condition that makes them tremendously influential in the life of the individual, despite the fact that the person is completely unaware of their existence. As an example, Little Hans, the subject of one of Freud's famous case studies, had a fear of horses (Freud 1909/1955). This fear, Freud surmised, was a displacement of his unconscious castration anxiety, which was derivatively expressed as a horse phobia.

As the Freudian vision matured, psychoanalytic theorists gradually began to incorporate the influence of the external world. The structural, or ego psychological, model (Freud 1923/1961), for example, placed emphasis on individual adaptation to the demands of living, a consideration that was almost completely absent from earlier psychoanalytic theorizing. Likewise, subsequent developments in psychoanalytic theory, such as object-relations (Kernberg 1976) and self-psychology (Kohut 1971) orientations highlighted the role of attachment and early relational experiences as formative parts of the meaning making process. Psychoanalysis, then, is a masterful and compelling theory that primarily situates the creation of meaning within individual minds. In keeping with the individualistic theme of psychoanalysis, subsequent twentieth century theorists introduced alternative helping orientations, which, like psychoanalysis, presumed that meanings were forged in the crucible of the mind.

Cognitive theories, for example, give a central and determinative role to thought processes in the creation of meaning (Mahoney 1991). If a person believes that all relationships inevitably end in betrayal, for instance, she may behave and process new information in a way that causes this inner programming to gain momentum and become thickly overlaid with experiences and memories that support the suppositions of the core thought. As a result, she might deliberately sabotage relationships for fear of betrayal. In a self-perpetuating loop, these relational troubles would be interpreted as evidence for the dysfunctional belief, thereby strengthening the core cognition and causing it to become more deeply ingrained. Cognitively oriented psychotherapists directly challenge client beliefs in an attempt to change inner cognitive programming, which they presume is responsible for problems of living.

Psychological humanism is another example of a highly influential orientation to counseling that highlights the individual meaning making process (Rogers 1980). Indeed, the hallmark of humanistic counseling is an appreciation for the unique perspective of the client (Hansen 2005). Although cognitive, psychoanalytic, and humanistic orientations are conceptually distinct (and arguably theoretically incompatible; Hansen 2002), each of these systems of thought locates the meaning creation process within the minds of individuals. Perhaps Rogers (1980), a leading advocate of humanistic counseling, best illustrated this assumption about the psychologically enclosed nature of meaning making when he noted that

> The only reality I can possibly know is the world as I perceive and experience it at this moment. The only reality you can possibly know is the world as you perceive and experience it at this moment. And the only certainty is that those perceived realities are different. (102)

This quote underscores the individualistic assumption about meaning making that formed the basis for traditional twentieth century psychological approaches to helping. In this regard, Frank and Frank (1993), in an attempt to summarize the key ingredients of extant psychological orientations, noted the importance of the individual "assumptive world" (24) as a theoretical postulates that is integral to the healing process.

The axiom of individual meaning making can only be taken so far, however, before it runs into solipsistic dead ends (Hansen 2004; 2010b). People are quite obviously influenced by each other. Research and theories that emphasize the social creation of meaning, then, were an inevitable development in the ongoing search to understand the nature and treatment of psychological suffering.

Social Meaning Making

Imagine you suddenly wake up in a strange room and have no recollection of how you got there. You are in severe pain and a person is standing over you holding a sharp instrument. In one hypothetical scenario you are told that this person is a surgeon who is coming to your medical aid after an accident. In an alternative scenario, however, you are informed that the person is a torturer who is intent on gathering information from you. It is quite obvious that these situations would create radically different structures of meaning, even if the level of pain you experienced was exactly the same in both instances. These contrasting vignettes illustrate that isolated, individual experience cannot possibly account for the whole story of meaning making. People are embedded in relational matrices, which have a tremendous influence on the meaning creation process.

As noted above, even psychoanalysis, a theory that began with a strong axiomatic assumption that meaning making occurs within enclosed, isolated minds, eventually integrated theoretical developments that incorporated (or at least begrudgingly accepted) the role of social processes. Assumptions about individualism cannot be sustained for very long before they give way to the commonsensical idea that other people influence the way we think about ourselves and the world. People are not enclosed, solipsistic containers. We are relational actors, who actively participate in the creation and maintenance of social realities.

Social constructionism is an intellectual movement that has positioned the meaning creation process between people, not within them (Gergen 1999). The conceptual details of social constructionism are reviewed in a later chapter. For purposes of the current discussion, however, it is important to note that the social constructionist point of view has had a tremendous influence on mental health ideology over the past several decades. Traditional helping orientations have been revised to incorporate a relational element. Under the influence of social constructionist principles, clinical psychoanalysis, for instance, has been transformed from a one-person psychology, which, posited that the meanings that emerge in the clinical scenario emanate exclusively from clients, to a two-person psychology, which recognized that the therapist and client are always mutually engaged in the co-construction of meaning (Gill 1994). Humanism is another example of a helping orientation that has been influenced by a relational perspective. Although humanism historically emphasized isolated individualism, contemporary humanists recognize that psychological development occurs within relational and cultural contexts (Comas-Diaz 2015; DeRobertis 2015; Hoffman, Cleare-Hoffman, and Jackson 2015). As evidence of this theoretical transformation from strict individualism to an acknowledgment of the social factors that contextualize development, Lemberger (2012), in his description of humanism, noted that "the individual self is indivisible from the cultural self" (180). New helping orientations have also made use of insights from social constructionist epistemology. Narrative therapists, for example, deliberately partner with their clients to create novel, co-constructed perspectives, which are designed to ease the psychological pain caused by old storylines (White and Epston 1990).

Meaning making, then, can be viewed as a social process. Certainly there is merit in exploring the ways that people create meaning in their own minds. However, the social vantage point is an extraordinarily useful, and arguably conceptually necessary, addition to an exclusive focus on individualism. One example that highlights the necessity of the social view is the recovered memory movement, which occurred primarily during the 1980s. During this era, certain influential therapists (e.g., Fredrickson 1992) believed that they had the ability to detect when clients had been subjected to severe childhood abuse, even when clients initially denied that they had ever been abused. After therapists continually coaxed them to further explore their histories, many clients began to recall the traumatic mistreatment they had endured, which had previously been forgotten. Formerly benign fathers, for example, were suddenly remembered as sadistic monsters that had inflicted horrific abuse on clients, who, before entering therapy, had no recollection that they had been mistreated. Therapists congratulated themselves on recovering the memories they believed to be responsible for their clients' problems.

Note that the recovered memory movement depends on an isolated model of the mind. That is, this treatment method presumed that memories are true, static copies of events, stored in pristine form. Therapists simply access these memories; they do not change, transform, or implant them. This concept of memories as static entities was successfully challenged by memory researchers, particularly Loftus (Loftus and Pickrell 1995), who used a clever experimental method to demonstrate that false memories could, indeed, be implanted. In short, after obtaining information about an adult subject's childhood from a family member, Loftus constructed a series of vignettes for each subject based on events that had actually occurred. However, one of the vignettes was a story about being lost in a mall, an experience that none of the subjects were reported to have had. The lost in the mall story contained contextual cues from the subject's childhood (e.g., naming a mall that the subject had visited), but the story itself about being lost never occurred. The subjects were then asked whether they recalled the various stories. A significant number of subjects recalled the false lost in the mall story as a true event. In other words, the false story, because of its contextual clues, and presentation alongside of other true stories, was *remembered.*

This finding, of course, undermined the central premise of the recovered memory movement, specifically that true memories lie buried in the psyche, like ancient archeological artifacts, waiting to be dug up in pristine form by a neutral party. Loftus' research clearly demonstrated that false recollections can be implanted, and that memory is a highly dynamic process, not a static one. The central point for purposes of this discussion is that memories, and the structures of meaning they contain, are strongly influenced by social, relational processes. Meaning making, then, cannot be conceptualized as occurring exclusively within the mind. Relationships create, transform, and maintain meaning systems.

Another example of the creation of meaning through social processes is diagnostic labeling. Diagnosing someone is not merely an act of identifying a supposed disorder. There are tremendous psychological consequences to telling someone that they have a diagnosable mental health condition (Frances 2013; Greenberg 2013). Under the medical model, which is currently predominant in mental health culture, these consequences are seldom considered. However, when a client is told by an expert that he or she has a mental disorder, this information can have a significant impact on self-concept, the explanations the client constructs for her or his own behaviors, and the types of life goals the client believes are achievable. Indeed, diagnostic labels, themselves, create meanings and experiences (Frances 2013). Drawing from my own experience, I have heard many clients dismiss their angry outbursts as simply being due to "my bipolar disorder." This explanation, which is fully supported by the medical model and current diagnostic practices, automatically forecloses on any meaningful psychological discussion about the anger. The rage was simply a product of the disorder, period.

People also fulfill the prophecies foretold by their disorders. Clients naturally begin to think of themselves in new ways when they are told that they have a diagnosable mental health condition (Frances 2013). As an analogy, imagine that an expert determines that you have an unusually high degree of intelligence. This expert opinion would almost certainly create new psychological structures of meaning related to your self-concept, which may cause you to formulate novel explanations for your behaviors, have greater confidence in your opinions, seek out more intellectual stimulation, or pursue higher education, to name a few examples. In short, you would probably begin to live up to the label. Alternatively, now imagine the psychological consequences of being told by an expert that you are psychiatrically broken or defective. As a consequence, you might determine that your goals are unachievable, attribute your behaviors to the disorder instead of taking responsibility for them, and begin to see yourself as a passive victim of your psychiatric disability rather than as a willful creator of new possibilities.

Meaning making processes, then, can be understood at both individual and social levels. The social realm can be further subdivided into micro-social processes, which were discussed above, and the overarching culture in which these social processes are situated. The cultural influence on meaning systems is a useful avenue to investigate because people ordinarily come to value the meanings that constitute their cultural surround. Therefore, the intersection of meaning systems, mental health, and culture is a fascinating and extraordinarily fruitful intellectual crossing to explore.

Cultural Meaning Making

Consider the values that are important to you. Perhaps you believe that hard work builds character, people should pursue higher education, democracy is a superior and enlightened political system, or that women should have the same rights and privileges as men. Whatever your core values, you certainly were not born with them hardwired into your neural pathways. People internalize the values of the larger culture in which they participate. Personal independence and autonomy, for example, are prominent Western ideals. However, people who have adopted the values of a collectivist culture are often shocked and appalled at the socially disconnected individualism that constitutes American society. Likewise, people raised in individualistic cultures may be unable to fathom the reasons that residents of other regions of the world regularly consider the impact of their decisions on their extended family. As another example, arranged marriage may seem completely natural to those who were raised in a culture that supports this practice, but people from other cultures may regard it as a primitive ritual, which undermines love, romance, and personal decision making. Clearly, the cultural level of analysis cannot be ignored when considering meaning systems.

Regarding mental health, contemporary practices generally do not consider the impact of culture on symptomatology. Cultural factors are largely ignored in modern mental health ideology because of the widespread adoption of the medical model of practice. As noted above, when the medical model is applied to formal medicine, disorders are identified and specific treatments are prescribed. Although culture should be a consideration in all healthcare professions, it is arguably far less important a variable in formal medicine that it is in mental health. After all, in formal medicine, instances of smallpox are essentially the same, regardless of the culture in which they appear. Granted, there may be cultural differences in the way medical conditions are perceived or expressed. However, medical disorders are physical, bodily conditions, and human bodies have universal commonalities, regardless of culture.

It is a completely different story with mental health problems, though. Psychological suffering is absolutely shaped and determined by cultural variables. The medical model has little provision for cultural influences; it emphasizes discrete disorders and prescriptive treatments. When the medical model is superimposed onto the mental health domain, it naturally minimizes the role of cultural factors (just as it does in formal medicine), an ideological situation that may be somewhat appropriate for the diagnosis and treatment of physical problems, but grossly inappropriate for practices that are designed to alleviate psychological suffering. In short, the medical model is ideologically structured to focus attention on certain variables (i.e., discrete disorders and prescriptive treatments) and ignore or minimize others. When mental health practitioners adopt the medical model, then, they inadvertently don ideological blinders that cause them to minimize the importance of cultural variables because these variables are outside the purview of the medical model.

As an illustration of the medical model view of culture, the current version of the DSM contains a standard *culture-related diagnostic issues* section as a part of the template that is used to describe disorders. The following language typifies the content of this section: "there is considerable cultural variation in the expression of generalized anxiety disorder" (American Psychiatric Association 2013, 224). Note that this statement presumes that generalized anxiety disorder is a condition that precedes culture (i.e., the disorder exists prior to its cultural expression). The statement rests on the assumption that disorders are internal, free-standing entities, waiting for the expressive medium of culture to give them a voice. There are only two ways that this claim could be verified: a) if detectable biomarkers for disorders are established; two people with the same brain lesion, for example, might have very different expressive features, depending on their culture (e.g., one might regard his confusion as a curse from a supernatural entity, the other may become preoccupied with his ability to achieve and maintain a role as a provider, etc.); and b) if the authors of the DSM were able to completely transcend the boundaries of their own cultural influences and accurately ascertain raw disorders in pristine, culture-free form. There are virtually no biomarkers for DSM disorders (they are merely lists of symptoms), and the second scenario is ludicrous. Therefore, the medical model based cultural commentary in much of the DSM, when deconstructed, is often revealed to be contradictory and illogical, merely a superficial, politically correct nod to the importance of acknowledging culture but, in the end, logical gibberish.

In fact, multiple lines of evidence suggest that symptom patterns are determined by culture, not that culture is simply a medium for the expression of pre-existing disorders. Hysterical conversion reactions, for instance, were prominent in turn of the century Vienna, but are an extraordinary rarity in modern times (Shorter 1992). Likewise, asylum patients were regularly afflicted with catatonia in the mid-twentieth century, but this condition has virtually disappeared (Stompe, Ortwein-Swoboda, Ritter, Schanda, Friedmann 2002). Different regions and eras are regularly stricken with unique patterns of mental health symptoms. A reasonable explanation for this phenomenon is that culture plays a highly influential role in determining psychiatric symptomatology. Indeed, there is abundant evidence for this hypothesis.

In his enlightening book, *Crazy Like Us* (2010), Watters described multiple case studies, which illustrated the role of cultural forces in mental health. Indeed, in contrast to the view posited by the DSM, Watters asserted that "mental illness cannot be separated from culture" (9). The primary thesis of the book is that so-called disorders can be transmitted from one culture to another. Multiple case studies are presented as evidence for this cultural contagion hypothesis. For instance, the victims of the tsunami in Sri Lanka had no concept of post-traumatic stress disorder (PTSD) prior to the well-intentioned interventions of teams of aid workers, who taught the local residents the symptoms they should expect to experience after the tsunami. Eventually, having been indoctrinated into the expectation that they would experience certain symptoms, PTSD spread among the locals, although there was no evidence that they ever suffered from PTSD symptoms subsequent to prior traumatic events.

As another example of the role of cultural factors in mental health, there was no concept of everyday, mild depression in Japan prior to the deliberate, cultural interventions of the pharmaceutical industry (Watters 2010). With the goal of selling anti-depressants to the untapped market of Japanese citizens, manufacturers of psychiatric medications hired cultural specialists, who, based on their knowledge of the Japanese worldview, devised plans to spread the concept of depression to the locals during the early 2000s. This cultural intervention was an incredible success, as Japanese citizens came to endorse the idea of mild depression in droves, thereby creating a sudden "epidemic," which the pharmaceutical industry was ready to treat with their pills.

Cultural factors, then, have a tremendous influence on the types of symptom patterns that emerge in particular locales. Note that this is the opposite of the view implied by certain language in the DSM (i.e., that *pre-existing* disorders may manifest themselves in different ways as a function of culture). There was no evidence of any pre-existing potential to acquire PTSD symptoms after a trauma in the Sri Lankans, or signs that mild depression had been a problem in Japan before the targeted cultural interventions of the pharmaceutical industry.

In this regard, Shorter (1992) posited the idea of a "symptom pool" (5) as an explanatory concept to account for cultural differences in mental health symptoms. According to Shorter, cultures and historical eras have particular, acceptable ways (i.e., symptom pool) of manifesting psychological distress.

Hysterical conversion reactions were part of the cultural symptom pool in Vienna during the late nineteenth century. Sudden, inexplicable paralysis of the hand (i.e., glove paralysis), for instance, was a culturally acceptable option for expressing distress during the early part of Freud's career. Likewise, mild depression was not a component of the Japanese symptom pool until the pharmaceutical industry paved the cultural way for it to become an acceptable mode of expressing psychological pain. Cultures play a strong role in determining which symptoms are acceptable for people to adopt.

Perhaps an analogy might make the concept of a cultural symptom pool seem very commonsensical. That is, what one chooses to eat is, at least somewhat, a function of the options that the cultural provides. Hamburgers, moussaka, or goi cuon are part of the food pool of various cultures. The inner state of hunger is a constant in the human species. However, the food one selects when experiencing hunger is partially determined by the cultural food pool. Likewise, according to Shorter (1992), the symptoms one adopts when in a state of psychological suffering is dependent on the menu of options in the cultural symptom pool. Thus, the idea of a symptom pool is a powerful explanatory concept that would seem to account for many of the cultural variations in symptom expression.

Meaning systems, therefore, can be understood from individual, social, and cultural points of view. These three vantage points are vitally important to appreciating meaning systems and psychological suffering. However, when discussing the meanings that people adopt, it is important to note that everyone does not have an equal opportunity to express their perspective. Indeed, the environment in which meanings breed is arguably infused with the dynamics of power.

POWER, MEANING SYSTEMS, AND MENTAL HEALTH CARE

I was probably first struck by the realization that power played an important role in meaning systems and mental health care on a particular day during my employment at a psychiatric hospital. The morning started with loud, angry protests from an African American resident, who had been told that she was going to be discharged from the hospital within a few hours. This resident felt psychologically unprepared to face the challenges of her life, which included poverty, homelessness, and numerous other stressors. Her protests escalated until she became aggressive and destroyed unit furniture. She was subsequently held down by several workers and given a sedative shot. The outburst was interpreted as a sign of her mental illness, her dosage of psychotropic medication was increased, and she was mandated to stay on the unit for an extended period.

After this incident, I went to lunch with several co-workers, who told me about another incident that had occurred that same morning. Two burly, psychiatric residents got into a fight in the resident break room, which resulted in much of the room being destroyed. As a consequence of their actions, the chief psychiatrist ordered them to seek counseling so that they could explore the reasons for their anger and find better ways to manage it. The events of that day forever changed the way I thought about power, meaning systems, and the dynamics of mental health care.

The African-American woman, whose outburst could be easily understood in light of the extreme stressors she faced, was silenced with medication. Any meanings that she struggled to express were dismissed as being the result of her mental illness. No one even thought to listen to her; she was simply ill. Alternatively, the two Caucasian, male residents, who had privileged lives, were not diagnosed but encouraged to express themselves in counseling. They were invited to talk about the meanings that gave rise to their anger. Arguably, if anyone should have been medicated and diagnosed, it should have been the psychiatric residents, who clearly had a much lower threshold for the expression of anger than the woman. Boiling over into a violent state when one has a safe, secure life, with multiple support systems would seem to indicate a far more severe problem with anger than an outburst from someone who would soon be facing severe psychosocial stressors that few people can even imagine. Upon encountering him later in the day, I asked the chief psychiatrist why he had not treated the residents with medication. He just looked at me quizzically, as if I had asked a bizarre question.

In this regard, the philosopher Foucault (1980) has noted the relationship between truth claims and power. For instance, if heterosexuality is regarded by the majority as the true, moral expression of sexuality, then people with alternative sexual orientations will be disempowered. As another example of the relationship between truth and power, people whose meaning systems are regarded as signs of mental illness are often silenced by the mainstream. Furthermore, in my observation, minority groups, the poor, children, and other disenfranchised members of society are disproportionately muted by diagnostic labeling, psychiatric medication, and involuntary hospitalization. The meaning market is clearly not free; it is highly regulated by powerful meaning monopolies. These hierarchies are so knit into the fabric of society and mental health care that people often do not even notice them. The unit staff and chief psychiatrist cited in the previous vignettes were not evil, prejudiced people who consciously chose to behave in discriminatory ways. On the contrary, they were decent clinicians who reflexively responded to the unspoken hierarchies of the culture in which they operated. Indeed, the only reason that I probably considered the differences between the treatment of the residents and the hospitalized woman is because they occurred on the same day, and I happened to become aware of them at about the same time. I was jarred into awareness after being confronted with a sudden contrast that I was unable to ignore. If the incidents with the woman and the residents had not occurred on the same day, I probably would not have given any thought to the power disparities inherent in these events.

Because of these hidden hierarchies regarding the expression of meaning, it is important for counselors and psychotherapists to engage in continual reflective examination about the interplay of meaning systems and power dynamics in their work. Indeed, talk therapists have an embarrassingly bad history of disempowering clients (Masson 1994). I believe that truly malevolent counselors who are deliberately out to use their clients are a relative rarity, though. I suspect that the vast majority of power plays in psychotherapy are subtle and beneath the psychological radar of the practitioners who engage in them. The counselor who attempts to silence the voice of the battered woman with cognitive-behavioral techniques aimed at alleviating her depression, for instance, is simply operating according to the dictates of the culturally dominant medical model. Likewise, a minority person who is legitimately angry about discrimination and unfair treatment may be seen as having a personal problem that warrants the use of anger management techniques. Again, practitioners must actively consider the power dynamics inherent in their practices to minimize the risk of reflexively operating in accordance with hidden, culturally mandated power hierarchies.

SUMMARY

People are prolific creators of meaning systems. The ability to make sense of the world has provided the human species with a tremendous survival advantage. However, there is a steep price that is paid for this ability. People suffer immensely because of the meanings they endorse. Not only have warring groups killed and tortured each other throughout history because of perspectival differences, battles related to meaning systems are regularly fought out within individual minds. Worries about the future, regrets about the past, and sorrow for not having lived up to certain ideals could not exist as experiential states without the ability to generate and endorse meaning systems. Fortunately, meanings can also serve as an antidote to suffering by inspiring hope. Given their tremendous power to cause suffering and healing, counselors and psychotherapists should place meaning systems at the center of their work.

Unfortunately, the medical model has come to dominate mental health culture. With its exclusive focus on disorders and their treatment, the medical model has virtually banished meaning systems from contemporary helping practices. As a result, talk therapists, en masse, have endorsed a treatment paradigm that regards the unique perspectives and values of their clientele as largely irrelevant to the counseling and psychotherapy process. Furthermore, a core assumption of the medical model is that problems reside within individuals. This conceptual emphasis diverts attention from social and cultural influences, which are tremendous contributors to the meaning making process.

Meanings exist within an environment of power. When dominant groups decide that certain worldviews are true, minority groups often suffer. However, what are the criteria for determining whether a meaning system is true? Are some perspectives true and others false? How should the worthiness of a belief be judged? How have these conceptual issues related to meaning systems manifested themselves in theories of counseling and psychotherapy? These topics, and others, are discussed in the following chapter.

Chapter Two

Conceptualizations of Meaning Systems

As noted in the previous chapters, meaning systems are vitally important to understanding and helping people. It is, therefore, shockingly counterintuitive that contemporary mental health professionals have embraced the medical model, a paradigm that ideologically eradicates the rich meanings that animate human lives. Indeed, there is abundant empirical evidence that meaning systems, and the strong therapeutic relationships that emanate from an appreciation of client perspectives, should be at the heart of the practice of counseling and psychotherapy.

Up to this point, I have not offered a unified definition of meaning systems, preferring instead to first impress the reader with the importance of an appreciation for human experience when engaged in the task of relational helping. To gain greater clarity about, and conceptually advance, the topic of this discussion, however, I offer the following definition: *Meaning systems are the ways that people structure and make sense of the world on individual, social, and cultural levels*. As part of this fundamental definition, I also include: a) creative or other endeavors that may not directly serve any survival or adaptive function; and b) the phenomenological flow of individual experience. Both of these secondary considerations arguably emanate from the primary definition.

Note the wide-ranging inclusiveness of my definition of meaning systems. Essentially, it includes every thought, feeling, fantasy, and perspective that people experience or endorse, including systems of meaning that serve to disempower or eradicate other perspectives (e.g., medical model). This broad definition might seem too conceptually unwieldy to serve as a useful construct. Indeed, how could the incomprehensibly diverse and raucous elements of my definition possibly be conceptually corralled under a single construct, particularly one that would have the theoretical nimbleness to survive the quick conceptual twists and turns necessary for further philosophical exploration? In this regard, however, consider that precedents for massively inclusive explanatory definitions have been set in other fields. Physicists, for instance, make excellent use of the unifying ideas of gravity and atoms, which are constructs that encompass the entire universe. In principle, then, the broadly inclusive nature of my definition of meaning systems is not necessarily a problem that would forestall further investigation.

As further support for my decision to include many diverse elements under a single definition, consider that there is a unifying, common denominator to the vast, seemingly incomprehensible territory of meaning systems. This golden thread, which runs through all human perspectives, provides additional justification for grouping such a seemingly varied array of elements under a single construct. This unifying common denominator is language (Rorty 1999).

Think about any experience, value, or belief that is important to you. Now consider the roles you play in your social life. Review, last, some of the tenets of the culture you inhabit. The only means to think about or communicate any of the above meaning systems is through the vehicle of language. Even our internal flow of inner experiences is often referred to as *self-talk*. Meaning systems are constituted by language; without language, they could not exist. Again, even the unshared experiences and meanings that reside exclusively within the realm of individual psychologies are linguistically based. Language symbolizes experience and allows meanings to be stored, recalled, altered, and communicated. Linguistic symbols are analogous to programming languages for computers; without them, processing could not occur.

During the course of evolution, humans developed the ability to symbolize their experiences in "grunts and squeals" (Frederickson 1999, 252), which were gradually refined into systems of language. The ability to create and communicate meanings allowed people to structure relationships, and eventually cultures, around roles, values, beliefs, and norms. Civilization, then, is arguably a byproduct of language.

The unifying, common denominator of language makes the construct of meaning systems a useful theoretical construct, not a mammoth, hodgepodge of unrelated elements that would bog down and hinder further philosophical exploration. Defining meaning systems as linguistic structures is also an excellent conceptual fit for advanced investigations into the work of psychotherapists and counselors. In this regard, therapy was aptly described as the "talking cure" (Gay 1988, 65) in the earliest days of the profession. If you were to hop into a time machine and throw open the door of any therapy session over the past century, you would simply see people talking and listening to one another (Hansen 2014b). Of course, if you threw open enough doors, you would also witness an unseemly variety of grossly unethical behavior. Putting these latter observations aside, though, ethical, customary therapeutic practice consists of a series of conversations between parties who are united by a helping contract.

Although it is reasonable and conceptually useful to define meaning systems as linguistic structures, this definition also brings a number of puzzling philosophical questions to the forefront of inquiry. For instance, do certain meaning systems represent an objective reality beyond language? If so, what would be the criteria for determining which perspectives are correspondent with nature's truths and which ones are not? Throughout history, people have used language to make sense of the world, but how do we understand the sense that people make? Can language represent the world as it is or is language simply just a bunch of "grunts and squeals" (Frederickson 1999, 252)? Indeed, when dogs bark, hens cackle, or dolphins squeal no one regards a subset of these noises as embodying transcendent truth. When human animals make linguistic noises, alternatively, people generally believe that some of these noises are potentially correspondent with an objective reality that exists beyond the utterances. Are these radical differences in the appraisal of animal noises justifiable? If so, on what grounds?

Questions about language, what it symbolizes, and how it should be conceptualized are at the conceptual heart of the talk therapy professions (Hansen 2014a). Counselors and psychotherapists are conversational engineers; they cultivate, direct, and shape the interactional flow of words that unfold in their offices to meet the goal of alleviating the psychological suffering of their clientele. The psychotherapy literature is replete with ideas about how to selectively attend to and manipulate words in order to bring about a healing impact. Cognitivists, for instance, advocate paying particular attention to the linguistic structures that are deemed thoughts. Psychoanalysts, on the other hand, pull up language like rocks in a field, looking for hidden sentences that lie underneath the manifest ones. For all of the theoretical and research efforts that have gone into conceptualizing client problems and how to respond to them, however, relatively little attention (within the helping professions) has been paid to examining the nature, role, and function of the expressive vehicle in which problems and interventions are communicated. To gain a conceptual understanding of meaning systems, language, itself, must be subject to philosophical scrutiny.

A review of philosophical understandings of language lays the groundwork for an exploration of issues related to meaning systems in theories of counseling and psychotherapy. For instance, psychoanalytic theory, over the course of its evolution, has arguably had an ambivalent relationship with meaning systems, alternating from open acceptance, to diagnostic judgment, to funneling all client free associations into a set of rigid theoretical categories. Furthermore, various theories emphasize different components of experience, such as thoughts or emotions. To begin an analysis of systems of counseling and psychotherapy as they are related to meaning systems, it first is important to investigate the relationship between language, meaning, and truth.

LANGUAGE, MEANING, AND TRUTH

Suppose one person claims that elephants are land animals and another argues that elephants can fly. Both claims are symbolically expressed in language, the vehicle through which meanings are communicated. Most people would probably consider the former claim correspondent with the reality about elephants and the latter utterance as absurdly disconnected from truth. This example is illustrative of the fact that the Western mindset tends to categorize meaning systems dualistically (i.e., whether or not they are a good match for the intrinsic nature of reality) (Hansen 2008; Rorty 1999). This dualistic system of categorization often leads people to conclude that the utterances of scientists, for example, should be valued over the words of poets. In this regard, a poet might, indeed, characterize elephants as having the ability to fly. This is only an artistic musing, most people would probably argue, which, at best, has the potential to bring about a pleasurable aesthetic experience. Alternatively, by using a method that incrementally reveals the laws of the universe, scientists can gradually come to acquire objective knowledge about reality. Is this view of science, particularly as it relates to other disciplines, justifiable, though? After all, the end product of both poetry and scientific investigation is simply a bunch of human "grunts and squeals" (Frederickson 1999, 252). What makes one set of marks epistemologically superior to another?

This idealization of the scientific method as the supreme route to revealing nature's truths has been in Western cultural vogue for several centuries. However, for thousands of years before the cultural coronation of science as the king of truth, divine revelation was regarded as the way to cut through the static of human ideas to the eternal laws of the universe (Tarnas 1991). Historically, truths revealed by God were naturally considered superior to any sketchy guesses about reality that mere humans might come up with. Soon after the scientific method was introduced and began to be employed, science and religion often came to a head, such as in the trial of Galileo (Tarnas 1999). However, science eventually won the cultural blue ribbon for truth detecting method, although many people continue to regard religious revelation as supreme. Debates about whether evolution or creationism accurately represent the origins of humankind, for instance, illustrate current tensions between those who idealize science as the route to truth and those who regard divine revelation as the last word about reality.

Dualistic categorization of human claims, then, has been a core element of Western culture for thousands of years. Whether the arbiter has been science, religion, or philosophical logic, certain sets of words have been regarded as correspondent with reality while others have been deemed to have missed the mark. This dualism is present throughout traditional orientations to counseling and psychotherapy (Hansen 2002; 2008). Freud, for instance, thought that psychoanalysis could alleviate psychological suffering by revealing the true nature of the unconscious processes that were causing it (Freud 1916/1963). Behaviorists, alternatively, aimed to eradicate the messy subjectivity of psychoanalysis by exclusively focusing their efforts on behaviors (Watson 1919). Behaviorist ideology proved highly compelling in an intellectual climate that regarded subjectivity as a fog that interfered with the ability to view objective reality clearly.

The process of sorting meaning systems according to whether or not they are a match for the intrinsic nature of reality seems natural and intuitive to people who have been indoctrinated in Western intellectual culture. Indeed, most people probably regard the assumption that some meanings are correspondent with nature and others are not as an unquestionable given, a natural starting point for all intellectual inquiry. However, this epistemological assumption about the potential of meaning systems to represent nature's truths is not, itself, an objective fact that was found pristine in nature. Like all ways of thinking about the world, it was constructed by people. To achieve greater conceptual understandings of meaning systems, it is important to review the philosophical origins of this epistemological dualism, which has been knit into the fabric of Western thought.

Modernism

The intellectual movement that presumes meaning systems can be sorted according to whether or not they are correspondent with objective reality is generally referred to as *modernism* (Hansen 2004; Sexton 1997). Using the above example to illustrate the central tenet of modernism, the claim that elephants are land animals is presumably correspondent with objective reality, whereas the proposition that elephants can fly is not a match for nature's truths, unless, of course, scientists discover a species of flying elephants. In modernist ideology, then, human claims can be dualistically sorted (at least potentially) according to whether or not they match the intrinsic nature of reality.

Again, to people who have been indoctrinated in the tenets of Western intellectual culture, this modernist mindset probably seems unassailable. Within the scope of the Western worldview, it is commonsensical to presume that some meaning systems are true representations of reality and others are not. Human progress is arguably dependent on the identification of objective truths. Indeed, the truth-finding, scientific method has resulted in the eradication of deadly diseases and invention of new technologies, which have elevated humankind far above the brutal living conditions of our ancestors. To extend this modernist vision, one might also argue that it would naturally be in the best interests of the professional helping enterprise to discern which systems of psychotherapy and counseling are true representations of human psychology and which ones are off the mark. How, then, one might ask, could the tenets of modernism possibly be questioned?

In order to appreciate critiques of this true-false dualism it is important to understand its philosophical origins. A good starting point for this understanding is, perhaps surprisingly, an ancient, imaginary cave. Specifically, the Greek philosopher Plato (1968) presented the idea of a cave, which was inhabited by people who had always been locked, by chains, into the position of facing one of the cave walls; they had never been able to turn their gaze away from the wall. Behind them a fire burned at the entrance to the cave, so anything that passed between the fire and the cave opening was cast as a shadow on the wall that the dwellers faced. The people in the cave, then, were only able to see shadows, not the real entities that were casting them. Using this allegory, Plato, through Socrates, argued that the cave dwellers, because they had never seen anything other than the wall, would naturally mistake the shadows for reality. By using the careful reasoning of philosophers, however, the cave dwellers could cast off their chains, turn around, and see the true entities that were casting the shadows, thereby ending their illusionary state.

Note the true-false dualism inherent in the allegory of the cave. People can either be correct or mistaken about the essential nature of reality; the goal of intellectual inquiry is to ascertain the true essence of phenomena and not be fooled by the shadows. This epistemological dualism shaped Western intellectual culture for millennia. Indeed, the early twentieth-century philosopher Whitehead (1979) noted that the history of philosophy "consists of a series of footnotes to Plato" (39). This Platonic vision received a strong ideological boost, along with some added intellectual features, during the Enlightenment.

In medieval Europe, citizens generally followed royal dictates or papal decrees. However, due to certain political events, people began to challenge these authorities during the late 1600s. These challenges widened, gained intellectual momentum, and grew into a movement called the Enlightenment (Hicks 2004; Rosenau 1992; Tarnas 1991). Instead of abiding by external powers, European intellectuals increasingly began to rely on individual reason as the route to truth. The iconic hero of this age thereby became the courageous intellectual, who reasoned his way to new understandings about political systems, religious matters, and the very nature of reality. The French philosopher Descartes is a good example of an intellectual who set the stage for Enlightenment thought.

Descartes (1988) worried that everything he had been taught might be false. All of his philosophical conclusions would be wrong if they had been based on teachings he had mistakenly assumed to be correct. In an effort to find the truth, he reasoned that he would have to start at the very beginning by discarding all of the supposed facts he thought were true. By engaging in this process of radical doubt, Descartes hoped to arrive at truth through the process of careful reasoning, from the ground up. It is not hard to appreciate this Cartesian strategy. That is, if you suspect that you might have been given inaccurate information, a logical route to accurate knowledge would be to purposefully discard everything that you had been taught and figure things out for yourself. People who lose their faith in the religions that they grew up believing, for instance, sometimes start their search anew and struggle to find a personally satisfying worldview.

For Descartes (1988), the starting point of his inquiry was, indeed, the very beginning. In a series of meditations, he began by doubting everything, even his own existence. Eventually, Descartes concluded that the very fact that he was thinking must surely mean that he existed in some form. From this central conclusion, Descartes eventually reasoned his way to a series of ideas that helped to shape modern Western culture, including mind-body dualism, which is the tremendously influential metaphysical distinction between material reality and the immaterial realm of the mind.

Enlightenment thought has had a profound and lasting impact on Western intellectual culture (Hicks 2004). In this regard, the ability to reason is a property of individuals. Therefore, the Enlightenment idealization of reason resulted in a Western emphasis on individualism. Individualism, in turn, naturally gave rise to political movements founded on individual rights and fortified the idea that people have a cohesive, internal self-structure that guides their actions. The Cartesian distinction between material and immaterial realities encouraged objective, scientific investigation of the material world, which has led to remarkable advances in medicine and other fields. The Enlightenment, then, created strong cultural waves that have flowed throughout Western thought.

Note that traditional theories of counseling and psychotherapy are founded on Enlightenment ideals (Hansen 2002). Specifically, helping orientations generally view the individual as the unit of change. The willful individual, with an internal self-structure, is the theoretical starting point of humanism, for example (Maslow 1968; Rogers 1951; 1957). Furthermore, the accompanying Enlightenment ideal of finding objective truth also pervades traditional theories of helping (Hansen 2002). Psychoanalysts endeavor to find the true unconscious conflicts of their clients; accurate (i.e., true) empathy is the linchpin of humanistic practice; and traditional cognitive therapists emphasize the importance of objectively apprehending and correcting irrational cognitions. Therefore, conventional systems of psychotherapy and counseling were not created in an ideological vacuum. Every conceptual structure arguably bears the marks of the culture that produced it. Orientations to helping were forged in the ideological fires of modernism, wherein foundational assumptions about objective truths and inner selves burn bright.

The identification of the modernist foundations of traditional orientations to talk therapy naturally leads to some interesting questions. For instance, are there alternative conceptual foundations that could be used to understand the meaning systems that emerge in the helping encounter? Could a nonmodernist ideological ecosystem perhaps yield theories that would be superior, in certain respects, to theories that were built upon a modernist foundation? Is there a compelling, logical structure that can jar us away from the hypnotic, cultural hold that modernist ideals have on us, so that we can view the world through a different ideological lens? To address these questions, it is necessary to examine critiques of modernist ideology. These critiques have coalesced into a movement called postmodernism.

Postmodernism

As the centuries after the Enlightenment unfolded, problems with the modernist vision became increasingly apparent. For instance, the Enlightenment association of the acquisition of truth with human progress has arguably not resulted in humankind coming closer to some kind of utopia (Anderson 1990; Hillman and Ventura 1992). Indeed, supposed Enlightenment style progress has brought us the global threat of nuclear weapons; technological advances that have created a widespread sense of malaise and isolation; and industries whose sole purpose is to manufacture drugs designed to anesthetize uncomfortable feelings before their meanings can be usefully considered. Furthermore, truth proclamations have clearly had deleterious consequences for disempowered groups. The traditional psychiatric truth that homosexuality is a mental disorder, for instance, has caused untold suffering to people with same-sex attractions. Perhaps, then, the path to utopia is not paved with truth.

During the mid-twentieth century, critiques of modernism began to strengthen, gain momentum, and coalesce into an ideological movement known as postmodernism (Rosenau 1992). In addition to noting the failure of the Enlightenment vision to come to fruition, postmodern philosophers critiqued the logical structure upon which the modernist project was built. Far from being solid and firm, the modernist foundation of Western intellectual culture, according to certain critics, had severe structural defects. Rather than continue this construction project, perhaps it would be better to work from a new foundation, one that would overcome the logical problems inherent in the modernist vision. Notably, philosophical critiques of modernism are voluminous and complex. For purposes of this discussion, I confine the following discussion to the critique of a defining ideal of the Enlightenment: the association of human progress with the gradual acquisition of nature's truths.

There are various philosophical conceptualizations of truth. The relevant definition of truth for this overview of postmodern thought is called the *correspondence theory of truth* (Schmitt 1995). According to the correspondence theory, truth is defined as a match between human statements about reality and the intrinsic nature of reality. This is probably the way that most people think about truth. For instance, consider the following statements: a) influenza is caused by a virus; b) influenza is caused by evil spirits. Most people would probably consider the first statement correspondent with reality. That is, it is a match for the true reality that exists beyond the statement. The latter utterance, however, would ordinarily be deemed as an inaccurate match for the truths of nature. To put these statements in the allegorical language of Plato's cave, the second statement is the shadow and the first is the essential truth that is casting it. The scientific method, which was idealized by the Enlightenment as the tool for discovering objective truth, is the primary instrument for distinguishing truth from shadows. As mentioned above, if you have been indoctrinated in the assumptions of Western intellectual culture, you may wonder what could possibly be illogical about the correspondence theory of truth. Actually, however, there are a number of problems with the correspondence theory that have been noted by postmodern philosophers. I manage the complexity of these postmodern critiques of truth by limiting the discussion to three central arguments.

First, there are usually various perspectives about the same entity or phenomenon (Hansen 2002; 2004; 2014a). Consider a pen, for example. To some, it is simply a writing instrument. Others may regard the pen as a highly valued collectible item. The engineer who designed it may have an entirely different view of the pen, perhaps only considering it from the vantage point of its mechanical design. The pen may have been a gift to someone, who might come to regard it as a highly sentimental item, full of meanings that remind the person of a special relationship. To a physicist, who views physical objects as reducible to subatomic particles, the solidity of the pen is an illusion. The pen is actually comprised of vast empty spaces between invisible specks of matter. Of course, there are numerous other perspectives and, in the future, many other points of view about the pen may be introduced (e.g., it is an antique; a symbol of simpler times; representative of writing instruments in parallel universes, etc.).

Returning to the Platonic cave, which of the above perspectives accurately represents the essential pen and which views are shadows? In other words, what is the truth about the pen? Which view is correspondent with the real, true reality? These questions, of course, are highly problematic because all of the perspectives about the pen are defensible, depending on the individual or community from which the viewpoint was derived. Indeed, who could arbitrate these views and decide which one is the supposed correct perspective? Anyone selected as an arbitrator would be subject to his or her own individual and communal influences, which would inevitably bias the decision. Could anyone really adopt a "view from nowhere" (Nagel 1986, 70) and somehow determine the hypothetical true essence of the pen? Therefore, as postmodern philosophers have argued, taking the Platonic idea of true essences to its natural conclusion leads to logical problems (Rorty 1999; 2000). Indeed, even twentieth century physicists noted that the act of observation could alter what is being observed.

The obvious legitimacy of multiple perspectives, the seemingly incontestable assumption that people can never escape their influences, and the recognition that observers influence whatever realities are being observed all served to undermine the Platonic view that we should conceptualize phenomenon as having singular essences. The postmodernists, then, have been described as *anti-essentialist*, which means that they generally do not endorse the view that inquiry should be aimed at uncovering essential, true realities (Muran 2001; Rosen 1996). Instead of the essentialist view, different meaning systems should be appreciated and honored, not judged according to their correspondence with some essential reality.

What about science, though? Some might argue that the scientific method cuts through the fog of human subjectivity, thereby enabling increasingly clear views of the intrinsic nature of reality. After all, objectivity is the defining element of scientific investigation. Scientists endeavor to remove themselves and their biases from their research by using double-blind and other methods, which are designed to subtract the influence of the investigator. As further evidence for the ability of science to reveal nature's truths, some might cite the incredible progress that has been made with the scientific method, including the eradication of deadly diseases, development of sophisticated technologies, and increased understandings of the laws of the universe. Are the meaning systems produced by scientists, then, epistemologically superior to meaning systems generated in other realms? The postmodern response is that they are not.

Fundamental to the postmodern view of science is the work of Kuhn (1996), a philosopher of science. Kuhn argued that science is essentially a communal activity. To illustrate this point, consider the training that is necessary to become a scientist. One is gradually indoctrinated into a communal point of view, wherein certain questions and conclusions are acceptable and others are not. For instance, a researcher who specializes in neurochemical investigations of psychiatric disorders has undergone decades of training, countless efforts to gain acceptance and notoriety in the field, personal sacrifices to master the craft, and indoctrination into the perspectives and values of her or his scientific community. When operating within the bounds of her professional life, the researcher will never draw the conclusion that depression is the result of early developmental conflicts, social injustices, or relational problems. These conclusions, or even the questions that might lead to them, are not admissible to the community in which the researcher participates. Having spent years being immersed and indoctrinated in a scientific community that views psychiatric problems as brain-based, the researcher will inevitably draw conclusions about depression that are based on neurochemistry. According to Kuhn, scientific progress is made in bursts when maverick scientists violate communal rules and draw novel conclusions, which at first might be rejected by the community, but may gradually come to be regarded as brilliant observations, which are subsequently integrated into the new communal view.

From a Kuhnian perspective, then, science is a puzzle solving activity (Kuhn 1996). Scientists solve puzzles that are important to particular scientific communities. Simply because a solution to a puzzle meets a communal goal, or even when the solution advances interests beyond the community (e.g., a cure for a deadly disease), it does not logically follow that the solution is correspondent with some transcendent reality that hypothetically exists beyond the bounds of all communities. As an illustrative example of this point, when a beaver builds a dam, the beaver is solving a problem related to its adaptation. It would, of course, be absurd to characterize this solution to a particular adaptive problem faced by beavers as somehow representative of the intrinsic nature of reality. Following naturally from this beaver example, it would be just as absurd to characterize the solutions that human animals formulate for their unique problems as being correspondent with nature's truths. Within this Kuhnian critique, then, science is a puzzle solving activity, which is devoted to solving problems that are important to various scientific communities. There is no compelling reason to believe that the solutions to problems that uniquely serve the interests of human animals are any more connected to a transcendent reality than are the puzzles solved by nonhuman animals. In this respect, the polio vaccine is analogous to bear hibernation. Both are unique, adaptive solutions, which address the concerns of particular animal species; they are adaptational solutions to species-specific problems, and there is no reason to regard them as representations of the eternal truths of nature.

To summarize the above, first critique of modernism, people have various perspectives on the same phenomenon. There is no way to arbitrate these perspectives to determine which ones are correspondent with nature's truths. Furthermore, scientific perspectives, as communally based attempts at puzzle solving, do not have any special ability to reveal reality in a pure form. With this first critique in mind, postmodernists have generally argued that the Platonic ideal of an essential, true reality should be abandoned.

The second postmodern critique of modernist assumptions about truth is related to language. As noted above, any meanings that people express (even privately to themselves) must be transmitted in the vehicle of language. Humans, of course, invented language and the particular categories of meaning that are inherent in different linguistic systems (Rorty 1999). For instance, I might describe a certain stretch of land in terms of its roads; the same area might be described according to rock formations by a geologist; and a politician may speak of the political preferences of people who reside in the area. Each linguistic system, even within the same language, has different ways of describing and categorizing the identical area. This example naturally leads to intriguing questions: What is the true reality of the area, beyond language? If language always imposes linguistic meanings and categories on any phenomena that is described, can hypothetical, true phenomena beyond human description ever be accessed?

The postmodern answer to these questions is that it is impossible to get outside of language to obtain a language-free view of reality (Hansen 2007; Rorty 1999). Whenever people describe anything, they must use the tool of language; the only descriptions that can be generated are linguistic ones. People are thereby epistemologically trapped within their ways of speaking about the world. To break down the logic of this critique: a) humans invented language; b) any conclusions about reality that humans formulate must be expressed in language; therefore, c) all human conclusions are tainted by the categories inherent in linguistic systems. As soon as anything is described, it is contaminated by the human-invented descriptive categories of the language that is used to describe it. This reasoning led the philosopher Derrida (1995) to declare "there is nothing outside of the text" (89). Like the first critique of the modernist conceptualization of truth, the second critique also rejects that Platonic ideal of ascertaining essential truth. As soon as any supposed essential truth were subject to a description, it would be contaminated by the categories inherent in the language that was used to describe it.

The third postmodern critique of the modernist ideal of truth is also related to language. This critique, however, considers language from a Darwinian perspective. In this regard, language evolved, like other traits, because it served an adaptive function (Dennett 1995). It is not difficult to understand the reasons that language ability was naturally selected as a human trait. Our distant ancestors who were able to communicate and use symbols to represent natural phenomena would have clearly had a strong survival advantage over those who lacked this ability. From an evolutionary perspective, then, the ability to use language is a type of adaptive tool, which was naturally selected for because it strongly contributed to the survival of the species.

If language is a tool, akin to a hammer, which helped the human species adapt to their environmental circumstances, when did this tool become capable of embodying the pure essence of the phenomena it describes? It would be absurd to say that a hammer, as a tool, is capable of representing the true essence of carpentry, for example. A tool can only be used to manipulate the environment. By extension, language, as a tool, is also used to manipulate the environment. Language can be used to tell someone to run from a threat, convey instructions about how to build a house, or symbolize future dangers so they can be anticipated and avoided. Clearly, language is a powerful tool. However, under the modernist vision, essential truths about reality are capable of being embodied in language. Certain strings of words are presumed to potentially represent pure truth, while others are not. However, if language is merely a tool, regarding it as having the ability to embody truth is as absurd as supposing that a fork, as a tool, is capable of embodying the essence of eating. Tools cannot represent the intrinsic nature of reality; they are merely tools (Hansen 2008; Rorty 1999). To summarize this line of reasoning, the following are the logical steps of this third, postmodern critique of modernist assumptions about truth: a) language ability exists in humans because it was naturally selected for; b) language, then, is a type of tool that helped our distant ancestors adapt to their environmental circumstances; c) as a tool, language can be used to manipulate the environment; d) however, tools cannot magically transcend their tool function and suddenly become capable of embodying the true essence of reality; therefore, e) language, as a tool, can never embody the true essence of reality. By definition, then, nothing that is ever put into words can be true (in the sense of representing the intrinsic nature of reality).

The correspondence theory of truth, and its accompanying modernist ideology, has been compellingly critiqued by postmodern philosophers. To review, the first critique notes that there are many legitimate perspectives on reality. There are no unbiased authorities who could arbitrate various points of view to determine which one represents the intrinsic nature of reality. Second, language is a human invention. Therefore, anything that is described in language must be tainted by the linguistic categories that people invented. Last, humans have the ability to use language because language served as a powerful adaptive tool in their evolution. As a mere tool, though, it can only manipulate realities, not embody pristine, essential truths.

Postmodernism, then, provides a thorough critique of Enlightenment, modernist ideology. Once modernism is rejected, however, what might replace it? The search for the intrinsic nature of reality has guided Western intellectual culture for thousands of years. With the Enlightenment, this search became strongly associated with human progress and idealized the scientific method as its guide. Indeed, traditional systems of counseling and psychotherapy were also based on these ideals. That is, it was generally presumed by traditional theorists that if the therapist helps the client see the truth, the client will be set free from his or her symptoms (Hansen 2002; 2004). Whether the goal was to discern unconscious process, correct irrational cognitions, or identify stimulus-response contingencies that created and maintained symptoms, a strong, Enlightenment-based association between truth and progress animated the foundational orientations to professional helping. If the rug of truth is pulled out from under Western culture and systems of counseling, where would that leave us? What would we do then?

The European postmodernists were generally not concerned with providing a replacement for modernist ideals. Broadly speaking, they spent their intellectual time deconstructing Western culture without providing useful ideological replacements for the modernist ideals that their critiques destroyed. Perhaps it is fine to simply play in the rubble of modernism after you have blown it up if your interests are exclusively in literary studies or other areas of the humanities (Rosenau 1992), as was the case with certain European postmodernists (e.g., Derrida 1995). However, for psychotherapists and counselors, who are interested in the practical application of their theories to helping people, modernism arguably must be replaced by a new overarching ideology. It is not enough to simply take away the foundations of traditional models of helping; in order to help people, theories have to stand on new ideological pillars. According to critics, then, postmodernism creates the problem of relativism (e.g., Held 1995). That is, if truth is taken away as a guide to action, there is no justification for making one choice over another.

American philosophers, particularly Rorty, have proposed an ideological replacement for the modernist search for truth. In short, Rorty (1979) resurrected pragmatism and conjoined it with postmodern philosophical insights to resolve the problem of relativism that is associated with postmodern ideology. To understand this conceptual strategy, the tenets of pragmatism must be reviewed.

Pragmatism is a uniquely American philosophical system that first emerged during the latter part of the nineteenth century (Menand 2001). Although pragmatism is an ideologically diverse movement, it is conceptually unified by the central premise that ideas and beliefs should be evaluated according to their practical applicability, not by their relative proximity to the intrinsic nature of reality. James (1995), a founding pragmatist, summarized the key assumption of pragmatism: "true is the name of whatever proves itself to be good in the way of belief" (30). In other words, a true belief is one that advances human interests. Instead of viewing theories as potential representations of nature's eternal truths, "[t]heories thus become instruments, not answers to enigmas, in which we can rest" (21). This pragmatist view of truth is consistent with, and was strongly influenced by, Darwinism, which became a prominent intellectual movement in the decades prior to the emergence of pragmatism (Menand 2001). To Darwin, humans are simply another species of animal that have evolved to adapt to the conditions of their environment. Language, as mentioned above, is one of the human animal's most powerful adaptational tools. Theories, ideas, and beliefs are comprised of language. Therefore, according to pragmatists, human systems of thought should be evaluated exclusively according to their tool function (i.e., the degree to which they advance human interests), not by abstract, epistemological criteria (i.e., whether or not they are correspondent with the intrinsic nature of reality).

As the twentieth century unfolded, pragmatism began to lose prominence as new philosophical systems came into vogue. Rorty (1979), however, revived pragmatism during the 1970s to resolve the problem of relativism that is created by postmodern ideology. This pragmatist resolution meant that meaning systems should be evaluated according to their potential use value, not according to whether they are mere shadow appearances or the truth about reality. To say this succinctly, "the appearance reality distinction should be dropped in favor of a distinction between less useful and more useful ways of talking" (Rorty 1998, 1). This new pragmatism, which was injected into postmodern ideology, is called *neopragmatism* (Polkinghorne 1992).

To illustrate neopragmatic thought, consider the statements regarding the cause of influenza noted above. Within the modernist vision, the idea that influenza is caused by evil spirits should be rejected because this statement is not correspondent with the true nature of reality. However, if postmodern critiques of modernism are taken seriously, the statement cannot be rejected on the grounds that it does not conform to the intrinsic nature of reality. In fact, no statements can be rejected using the criterion of their relative correspondence with nature's truths. This failure of postmodern ideology to presumably reject any ideas creates the problem of relativism. However, using the neopragmatic criteria of usefulness, the idea that influenza is caused by evil spirits can easily be rejected because it is not a useful idea to endorse. Physicians have found great use for the assumption of viral causation and no use for the concept of spiritual possession. Therefore, the use value of ideas is the neopragmatic criterion for determining whether a system of thought should be endorsed. Incidentally, within neopragmatic thought, the statement that elephants can fly should be rejected because no one has found a use for it, not because it fails to match transcendent truth. Indeed, perhaps one day people might find a use for regarding elephants as flying creatures. This idea, to the twenty-first century ear, is arguably no more bizarre sounding than the premise that solid appearing objects consist primarily of empty space would be to a person living in the fourteenth century. However, as it turns out, the community of physicists has found it extraordinarily useful to conceptualize the world as being comprised of invisible, subatomic particles.

There are two important points that should be noted about neopragmatic thought. I know to address these issues because people regularly bring them up when I provide an overview of neopragmatism. Perhaps you, the reader, thought of them when you were reading the above section. The first point is a challenge to postmodernism, which frames the movement as ideologically hypocritical. This point is summarized by the following question: If postmodernism (including neopragmatism) rejects the idea that humans can access a transcendent truth, how can the proponents of postmodernism and neopragmatism make the seemingly hypocritical claim that their ideology is true? The answer is that postmodern philosophers do not generally regard their ideology as true; they simply frame it as an alternative to modernism. They argue that the postmodern alternative may bring about desirable benefits that are not available when operating within a modernist ideology. However, they regard their ideologies as potentially useful conceptual options, not as truths.

The second issue is not a critique of postmodern thought, but an understandable conceptual confusion, which is represented by the following question: Are postmodernists saying that there is no truth, that objective truth does not exist? I can certainly appreciate this question. Indeed, some postmodern writings can be interpreted to mean that objective reality does not exist. In this regard, I favor the neopragmatic response to this question. Specifically, Rorty (1998) argued that the dualism between true reality and mere appearances should be eradicated; the dualism, itself, should no longer be endorsed. The question of whether or not truth exists is drawn from a dualism that neopragmatists reject. In other words, it is nonsensical to ask whether or not objective truth exists within an ideology that rejects the distinction between the intrinsic nature of reality and mere appearances. As an analogy, this question would be tantamount to asking an atheist whether she is worried about what God might think of her rejection of Him. The question is nonsensical to the atheist because it is based on a premise that she rejects. So, the answer I usually give to the question about whether or not objective truth exists within the neopragmatic frame of reference is that this question is nonsensical to neopragmatists because they reject the dualistic premise on which the question is based.

In summary, I have provided an overview of two fundamental ways that meaning systems can be conceptualized: a) according to their correspondence with objective truth; and b) according to their usefulness (i.e., postmodernism and neopragmatism). These ways of conceptualizing meaning systems have implications for the helping professions. Indeed, counseling and psychotherapy are virtually defined by systems of meaning, which include the theories that guide professionals and the numerous meanings that arise during every helping encounter. Therefore, it is arguably useful to import philosophical concepts about meaning systems into the domain of the helping professions, so that counselors and psychotherapists can consider various ways of conceptualizing the rich layers of meaning that constitute their professional lives.

LANGUAGE, MEANING, AND TRUTH IN COUNSELING AND PSYCHOTHERAPY

Counselors and psychotherapists spend their professional days immersed in meaning systems. Clients talk about their problems, interpretations of events, recollections from childhood, relationships, worldviews, and various perspectives on living; therapists struggle to make sense of it all. The type of sense that therapists make, of course, depends on how they conceptually regard the complex, seemingly infinite webs of meanings that emerge in the helping encounter. In this regard, there are at least two sense-making levels of abstraction from which counselors and psychotherapists can draw.

First, at a relatively high philosophical level of abstraction, talk therapists can appraise meaning systems according to whether or not they are true, in the sense of being correspondent with some reality beyond the meaning system. From a modernist perspective, as noted above, therapist theories and client utterances are presumed to have the potential to be correspondent with the intrinsic nature of reality. Theories can be correct or not, and client utterances may or may not be an accurate representation of the external world and a client's inner, psychological life. If operating from a postmodern perspective, alternatively, the meanings that animate the helping encounter are appraised according to whether they are useful or not; within this ideological framework, the idea of correspondence with reality is nonsensical, and, is therefore, not considered.

Second, moving down a rung on the ladder of abstraction, are helping orientations, such as cognitive-behavioral and psychodynamic theories. These orientations help practitioners select which types of meanings are important, how to conceptually regard them, and potentially useful ways to intervene. Cognitively oriented practitioners, for instance, are selectively attentive to client thoughts, appraise them according to the degree to which they contribute to problems, and challenge the thoughts that are causing psychological suffering. This second rung of abstraction can be influenced by the first. For instance, early psychoanalytic theorists were generally modernist in their thinking, presuming that Freudian maps of the mind were correspondent representations of the psychic territory. Certain later psychoanalysts, however, were influenced by postmodern philosophers (e.g., Spence 1982). This influence led them to regard psychoanalytic theories and patient verbalizations as narratives, not objective truths.

Both levels of abstraction (i.e., truth orientation and theoretical perspective) have implications for the conceptualization of meaning systems in the helping encounter. Whether one sorts meanings according to truth or by use has broad consequences for the practices of psychotherapy and counseling. Likewise, theoretical orientations strongly influence the ways in which the information that emerges in therapy is considered. The implications of both levels of abstraction are considered in the sections below.

Modernism and Postmodern Conceptualizations of Counseling and Psychotherapy

The helping professions were forged in the fires of modernism. At the beginning of the twentieth century, the scientific method was responsible for numerous advances in physics, chemistry, and medicine. The cultural air was thick with excitement about advancements that could be made by discovering nature's truths. Sigmund Freud, the inventor of the talk therapy scenario, was indoctrinated into this scientific, intellectual culture. Indeed, Freud considered himself a scientist and only reluctantly went into outpatient practice after he failed to secure a position as a research neurologist (Gay 1988). Freud and his followers viewed their psychoanalytic maps as correspondent with the psychic terrain, thereby allowing psychoanalysts to objectively come to know the unconscious conflicts of their clientele. In this regard, the early Freudians saw themselves as scientists of the mind. Behaviorists and other twentieth century theorists also operated within a modernist, scientific paradigm, which they believed would allow them to have an objective view of client problems and effective treatments (Watson 1919). In addition to theories that were directed at helping people, academic psychology also adopted the paradigm and methods of the natural sciences. As psychology began to emerge as a separate discipline, psychological laboratories used the scientific method to explore psychophysiological phenomena (Titchener 1921). From the beginning, then, clinical and academic psychology were based on a modernist view of the world, which placed the highest value on the ideals of truth, objectivity, and the scientific method (Polkinghorne 1992).

During the first part of the twentieth century, it probably seemed unquestionably obvious to theorists and researchers that the social sciences, both clinical and academic, should adopt the investigative paradigm of the natural sciences. At the time, the intellectual culture did not really offer any alternatives. However, with the emergence of the postmodern critique in the past several decades, an alternative paradigm has begun to emerge. The presence of dual paradigms now allows us to consider whether the investigative methods of the natural sciences were a good fit for the study of people, particularly for the theories and research that drive the helping professions.

There are certainly compelling reasons to question the appropriateness of the modernist, scientific model as a paradigm to advance the helping professions. Medicine and other natural sciences have made tremendous strides over the past century. The social sciences and the helping professions, in contrast, have arguably made little progress with the use of the scientific method (Anderson 1990; Hillman and Ventura 1992; Rosenau 1992). Unlike smallpox and other diseases, crime, poverty, child abuse and other social ills have not been eradicated with the methods of the natural sciences. It is also questionable whether psychotherapy and counseling have made significant advances over the past century, or whether practitioners have simply endorsed and idealized various helping orientations, as they have historically come into and out of vogue, with little progress to show for it.

In addition to this lack of progress, there are other reasons to suspect that the scientific method might not be a good investigative paradigm for the helping professions. Investigators operating in the natural sciences seek universal laws about the objects they study (Hansen 2004; Polkinghorne 1992). Chemists, for instance, attempt to uncover the true, essential properties of chemicals, the rules that govern their interactions, and the uses that can be made of them. Because it is designed to objectively uncover the enduring laws of natural phenomena, the scientific method has proven to be an excellent tool to advance the goals of chemists and other natural science professionals. People, though, are fundamentally different from the physical hunks of matter that scientists study. Human beings are not only determined by laws that govern their physical bodies, they are also influenced by values, the sense they make out of the world, culture, families, and other sources of meaning. In short, people are influenced by the meaning systems they create; chemicals (and other physical matter) are not. It is arguably misguided, then, to attempt to uncover the eternal laws of human behavior because people follow the laws that they create.

Given the shortcomings of the use of modernist ideology as applied to the study of people, it is not surprising that modernism also has significant drawbacks for the theories and practices of human helping. With regard to theories, there are hundreds of orientations to psychotherapy and counseling. Many of these theories have completely incompatible assumptions about human nature (Hansen 2002). Traditional psychoanalytic theory, for instance, begins with the assumption that humans are sexual and aggressive animals who are eventually tamed by society (Brenner 1973). The untamed elements of experience are relegated to the unconscious, wherein they continue to be a driving, yet hidden, force in the personality. Humanism, alternatively, begins with the assumption that people have an inborn drive toward actualization (Maslow 1968), a theoretical position that is arguably the complete opposite of the psychoanalytic starting point. Furthermore, unlike psychoanalysis, humanism makes no presumptions about an unconscious mental life (Hansen 2000). To complicate matters, all popular systems of psychotherapy, regardless of their gross conceptual incompatibilities, are about equally effective (Wampold 2001). How can theoreticians, researchers, and practitioners make sense of this theoretical situation?

From a modernist point of view, if two theories were equally effective at explaining a phenomenon, it would likely be presumed that each theory was reflective of a part of the truth about the phenomenon. If two explanatory systems each provided explanations for the cause of a disease, for example, the assumptions of the two systems would be scientifically investigated, the true parts of each would be identified, and the accurate elements of both theories would be combined into a super-theory, an integrated theoretical structure that would presumably have greater explanatory power than either of the original singular theories. This is how the progression of knowledge operates in modernist ideology. With systems of psychotherapy, however, it is exceptionally difficult, if not outright impossible, to fashion such integrations because the theories are inherently incompatible (Hansen 2002). Humanism and psychoanalysis are very different at the level of their theoretical DNA. A Frankensteinian integration that retains the essences of each theory is, in all likelihood, an impossibility. Again, what makes this theoretical puzzle even more maddening is that the theories are about equally effective at helping people.

A solution to this problem of theoretical integration, however, is to drop the reliance on modernism and, instead, operate within a postmodern epistemology (Hansen 2002). Theories, under a postmodern ideological umbrella, are not considered representations, or even partial representations, of the intrinsic nature of reality. Rather, theories are narratives about the human condition. The test of their worth is their ability to bring about results, not their proximity to nature's truths. The integrative commonality of psychoanalysis and humanism, within a postmodern ideology, then, is that they are both explanatory narratives, which therapists can offer as alternatives to the life stories that cause client suffering. Depending on theoretical orientation, a counselor may tell a client that her sadness is due to erroneous thoughts, unconscious conflict, or the fact that her experience has never been properly validated and understood. From a postmodern perspective, the correct theory is the useful one, not the one that comes closest to the truth about human nature. The perplexing puzzle of theoretical integration of psychotherapy orientations, then, is solved with the adoption of a postmodern perspective (Hansen 2002). In this regard, it is arguably misguided for therapists to try to be correct about clients; they should, instead, try to be helpful.

Aside from resolving the problem of theoretical integration as applied to the practice of counseling and psychotherapy, adopting a postmodern perspective can also have other benefits. The modernist paradigm tends to encourage a relational scenario wherein the therapist, by virtue of training, has true knowledge about the human condition that clients lack. The key component of helping, within this modernist set of assumptions, is that the therapist can reveal some truth to the client that the client has not been able to detect (Hansen 2014a). If the client had not known, for instance, that irrational thoughts cause depression, the counselor can teach the client about the way pathological thoughts operate and use specialized, thought-altering techniques to bring about alleviation of the presenting complaint. The truth, which can only be detected by trained therapists, sets clients free.

As mentioned above, though, truth can have a dark side. For one, incredible abuses of power have occurred, throughout human history, when certain groups of people have claimed to know the truth (Foucault 1980). Indeed, throughout the history of the helping professions, psychotherapists and counselors have used the power inherent in their truth positions to disenfranchise, exploit, and abuse their clients (Masson 1988). I do not believe that most helping professionals are malevolent or predatory. Often, the damage that is caused by truth occurs under the psychological radar of the helping exchange. This damage does not always take the form of obvious, exploitive power plays; sometimes, it just manifests itself as a potentially damaging failure of the therapist to truly hear what a client is struggling to say.

To offer an example from my practice, I was referred an elderly client who was suffering from anxiety and panic attacks. Her husband of over forty years had died about five years prior to the time she came to see me for help. By her account, she had mourned the death for about a year, eventually recovered from the loss, and went on to a fulfilling, busy life that was full of activities she enjoyed and friends whom she held dear. Mysteriously, years after she had gained peace of mind about her loss, she began to have debilitating panic attacks along with reminiscences about her husband. Like a good psychodynamic practitioner, I let her lead the discussion and tried to learn about her life from her perspective. At first she described her marriage as happy; her husband had been her lifelong soul mate. However, as the sessions passed, she began to describe a seamier underside to their partnership. He had been an alcoholic for at least a decade of their marriage. His drunkenness had caused numerous problems and created painful periods of marital separation. Furthermore, her husband's death was largely caused by his refusal to initiate the lifestyle changes that his doctor had implored him to adopt. Eventually, she explained, his poor health habits caught up with him, and he died.

After listening to this material for several sessions, my suspicious, truth-detecting, psychoanalytic self was begin to fashion a new tale out of her old one. My client was unconsciously enraged with her husband, her rage was repressed because she felt guilty about it, and the panic attacks were a sign that these warded off feelings were threatening to burst, in all of their painful force, through the wall of consciousness. My formulation accounted for the material she presented and offered an explanation for her current difficulties. By virtue of my expertise, I had detected the truth about her and would use it to set her free from her from her symptoms. Only, it did not quite work out that way.

She repeatedly denied my suggestions that a part of her felt guilty when she thought about her husband in a negative light. Her denial was not a problem for me; I had dealt with resistance before, read plenty of books on how to handle it, and was fully prepared to help her overcome her stubborn insistence on avoiding the truth. After all, I was the expert in the room, and I had regularly observed her retreat into defensive idealizations of her husband whenever it started to occur to her that he may not have been such a great guy. My expert appraisal of her sequence of associations was far superior to any analysis of her own experience that she could come up with.

As we continued to meet, she continued to deny my interpretations. I noticed, however, that she seemed slightly amused (certainly not bothered or defensively irritated) by my repeated interpretations. Her denials came with kind, knowing smiles, an air of wisdom, and a polite, deferential courtesy that suited her age. Intrigued, and somewhat stymied, by her response, I began to listen more carefully to her description of her experience. Unlike the youth of today, she explained, she and her husband had never expected their marriage to be perfect. The tough times were simply an inevitable part of a beautiful, loving, life-long partnership. They had been together for decades, through good times and bad, and now she was just sad that he was gone.

I was touched by the raw authenticity of her description. However, I was now on the verge of a loss of my own. Perhaps I was not a highly trained expert who had learned the truth about human nature in graduate school. In fact, the biases of my truth had almost prevented me from hearing hers. For the rest of our time together, I decided to give up my narcissistic attachment to truth and try to hear what she was telling me. This was not easy. Who was I to her, if not an expert? What did I have to offer, if not the truth? Did I have any expertise at all? I was also uncomfortable with the themes of death and isolation that she wanted me to hear. It was psychologically easier for me to think of her in relatively distant, theoretical terms. Thankfully, I kept these questions and concerns in check and did not allow the anxiety caused by them to propel me back to the comforts of my old expert role. After meeting for several months, her panic attacks subsided. The therapy was a success; she met her goals, and was grateful for my help. At the time, I had no idea what I had done to help her.

Looking back on this experience, I think that the effective element of the therapy was that I eventually recognized that I was using the ideal of truth to be a distant expert instead of an emotionally involved witness to her pain. She needed time and a safe place to reminiscence about her husband and fully process the loss; I eventually provided this for her. For purposes of this discussion, my narcissistic attachment to truth, and the expert role that came with it, caused me to overlook the meanings that were important to my client. Truth, then, can be a toxic element in the counseling process, causing therapists to engage in power plays and dismiss entire realms of client meaning systems. Most importantly, a therapeutic attachment to truth can undermine the most vital element of any helping relationship: attentive listening.

As another example of the harm a modernist perspective can cause, consider the consequences of telling a client about the supposed diagnostic truth of his condition (Frances 2013). Telling a client that he has bipolar disorder, schizophrenia, or adjustment disorder, for example, has tremendous consequences for the ways he will judge his own meaning systems and how future professionals will regard him. The hidden, carrier wave in the communication of mental health diagnoses is that the client is sick, deficient, and disordered. By extension, the meanings that are formulated by the client are unimportant (both to the client and professionals), as they emanate from a broken brain. Therefore, modernist, truth-style diagnostics can silence the meaning systems that drive thoughts, feelings, and behavior.

In this regard, Polkinghorne (1992) made an important and compelling argument that the psychology profession is epistemologically split between academics, who operate from modernist assumptions, and practitioners, who intuitively draw from postmodern epistemology. Academic psychologists focus on discovering general laws of human behavior and use modernist ideology and the scientific method in the service of this pursuit. Practitioners, alternatively, develop a personal knowledge base about interventions that help clients. To help their clients, psychotherapists and counselors must be attentive to multiple truths, worldviews, and meaning systems. Tailoring interventions to individuals is a vital element of successful counseling practice. This appreciation of diverse truths and the pragmatics of helping emanates from a postmodern epistemology, not a modernist, singular truth ideological stance. Therefore, according to Polkinghorne, there is a natural divide between the modernist orientation of academics and the postmodern values of practitioners. Indeed, practitioners who adopted the universal truth, one-size-fits-all epistemology of academics would undoubtedly be unsuccessful due to their inability to adapt, and tailor interventions, to the needs and meaning systems of diverse clientele.

If the meanings that emerge during the helping encounter are considered from a relatively high level of philosophical abstraction, then, postmodernism appears to be a far better ideological fit for the practice of psychotherapy and counseling than modernism (Hansen 2014a). While the idea of universal truths may be a suitable one for academics, practitioners must struggle to consider the multiple meaning systems that their clients present. Modernism in the helping encounter poses risks related to the power dynamics of the talk therapy scenario. Furthermore, by focusing on supposed true meanings, practitioners who adopt a modernist mindset risk dismissing gross realms of meaning that are vital to understanding clients, encouraging their growth, and honoring their humanity.

Helping Orientations and Meaning Systems

Helping orientations are at a lower level of abstraction than the philosophical issues related to modernism and postmodernism discussed above. The theoretical preferences of counseling practitioners, however, exert a strong influence on the ways in which the data from the helping encounter is sorted and interpreted. Furthermore, helping orientations differentially value particular meaning systems and tend to disregard others. Therefore, when conceptualizing meaning systems in psychotherapy and counseling, it is important to consider the influence of counseling orientations.

Consider, for example, a simple phrase uttered by a client, such as, "My sister hates me." The theoretical orientation of the practitioner has consequences for the interpretation of this phrase, the subsequent questions that are asked by the therapist, and how this reported experience is conceptually understood in the context of other experiences the client has presented. A cognitively oriented therapist, for instance, would hone in on the structures of thinking in the phrase and consider how these cognitive schemas might be corrected or reframed in the service of lessening psychological suffering. Alternatively, a psychodynamic practitioner would speculate about the hidden, latent meanings, which were implied by the statement. Is the sister's hatred actually a projection of the client's self-hatred? Does the perception of hatred defend against some other feeling, such as guilt, envy, or fear of intimacy? Is this statement a metaphoric expression of the client's feeling about the therapist? Practitioners who endorse other orientations might think that the statement is unimportant or can be wholly reduced to something else. A strict behaviorist would consider the internal thoughts and feelings expressed by the utterance irrelevant because no quantifiable behaviors are revealed by it. A biological psychiatrist, alternatively, might conclude that the statement is not worthy of further investigation because it is simply the product of a diagnostic condition, such as paranoia. Clearly, theoretical orientations have tremendous consequences for the ways that meaning systems are perceived in the helping encounter.

Although there are differences between theoretical orientations in terms of the ways in which meanings are interpreted, there are also tensions within theories about how to regard meaning systems. The history of psychoanalytic theory, for instance, is an interesting case study that illustrates how tensions about meaning systems can arise, conflict, and evolve within a theoretical orientation. In this regard, Freud, at the beginning of the psychoanalytic movement, proposed an interesting, therapeutic technique, which he called free association (Gabbard 2010). Essentially, while lying on a couch, the psychoanalytic patient was instructed to describe whatever came into his or her mind without editing the content. By attending to themes, sequences, and slips of the tongue, the psychoanalyst could presumably infer the unconscious conflicts that were at the root of the patient's problems.

A method that instructs a person to give voice to whatever is on her or his mind seems like it pays the ultimate respect to meaning systems. However, while patients were instructed to speak without any filters, early psychoanalysts listened with strong, theoretical biases, with the assumption that psychosexual conflicts were at the heart of every matter. Ironically, then, Freud instructed his patients to engage in a kaleidoscopic outpouring of the meanings that constituted their inner life, but instructed therapists to limit their vision to monochrome. This internal, theoretical tension between openness to meaning systems and dismissal or reduction of meanings arguably continued as psychoanalytic theory evolved.

In this regard, Freud's (1923/1961) introduction of the structural model in 1923 had lasting implications for the way in which meaning systems were regarded by psychoanalysts. Prior to the introduction of the structural, or ego psychological model, psychoanalytic thought had relied on the topographic model, introduced in 1900 (Freud 1900/1953a), which divided the psyche into unconscious, preconscious, and conscious domains. Freud replaced this topographic model because of two fundamental problems: a) the topographic model could not account for the self-sabotaging, guilty part of self that Freud regularly observed in his patients; and b) there was no location designated in the topographic model for defense mechanisms, which are unconscious but psychologically distinct from the psychosexual wishes that resided in the unconscious portion of the topographic model (Arlow and Brenner 1964). The new, structural model solved these problems by introducing structures of the mind. One of these structures, the superego, represented the guilty part of self. Defense mechanisms resided in the unconscious portion of the ego, a core structural component of this model of the mind. Regardless of the theoretical details that inspired this new model, the important point, for purposes of this discussion, is that Freud added structures to his map of the mind in 1923.

The structural model framed psychological conflict as occurring between the unconscious wishes of the id, the harsh judgments of the superego, and external reality (Arlow and Brenner 1964). Conflict resolution, which is brought about by the ego, can either be adaptive or maladaptive. For example, suppose a husband acts abusively toward his wife, the wife is unconsciously angered by this treatment, but she has a strong superego prohibition against becoming consciously angry. One possible resolution to this dilemma is for the wife to defensively attribute fault to herself instead of to her husband, thereby keeping her anger unconscious. This resolution, however, would likely cause a maladaptive, depressive response, as the wife would be beating herself up instead of directing her anger at the original target. This example illustrates that, from the vantage point of the structural model, life is a series of ego compromises between the id, superego, and external reality (Arlow and Brenner 1964). When these compromises create psychological symptoms, they are maladaptive. Compromises can also result in happy adaptations to the demands of living, such as when a sadistic wish to witness the suffering of others is defensively transformed into an adaptive, fulfilling career (e.g., psychotherapist, medical worker), which allows the wish to be simultaneously gratified and denied.

Whatever one thinks of the structural model, note the prominent role that external reality plays in this map of the mind. The earlier, topographic model, in contrast, was restricted to the psyche. The structural model exposed the psyche to the external world, with the assumptions that the mind factored the demands of reality into its compromise formations and that resolutions to conflict could have varying degrees of adaptation to life. With the structural model, Freud opened a giant cranial window that potentially allowed the meanings of mind and world to interact and influence each other. Imagine the potential of this model to allow personal, family, group, and cultural meaning systems to be considered as an integral part of psychological life. Indeed, certain theorists (e.g., Erikson 1950) widened psychoanalysis to include psychosocial phenomena, for example. Generally speaking, however, psychoanalytic thought did not evolve in ways that honored these new realms of meaning. In fact, they were arguably shut down.

In this regard, the structural model gave rise to two, dominant theoretical trends, each of which had its own way of limiting the meanings that would be allowed into psychoanalytic ideology and practice. The first trend emphasized the role of psychological deficiency (Pine 1990). The proponents of deficiency theorizing reasoned that if the mind had structures, then it was logical to presume that the structures could be defective. Perhaps, then, if someone regularly had angry blow ups, it was because they had an ego deficit with regard to their ability to regulate emotions. To say this in another way, the anger does not really have any meaning; it only indicates a psychic deficiency. Psychological abnormalities were due to faulty internal structures; the ego or superego could have holes, like psychic Swiss cheese.

The second, prominent trend that arose from the structural model was conflict theorizing (Arlow and Brenner 1964). Conflict theorists argued that deficiency theorizing was mistaken; all psychological abnormalities, indeed everything in life, was a product of conflict resolution. One of my professors was a strong conflict theorist. As an interesting example of this point of view, he announced to my classmates and me that we must enjoy looking into books; otherwise, we would not have advanced so far in our education. "However," he asked, "what do you really want to peer into? Your parent's bedroom at night?" None of us knew how to react to this interpretation, but, apart from my professor's bizarre sounding hypothesis about our educational interests, he was making an interesting point about the conflict model. That is, all behavior, even acts that appear entirely benign, are the product of a psychic negotiation between warded off wishes, guilty prohibitions, and the demands of reality. Conflict is at the root of everything. Note, however, that even though the ego psychological model opened the door to external reality, the conflict perspective that emanates from this model, ironically, only considers meanings systems that are derived from internal, psychological negotiations. For instance, I thought I went to graduate school because education was valued in my family; I was sincerely curious about psychological topics; I wanted to help others; the wider culture supported my choice; and I wanted a job that I would enjoy and find meaningful. None of these external meaning systems, which the structural model arguably had the theoretical potential to highlight, would have been considered by conflict theorists. The conflict version of the structural model, then, truncates whole realms of meanings and solipsistically funnels reality back into conflicted, individual minds.

The evolution of psychoanalytic theorizing, then, can arguably be interpreted as an ongoing struggle with ambivalence about meaning systems. Developments in theory and practice, such as ego psychology and free association, invited new realms of meaning into psychoanalytic thought. However, after the floodgates of meaning were opened, they were theoretically limited or shut down. As I argue in a subsequent chapter, there are multiple possible reasons that an openness to meaning systems is regularly met with a counterforce that limits their expression. One likely reason is that taking client meaning systems seriously can undermine the authority and supposed expertise of the counselor or psychotherapist. In the clinical example I offered above, my eventual openness to the widow's meaning systems threatened to undermine my status as an expert. My initial instinct was to view her unwillingness to accept my interpretations as an act of resistance, thereby allowing my status as a highly trained expert to be retained. However, once I decided to truly listen to her meanings, which were not the same as my supposed expert opinions, I had to give up my power and authority in the relationship. She was the expert, not me. Perhaps my initial reaction to hold onto my expert status by limiting the validity of her report has also been present at a wider professional level throughout the history of mental health care. Speculatively, then, the cycle is: a) a professional theory or technique that values client meanings gains traction in mental health culture; b) this openness to client meanings causes anxiety in professionals, as it risks undermining their status as experts; and c) counter ideological measures are proposed to limit the significance of client meanings, so that professional expertise is restored. Again, various explanations for shutting down meaning systems are proposed in the next chapter.

SUMMARY AND CONCLUSIONS

To review, I have provided a definition of meaning systems, which includes individual, group, and cultural ways of making sense of the world. Although this definition may seem very broad, language is a common denominator of all meaning systems, thereby unifying the seemingly diverse elements of this definition. All meanings, even the unspoken phenomenological flow of subjective experience, is constituted by language. Therefore, the role, function, and epistemological status of language must be clarified to achieve useful conceptualizations of meaning systems.

In this regard, I reviewed the basic assumptions of two, wide-ranging epistemological movements (i.e., modernism and postmodernism) in terms of their assumptions about language. Modernism presumes that language can be correspondent with reality. That is, certain combinations of words can be true in the sense that they match the intrinsic nature of reality, which exists beyond the words. Postmodernism, in contrast, does not support the assumption that words can be correspondent with some extra-linguistic reality. Language is a tool invented by people. Therefore, whenever something is described, it is automatically tainted by human-invented linguistic categories. Combinations of words, then, according to the postmodern movement known as neopragmatism, should be judged according to their usefulness, not by their correspondence with the intrinsic nature of reality.

I argued that there are compelling reasons to favor the postmodern perspective when conceptualizing the meaning systems that emerge in psychotherapy and counseling. First, the modernist paradigm in social sciences has arguably not resulted in many advances when compared to the natural sciences, such as medical research. Second, unlike chemicals, molecules, and cells, humans are not entirely determined by enduring laws of nature. People socially construct their own laws and follow them. Third, it is arguably impossible to advance the helping professions through a theoretical integration of various orientations within a modernist paradigm. Using postmodernism, however, seemingly incompatible theories can be integrated as narratives that have varying degrees of utility for changing lives. Last, abuses of power have occurred throughout history when one group claims to know the truth and another is accused of endorsing falsehoods. These abuses have also occurred in the helping professions, wherein, in modernist fashion, one member of the helping dyad is defined as the expert and the other is treated as an unenlightened sufferer. Perhaps, consistent with a postmodern paradigm, giving up the idea that therapists possess truth would result in fewer abuses of power in the practice of psychotherapy and counseling. Added to the above reasons to favor a postmodern epistemology over a modernist one when conceptualizing meaning systems in the helping encounter, the logic of the postmodern critique of modernism is highly compelling.

At a lower level of abstraction, beneath modern and postmodern epistemologies, counseling orientations play an important role in conceptualizing meaning systems. A cognitive practitioner, psychoanalyst, and behaviorist, for example, would likely interpret the same utterances in very different ways, perhaps with little agreement about the psychological implications of certain verbalizations and the potential meanings that should be considered important versus the ones that should be dismissed altogether. Using the evolution of psychoanalytic theory as a case study, I speculated that helping orientations perhaps reveal an ongoing ambivalence about being open to meaning systems that is enacted on a large-scale, professional level. Building on this ambivalence hypothesis, the next chapter reviews the history of mental health culture with particular attention to the value given to meaning systems during various eras. I make the argument that ambivalence about listening to clients is not only an underlying theme in the evolution of psychoanalytic theory, but that this ambivalence is an intrinsic part of the unfolding course of mental health culture.

Chapter Three

Meaning Systems and Mental Health Culture

In the previous chapters, I attempted to establish the importance of meaning systems to psychological suffering, healing, and the practice of counseling and psychotherapy. People construct systems of meaning on individual, group, and cultural levels. Unlike physical matter, which is exclusively subject to the laws of nature, humans continually construct the laws they follow. Inquiries into human behavior, then, require more than a strict scientific investigation aimed at revealing supposed universal principles of human conduct; the meanings that people create must also be appreciated and understood. With regard to the helping process, I have argued that the meanings that emerge during psychotherapy and counseling should be conceptualized in terms of their usefulness, not according to their supposed correspondence with the intrinsic nature of reality. By adopting the medical model, contemporary counseling and psychotherapy practice have severely minimized the importance of meaning systems in the helping encounter. This current professional trend of downplaying the significance of individual, group, and cultural ways of making sense of the world is completely counterintuitive, given the obvious importance of meanings to psychological suffering and behavior.

However, perhaps a counterargument should be entertained. In this regard, maybe I am just an old-style humanist who sentimentally longs for the days when therapy was an art, helping was necessarily an intimate process, clients had problems of living (not disorders), and empathy played a central role in the therapeutic process. Perhaps I should just get out of the way and stop trying to subvert the progress that the new brain-based, medicalized era can bring. I think that the above counterargument would have some merit if mental health care evolved in a stepwise, progressive fashion. If I were a medical professional arguing that bloodletting should be brought back as part of health care instead of these new-fangled vaccines and antibiotics, I would quite obviously be a misguided quack. This is because the practice of medicine, generally speaking, advances according to new scientific findings. Of course, the medical professions are subject to trends, fads, financial influences, power dynamics, and other factors. However, because the field of medicine is focused on intervening in the material, physical realm, a progressive understanding of the laws that dictate bodily functioning, via scientific research, generally results in incremental advances to the medical professions over time. Generally speaking, physicians are better able to help patients now than they were twenty years ago. There is no evidence that the same can be said of therapists.

Why, however, have the helping professions not progressed incrementally at the same rate as the natural sciences? Of course, progress has been made in the talk therapies, as contemporary counselors and psychotherapists have learned from research findings and the mistakes of their predecessors. For example, modern therapists hopefully know that they should not badger their clients to recall traumatic events (Wright 1994), schizophrenia does not likely result from schizophrenogenic parents (Lidz 1973), and no single treatment paradigm is inherently superior to all others (Wampold 2001), to name a few examples. Arguably, these and other findings certainly represent professional progress, although this rate of progress pales in comparison to the revolutionary advances made by the natural sciences during the past century.

As a suggested explanation for these differential rates of progress, the talk therapies are concerned with nonmaterial, meaning-based phenomena, while the natural sciences are focused on understanding material elements of the world. Counseling and psychotherapy, then, are arguably more akin to the humanities than the sciences (Hansen 2012). In this regard, assessing progress in the helping professions is at least somewhat analogous to assessing progress in the professions of poetry and music. Progress in these professions is gauged in terms of novel contributions, the ability to engage audiences, integration of alternative influences, and the potential to transform new generations. It would not be tenable to argue that hip-hop, for instance, is inherently superior to zydeco music. However, it would certainly be reasonable to claim that music tends to adapt to the times and integrate new styles based on current trends as it evolves; otherwise, it would lose aesthetic appeal and the power to engage listeners. Progress in music, then, is defined in entirely different ways than progress in the natural sciences.

Incidentally, these different definitions of progress became very apparent to me when I served on a university committee, which was charged with identifying professors who had made significant scholarly contributions during the previous year. The top nominees were a chemist and a theatre professor. Which one, we were asked, had done more to advance their respective field? To evaluate the chemist, the committee considered the number of refereed publications, how many times his work had been cited, and the influence of his research based on letters from eminent peers in his field. Evaluating the degree to which the theatre professor had advanced her profession, however, was a different task altogether. Her job was not to make discoveries or hone in on the laws of nature; she coordinated performances and wrote plays. Factors like originality and scope of her influence had to be considered. Both professors had clearly made major contributions to their respective fields, but the criteria the committee used to evaluate the representative from the material world of chemistry were necessarily very different from the criteria used to evaluate the theatre professor, who was engaged in the nonmaterial world of meaning systems.

So, are counselors and psychotherapists more like chemists or theatre professors? To broaden this question, do helping professionals primarily spend their careers investigating material or nonmaterial realities? The answer has implications for the way that progress in the helping professions is appraised and how the evolution of psychotherapy and counseling is understood. I think that the helping professions bear a much stronger resemblance to theatre than chemistry. The fundamental activity that takes place during a therapeutic encounter is talking (Hansen 2014b). Therapists spend their workdays delving into the realm of nonmaterial meaning systems, not material realities. Of course, the helping professions should absolutely be informed by scientific findings, particularly outcome research. Indeed, as noted above, scientific findings have advanced psychotherapy and counseling, just not nearly to the same degree as they have advanced medicine. Therefore, I am certainly not advocating for science to have no role in counseling and psychotherapy; indeed, science plays a vitally important role in the evolution of the helping professions. However, psychotherapy is primarily an art that deals with meaning systems, thereby making it much more akin to the humanities than to the sciences (Hansen, 2012). It is important to keep this humanities connection in mind when appraising the history, evolution, and progress of the talk therapy professions.

Indeed, in the material realm, science tends to reign in, focus, and narrow the evolutionary course of the various professions that are devoted to studying physical hunks of matter. In modern medicine, for example, a new treatment introduced by an influential member of the medical community would almost certainly not be adopted as standard medical practice unless the efficacy of the treatment had been scientifically verified first. Contrast this scientific standard with the historical introduction of treatment methods in the helping professions. Indeed, psychoanalysis (Freud 1916/1963), primal scream (Janov 1970), gestalt therapy (Perls 1969), and virtually every other treatment movement in the talk therapies became widely adopted primarily due to the persuasive appeal of their respective founders, not because of scientific evidence. As noted above, psychotherapy and counseling are more akin to the humanities than science. Therefore, persuasive appeal is certainly an important element in influencing and changing people's lives, just as it is in music or literature (Frank and Frank 1993). Psychoanalysis and primal scream were likely effective treatment paradigms during eras when they had widespread appeal and people had a strong sense of excitement and confidence about the potential of these methods to alleviate psychological suffering.

Indeed, I believe that those who would like the talk therapies to be entirely driven by scientific findings are misguided. If the round peg of psychotherapy is recklessly pounded into the square hole of science, the human element, the empathic appreciation of the meaning systems that drive the process, is necessarily lost. The aspiration to make the talk therapies entirely scientific is as silly as a hypothetical goal to make marriage entirely scientific. Certainly, there are scientific findings about the factors that constitute a good marriage, and married couples might benefit from learning about some of these findings. However, it would obviously be absurd to propose that courtship and marital relations should be manualized processes that are completely determined by scientific findings. Analogously, it is just as absurd to propose that science should wholly determine relational helping.

My central point, which is designed to prepare the reader for the next section, is that the evolution of the helping professions is not constrained by science, like medicine; indeed, this is the way it should be. However, this lack of scientific constraint makes the historical evolution of psychotherapy and counseling highly susceptible to trends, fads, and other nonscientific influences, just like fashion or music. In this regard, it is useful to view the history of the helping professions through a cultural lens, which is attuned to the values, norms, and ideals of particular eras (Hansen 2014a). Indeed, various insightful, cultural analyses of the helping professions have been conducted, including cultural factors related to treatment orientations (Fancher 1995), psychoanalytic institutes (Kirsner 2009), psychotherapy training (Davies 2009), psychiatric residencies (Luhrmann 2000), and the international spread of psychiatric disorders (Waters 2010). In a previous book (Hansen 2014a), I have also examined the history of mental health care from a cultural point of view.

In the following brief, historical discussion, however, I give particular attention to a central, organizing spectrum that can be used to understand the unfolding course of mental health culture. One end of this spectrum gives the highest priority to materialism and science. The other end prizes nonmaterial meaning systems. The evolution of mental health culture can be understood as a series of periodic alternations between the two ends of this spectrum (Decker 2013; Hansen 2009; 2014a). In this regard, reflection on other human activities suggests that it can be useful to posit a central spectrum to organize and give meaning to the unfolding historical evolution of particular subcultures. For instance, the cultural course of financial markets can be understood in terms of the bearish or bullish attitudes that have characterized particular eras. Likewise, the conservative versus liberal spectrum can be used to bring order and meaning to the culture of politics.

Because the talk therapies are situated somewhere between the material concerns of science and the nonmaterial subject matter of the arts and humanities, it should come as no surprise that a spectrum with material and nonmaterial endpoints can be used to understand the unfolding cultural course of mental health care. Indeed, like bears and bulls in the financial markets, when one end of the spectrum is dominant in mental health culture, the other is arguably suppressed (Hansen 2014a). During the heyday of excitement about internet stocks during the 1990s, bearish voices could scarcely be heard. In the midst of the financial crisis a decade later, however, the bulls were virtually silenced as the bears began to dominate financial culture. Analogously, mental health culture ping-pongs between material and nonmaterial value systems, and, when one side of the spectrum is dominant, the other is arguably suppressed (Decker 2013; Hansen 2009; 2014a). To understand the factors that gave rise to the suppression of meaning systems in psychotherapy and counseling during the current era, it is important to view the unfolding historical evolution of mental health culture through the lens of this spectrum.

A BRIEF HISTORY OF MENTAL HEALTH CULTURE

What is a mental health problem? How do you know if someone has been helped? What kind of help should be provided to people who suffer from psychological difficulties? These are some of the fundamental questions that have defined the course of the helping professions. Different answers to these questions have been offered at different points in history, depending on the values and perspectives that were dominant during particular eras. Viewing the history of mental health care through a cultural lens, then, can lead to new insights and understandings about the ongoing evolution of the helping professions. As mentioned above, framing this cultural analysis according to a spectrum with a material, biological perspective at one end and a nonmaterial, mental point of view at the other, can lead to new understandings about the devaluation of meaning systems in contemporary mental health culture.

When, though, did mental health care become a culture? Arguably, there have always been various, pocketed subcultures, which held certain perspectives about people who were afflicted with psychological problems, going back at least to ancient times when trepanning, or drilling holes in the skull, was practiced as a method to allow evil entities (the presumed cause of mental abnormalities) to escape (Porter 2002). Indeed, locating the source of mental health problems in the skull, and fashioning various skull-based interventions, has been a strong, recurring theme of mental health culture throughout history; this theme has become dominant again in contemporary times. Clearly, then, mental health culture is subject to ideological trends, which define particular eras. At what historical point, though, should a cultural analysis of these trends begin?

Psychotherapy was introduced during the late nineteenth century. In the mid-1800s, however, half a century before Freud invented the talking cure, psychiatry emerged as a distinct medical specialty, a historical marker which indicates that a professionalized culture of mental health care was underway at the time (Porter 2002). During the era when their profession was founded, psychiatrists worked almost exclusively as administrators of mental asylums. Asylums created the need for professional administrators, who eventually collaborated to form the distinct medical specialty of psychiatry (Shorter 1997). The asylum movement, then, as a strong, historical precursor to organized, modern, professional mental health care, set the stage for mental health culture for centuries to come. Therefore, the beginning of the asylum movement is a reasonable place to begin a historical, cultural analysis of mental health care, as particular values, norms, and attitudes about mental health issues began to coalesce around the collective goal of establishing asylums and treating asylum residents.

Numerous asylums for the mentally ill were founded during the late eighteenth and early nineteenth centuries (Dowbiggin 2011; Shorter 1997). Specialized residences for the mentally ill were established throughout the United States and Europe during this time. Some of these asylums were living quarters in private homes, while others took the form of large campuses. There are various hypotheses about the reasons that the asylum movement occurred at this point in history. Notably, Foucault (1965) speculated that the end of leprosy in Europe created a need for a new population to be defined as different or abnormal. The huge, empty leprosariums were eventually filled with the mad (i.e., the new lepers), thereby satisfying a societal need to exclude a particular group. Whatever one thinks of Foucault's speculation, the asylum movement gained traction in the late eighteenth century, as the mass introduction of specialized residences for the mentally ill set the stage for modern mental health care.

Once asylums were established, various ways of treating residents were proposed. As mentioned above, these treatment methods can be divided into two, general categories: a) materialistic, which regarded the physical body as central to the causes and treatments of mental abnormalities, and b) the nonmaterial perspective, which viewed psychological suffering as a phenomenon that should be understood and treated within the psychosocial realm (Decker 2013). Early materialistic, bodily methods of treating asylum residents included removal of their intestines, inducing sleep for multiple days at a time, and strapping residents in a hanging chair that was swung for hours (Shorter 1997; Whitaker 2002). Supposed medical treatments were often primitive, barbaric, and did nothing to promote cure. During the periods of the nineteenth century when biological interventions were in vogue, asylum residents usually lived in deplorable conditions and were sometimes even chained to walls. Thankfully, reformers, who were shocked and outraged by these living conditions, promoted *moral treatment* as an alternative to biological interventions (Dowbiggin 2011; Whitaker 2002).

Proponents of moral treatment argued that asylum residents should be treated with respect and kindness, analogous to the way that parents treat their children. With the moral treatment model, residents were kept busy with a daily schedule of duties and activities. Although the authoritarian structure of the asylum was still in place, patients and staff often participated in activities together. Love, respect, the guidance of wise authorities, and an orderly, scheduled day were the medicines of moral therapy. By using the institutional environment as a therapeutic tool, moral therapies were designed to bring about recovery through psychosocial (i.e., nonmaterial) means, not by intervening on a material, bodily level (Hollander 1981).

Biological and psychosocial treatments were used in asylum care throughout the nineteenth century. Notably, during the latter part of the 1800s, two highly influential figures proposed ideas that set the course for mental health culture for the twentieth century and beyond. The first, from the materialist camp, was Emil Kraepelin, a German psychiatrist who advocated a system of psychiatric classification based on symptoms (Greenberg 2010; 2013; Shorter 1997). The second, Sigmund Freud, was a Viennese neurologist who developed psychoanalysis, a theory of the mind and a psychological method of treatment (Gay 1988). These theorists, who proposed their foundational ideas during the same era, are iconic representatives of the material and nonmaterial visions of the helping process. Their central ideas continue to reverberate throughout mental health culture today.

Kraepelin proposed a model for categorizing mental health problems. Because the causes and cures for mental illnesses were unknown during his time, Kraepelin reasoned that a system of classifying varieties of psychological suffering would be a logical first step, which might eventually lead to important advances in the field. If conditions could be reliably identified, then professionals would have a common language to diagnose and investigate various mental health abnormalities. Asylum residents could not be classified according to the underlying causes of their conditions; the causes were unknown. Therefore, Kraepelin decided to base his diagnostic system exclusively on symptoms because there could presumably be a high level of agreement among professionals about observable symptomatology (Greenberg 2010; 2013; Shorter 1997).

Kraepelin's diagnostic model, which is called *descriptive psychiatry*, relies on descriptions of symptoms alone to categorize patients. Kraepelin reasoned that if co-occurring clusters of symptoms could be identified, then the course of an illness could be followed, and causes and treatments would eventually be discovered. Prior to making discoveries about mental health conditions, however, the conditions had to be reliably identified. Kraepelin thought that the best way to reliably identify mental illnesses was to classify them by observable symptoms. Note that Kraepelin's assumptions place him squarely in the materialist camp, as his diagnostic model had nothing to do with psychology or meaning systems; indeed, Kraepelin presumed that mental illnesses were caused by biological abnormalities (Greenberg 2010; 2013; Shorter 1997).

Kraepelin's ideas were influential during his time. However, decades after it was proposed, descriptive psychiatry would be revived and come to dominate mental health culture. As the twentieth century progressed, however, Kraepelinian thought was ideologically eclipsed by the nonmaterial, psychological theory of one of his contemporaries: Sigmund Freud.

From Freud's early life, pursuits, and interests, it seemed as if his course was set to make contributions in the material, biological realm, not propose ideas about psychology and meaning systems (Gay 1988). An aspiring research neurologist, Freud had hoped to secure a position as a professor. However, because of anti-Semitism and other factors, he was not able to obtain a professorial position. To support his family, Freud was forced to start an outpatient neurology practice. Turn-of-the-century Viennese neurology was, of course, very different from neurological practices today. Freud essentially helped people with nervous conditions, or bodily or emotional reactions that could not be explained by, or outright contradicted, what was known about physiology at the time. For instance, glove paralysis, a condition whereby the hand is unable to move but the arm functions normally, was known to be a neurological impossibility, yet people were afflicted with this symptom (McWilliams 1999). These type of conditions were seen by the nerve doctors of the time.

Freud experimented with various treatments for nervous conditions, such as hypnosis and cocaine. He eventually became fascinated with nervous conditions and turned his attention to helping people who suffered from these afflictions (Gay 1988). As an interesting material parallel to Freud's nonmaterial approach, Freud's friend and respected colleague at the turn of the century was Wilhelm Fleiss. Fleiss, a surgeon, believed that nervous conditions were caused by nasal abnormalities. Freud referred patients to Fleiss, who performed nasal surgery on them. There were eventual fallouts in the Freud-Fleiss relationship, however, and Freud became committed to a psychological approach to helping (Masson 1984). Notably, though, Freud thought that physical correlates to mental health conditions might be discovered one day (Gay 1988).

Although Freudian theory evolved over the years, the central postulate of psychoanalysis is that everyone has an unconscious mental life that is inaccessible to them (Pine 1990). Thoughts, feelings, fantasies, and memories that are too painful to be experienced consciously are disavowed and repressed in the unconscious. Although a person is unable to access her or his unconscious, the contents of the unconscious are libidinally energized, so they continue to have a strong force in the personality, albeit in derivative fashion. For instance, a person may be angry with a parent. If the anger is repressed because it is unacceptable to consciousness, it may make an appearance in a disguised form, such as the person displacing the anger on someone else, the anger turning in on the self, or the person becoming exceedingly gratuitous to the parent, as a way of hiding their true feelings from him or herself. Again, psychoanalysis is a complex theory that evolved in multiple stages. Even the brief example of a person experiencing anger noted above draws from both early drive and subsequent ego psychological theorizing (Pine 1990). However, unconscious motivation is a central postulate of all psychoanalytic theorizing.

Psychoanalysis spread throughout the world during the early- and mid-twentieth century. The spread of this formerly regional, mostly Jewish, Viennese movement was due to several factors. First, early in its evolution, psychoanalysis was a relatively open movement that attracted a variety of Viennese intellectuals. As psychoanalysis progressed, however, Freud began to define and enforce certain articles of psychoanalytic belief, such as the centrality of psychosexual motivation. No longer an open movement, Freud expelled former disciples who violated the party-lines of psychoanalytic thought. Although the loss of intellectual freedom in psychoanalysis was regrettable in one respect, the new, codified movement may have had wider appeal precisely because of its firm, graspable postulates (Makari 2008). Second, the looming Nazi threat caused many of the original psychoanalysts, most of whom were Jewish, to flee European danger areas to safe havens. Freud fled to England, but many sought exile in America where they established psychoanalytic institutes and took positions at universities. This dispersal of the original followers caused psychoanalysis to spread throughout the world (Jacoby 1983; Makari 2008; Shorter 1997). Third, some of the soldiers from World War I came home with a condition that, at the time, was called shell shock. Later referred to as Post-Traumatic Stress Disorder, shell shock was a strong selling point for the outpatient practice of psychiatry (Dowbiggin 2011). After all, if formerly normal people could endure experiences that caused them to have psychiatric symptoms, perhaps the vagaries of ordinary life could also cause people to have mental conditions, which could be treated by outpatient psychiatrists. Thus, the historical door to outpatient psychiatric practice was opened. At the turn of the century, psychiatrists almost exclusively worked as asylum administrators. With the public primed to accept psychiatry as an outpatient practice, psychoanalysis as the only extant outpatient treatment model was able to fill the need (Shorter 1997).

When psychoanalysis began to become acceptable and popular, the American psychiatric profession claimed it as their territory and actively banned other professionals from practicing it (Shorter 1997). Freud, a neurologist, was opposed to this psychiatric exclusivity (Freud 1926/1959). Despite Freud's protests, nonpsychiatrists were banned from being trained at American psychoanalytic institutes until the mid-1980s (McWilliams 2004). Defining psychoanalysis as an exclusive, psychiatric profession probably contributed to the rise and prestige of psychoanalysis in the mid-twentieth century. Indeed, to become an elite member of the psychiatric profession in the 1950s and 1960s, one had to become a psychoanalyst. The association with psychiatry, the newfound public need for outpatient treatment, and the fact that psychoanalysis was the only talk therapy available for decades, all contributed to the rapid spread of psychoanalysis. America, and much of the world, was overtaken by a nonmaterial understanding of psychological suffering: it was caused by unconscious conflicts and psychoanalytic psychiatrists could treat it.

Although the pendulum had swung to the nonmaterial side of the spectrum in the mid-twentieth century, new materialist, bodily treatments were also being proposed during this time. Some of these treatments were largely confined to asylums. Various types of shock treatments, for instance, were dominant in mental hospitals during the first half of the 1900s (Greenberg 2010; Shorter 1997). Indeed, to illustrate the way that mental health culture is subject to trends, shock treatments, after largely being abandoned for decades, have made a comeback in the form of electroconvulsive therapy. However, the most notable material, biological intervention of the mid-twentieth century, which spread beyond the confines of the asylum, was lobotomy.

Originally called leucotomy, surgical destruction of brain tissue to bring about relief from psychiatric symptoms was first conceived by Moniz, a Portuguese neurosurgeon who was eventually awarded the Nobel Prize for inventing lobotomy (El-Hai 2005; Whitaker 2010). Moniz's method involved anesthesia, cutting a hole in the skull, and other factors associated with traditional surgical procedures. These factors meant that the surgery required specialized expertise, was relatively lengthy, and required significant recovery time. Walter Freeman, an American neurologist, contributed to the spread of lobotomy as a treatment option by transforming the procedure into a relatively quick, minimally invasive method that could be performed in an outpatient practice.

While rummaging through his kitchen drawer, Freeman saw an ice pick, the perfect surgical tool for laborious lobotomies to be transformed into the relatively quick and simple procedure called transorbital lobotomy. Essentially, the icepick was inserted under the eyelid, where it could find a direct route to the brain. The instrument was subsequently tapped and moved in such a way that it destroyed brain tissue. Transorbital lobotomy was relatively simple, quick, and could even be performed as an outpatient procedure. Freeman spent his professional life actively promoting transorbital lobotomy and it spread throughout the world (El-Hai 2005). There were critics who thought that the procedure was barbaric and that it was an outrageous ethical violation to define the destruction of brain tissue as a medical procedure. During its heyday, however, these critiques did little to stop the momentum of the transorbital lobotomy procedure, which was heralded by its proponents as a medical breakthrough in the treatment of mental illness.

Interestingly, on the nonmaterial side of the spectrum, a new asylum treatment was also introduced in the mid-century. Jones (1953) formulated the therapeutic community as a treatment for residents of psychiatric institutions. Therapeutic communities bear a close resemblance to the earlier moral treatments (Hollander 1981). With therapeutic communities, however, the lines of authority are nearly dissolved. Patients and staff are virtually regarded as peers, have regular meetings, and can confront one another on relatively equal ground. Again, like the historically earlier moral treatment, treating asylum residents with dignity, respect, and valuing their opinions within the therapeutic community was thought to be a route to restoring their mental health.

Given the simultaneous presence of both material and nonmaterial approaches to the treatment of mental health problems, however, it would be inaccurate and too simplistic to describe mental health culture as grossly alternating between material and nonmaterial perspectives. Clearly, these perspectives have occurred simultaneously during historical eras. However, one side of the spectrum can arguably be seen as relatively dominant, particularly in certain regions. Even with the various material and nonmaterial currents running through mid-twentieth century mental health culture, psychoanalysis was arguably the relatively dominant, and perhaps most influential, ideology during that era. Notably, however, simply because a perspective advocates listening to patients instead of intervening on a bodily level, it does not necessarily mean that proponents of the perspective are entirely open to the vast realm of meaning systems. Indeed, psychoanalysis, as it evolved, arguably became increasingly closed to the nuances of what was on the minds of psychoanalytic patients (Fancher 1995; Kirsner 2009).

In this regard, the cultural evolution of psychoanalysis as it unfolded in America is an interesting study in itself. As mentioned above, psychoanalysis quickly became restricted to psychiatrists after it landed on American soil.

This professional restriction certainly narrowed the scope of the new ideas that were considered admissible to the psychoanalytic body of thought. Restriction on new ways of viewing people naturally resulted in defined, acceptable ways to interpret the free associations of psychoanalytic patients. Indeed, as psychoanalytic culture evolved in America, psychoanalytic institutes became very dogmatic, akin to religious institutions (Kirsner 2009). Proponents of alternative views of psychoanalysis, such as European object relations theorists, were actively excluded from American institutes. These restrictive, exclusionary practices severely narrowed the range of client meaning systems that practicing psychoanalysts were willing and able to hear. Indeed, it is extraordinarily ironic that psychoanalysts, who have spent more time (i.e., multiple days a week for years) listening to patients than any other professionals, kept seeing the laws of a very narrow version of psychoanalysis confirmed with virtually every patient they saw (Fancher 1995). Underneath it all, women were afflicted with penis envy and men with castration anxiety. Of course, it was a bit more complex than I am portraying it. However, listening to patients free associate for thousands of hours should arguably result in continual conceptual advances and unique, nuanced understandings of the numerous experiential and social factors that constitute life. Generally speaking, however, these developments did not occur. Simply because a nonmaterial system is dominant, it does not necessarily mean that professionals are really listening to their clients.

Regardless of whether they were truly attentive to the meanings systems of their clients, psychoanalysis was arguably the dominant force in mental health culture in the mid-twentieth century (Makari 2008; Shorter 1997). Several factors, however, resulted in the dethronement of psychoanalysis and simultaneously gave rise to a new material, biological psychiatry. First, new medications were introduced in the 1950s (Greenberg 2010; Shorter 1997). Thorazine, despite its severe side effects, helped to dampen the symptoms of schizophrenia. People who had resided in psychiatric hospitals for years and had chronic, debilitating schizophrenic symptoms, found new relief from their hallucinations and delusions with thorazine, thereby elevating them to a higher level of functioning. Lithium, introduced during the same era, was a godsend to people afflicted with manic depression. Nothing seemed to control alternations between psychotically energized highs and depressive, suicidal lows until lithium was introduced. In short, the material, biological psychiatrists scored a few wins in the mid-century. For the first time in history, biological treatments for mental health conditions were introduced that arguably did more good than harm.

Meanwhile, in the midst of this relative biological success, research psychologists were critiquing the effectiveness of psychoanalysis. Eysenck (1952), for instance, charged that psychoanalysis did not actually help patients. While, at first, these academic critiques were easily shrugged off by the psychoanalytic royalty, they began to negatively impact the dominance of psychoanalysis, particularly as new, competitive treatments were introduced. Systematic desensitization, a behaviorally derived treatment, was developed as a relatively brief method to cure phobias (Wolpe 1958). Instead of seeking five-day-a-week psychoanalysis for half a decade to uncover and work through the hidden psychosexual conflicts lurking behind one's fear of public speaking, for example, the fear could easily be cured in a dozen sessions by a practitioner of systematic desensitization. Other, new competitors in the mental health marketplace also began to appear. Rational emotive behavior therapy (REBT) practitioners, for instance, directly challenged the irrational thoughts that these practitioners presumed were driving symptoms (Ellis and Grieger 1977). Like systematic desensitization, REBT was a brief, focused treatment. These new treatments were an attractive alternative to the long-term, exploratory methods of psychoanalysis. With the introduction of competitors to psychoanalysis, psychologists, social workers, and counselors began to lobby to become licensed as psychotherapy treatment providers (Fancher 1995). These efforts were eventually successful. Therefore, in addition to the introduction of useful biological treatments, the dissolving monopolies of psychiatrists as sole treatment providers, and psychoanalysis as the only available method of talk therapy, also contributed to the decline of nonmaterial psychoanalysis and the rise of material, biological psychiatry from the mid-1950s onward.

One of these new psychotherapy treatment orientations deserves special consideration in the context of a discussion about meaning systems. Psychological humanism became a powerful force in mental health culture during the 1960s and 1970s (DeCarvalho 1990). Its early proponents, such as Rogers (1951) and Maslow (1968), rejected the reductionism of psychoanalysis and behaviorism, which were the predominant treatment orientations at the time (Davidson 2000; DeCarvalho 1990). Humanists charged that psychoanalysis reduced people to psychic structures, such as the ego, superego, and object representations. Behaviorism, according to humanists, advocated a different version of reductionism, reducing people to stimulus-response contingencies. Humanism, sometimes called a third-force in psychology for its emergence after psychoanalysis and behaviorism, idealized authentic, unreduced, relational encounters with clients. According to humanists, every client had unique meaning systems and perspectives that needed to be understood and appreciated as a key element of the helping process. Reducing clients to baser processes, then, was antithetical to helping them (Matson 1971).

During the 1960s, as biological psychiatry was beginning to ascend and psychoanalytic psychiatry was starting to decline, the humanistic movement was having a major impact on mental health culture. The seeds of humanistic ideals spread and related movements, such as Gestalt therapy (Perls 1969) and encounter groups, which valued meaning systems and authentic therapeutic relating, were launched. Therefore, in some respects, nonmaterial humanism and the new, material biological psychiatry were ascendant at about the same time. However, during the 1970s, the psychiatric profession endured challenges and underwent changes that would cause the material approach to become dominant in the subsequent decades.

Although, nonpsychiatric talk therapists were active during the 1970s, it is particularly important to note changes that were occurring in the psychiatric profession during that era. Psychiatry, even after the emergence of talk therapists from other disciplines, led mental health culture. Psychiatrists have the most power, prestige, and remuneration for services of the mental health professions. Professionals from other disciplines have historically tended to follow the lead of professional psychiatry in the hopes of gaining some of the privileges that psychiatrists have. Therefore, understanding the transformations that occur in organized psychiatry is crucial to understanding subsequent cultural changes in the talk therapy professions. In this regard, the 1970s were a tremendous era of challenges and transformation for the psychiatric profession that set the course for mental health culture, and the ways that meaning systems are regarded, through the present day.

During the 1970s, professional psychiatry was in a state of crisis. At least four factors were responsible for the state of the profession. First, there was an active and influential anti-psychiatry movement, which began in the 1960s (Shorter 1997). Represented in popular culture in the form of books and movies, such as *One Flew Over the Cuckoo's Nest* (Kesey 1962), the proponents of anti-psychiatry portrayed psychiatrists as brutal and authoritarian, indiscriminately robbing people of their liberty by locking them away in psychiatric hospitals, wherein patients were subject to sadistic measures, disguised as treatment, if they rebelled against psychiatric authority. Thomas Szasz, an influential psychiatrist and hero of this movement, even charged that mental illness is a myth (1961). This anti-psychiatry movement can be understood as one expression of the general spirit of the 1960s, which was virtually defined by rebellion against established authorities. When psychiatrists became the authority figures who were rebelled against, it severely damaged the public image of the psychiatric profession.

Second, Rosenhan (1973), a psychology professor, conducted a highly influential study about psychiatric diagnostics. In this study, Rosenhan and graduate students faked mental health symptoms and were subsequently admitted to psychiatric hospitals. Once admitted, the imposters acted normally and reported to hospital staff that they were not having any mental health symptoms. All of the pseudopatients continued to be identified as being mentally ill by hospital personnel, even after they had spent weeks in the hospital acting normally and denying any problems. To add insult to injury, staff at another hospital heard about the results of this study, believed that they would be able to distinguish mental illness from normalcy, and challenged Rosenhan to send them pseudopatients. Rosenhan agreed and, after the specified period of time, the hospital personnel presented Rosenhan with a list of imposter patients that they had identified as being normal. At that point, Rosenhan confessed that he never sent anyone to their hospital.

The Rosenhan studies were devastating for psychiatry's image as a medical profession. To contrast Rosenhan's findings with diagnostics in formal medicine, if someone were to come to a hospital deliberately faking a heart attack, they would be subject to a series of diagnostic tests, which would eventually reveal that they were not having any cardiac problems. Lacking objective tests, psychiatrists rely on observation, patient report, and clinical judgment to make diagnostic judgments. Rosenhan exposed just how biased diagnostic judgment in the mental health realm could be. Simply being admitted to a psychiatric hospital was evidence enough to convince psychiatric personnel that a person must be ill.

Third, the homosexuality vote also undermined public confidence in psychiatric diagnostics. Largely due to pressures from advocacy groups, in 1973 psychiatrists voted that homosexuality would no longer be considered a mental disorder (Shorter 1997). Although this highly contested, narrowly decided vote was a watershed moment for human rights, the decision publicized the fact that psychiatrists determine their diagnostic categories by professional consensus. In other words, they are simply winging it, making up diagnostic categories as they go along. Again, contrast this psychiatric approach to diagnostics in formal medicine. The medical professions cannot eliminate cancer or diabetes by voting to no longer consider them diseases. Psychiatrists, however, had eradicated one of their illnesses by vote.

In addition to the problems created by the anti-psychiatry movement and the shaky ground of psychiatric diagnostics, organized psychiatry, during the 1970s, was split between psychoanalytic practitioners and the new generation of biological psychiatrists (Decker 2013; Shorter 1997). These groups had opposing ideas about the origins of and treatments for mental health conditions. From the nonmaterial camp, psychoanalysts believed that psychiatrists should focus on the psyche. Their progressive, biological counterparts, however, wanted to do away with old-style psychoanalytic ideas and move the psychiatric profession into the material, biological realm. These opposing psychiatric factions, with their contradictory visions of professional progress, risked creating a professional paralysis, as neither side wanted to give up any ground to the other.

The psychiatric profession, then, was in a state of crisis during the 1970s. Given the enormity of their professional challenges, unifying the profession and restoring a positive public image would undoubtedly be a difficult task. The strategy that was put in place to resolve these problems was to fortify the medical identity of psychiatrists. After all, definitionally speaking at least, psychiatry is a medical profession, like pediatrics or surgery. Rallying around a medical identity, it was thought, might restore the tarnished image of the psychiatric profession and harmonize its disparate internal identities. To be perceived as a legitimate medical profession, however, psychiatry had to acquire an important symbolic tool, which would put to rest any doubts about whether psychiatry was a branch of medicine: a diagnostic guide.

The DSM-III and Beyond

It is difficult to overestimate the impact of the third edition of the Diagnostic and Statistical Manual (DSM) (American Psychiatric Association 1980) on mental health culture. Following its publication in 1980, psychotherapists and counselors gradually began to embrace the medical model (Hansen 2009; Shorter 1997). Understanding the odd devaluation of meaning systems in contemporary psychotherapy and counseling, then, requires an appreciation for the professional, historical, and cultural factors that gave rise to the DSM-III. Notably, the 1980 version of psychiatry's diagnostic guide was preceded by the first edition of the DSM in 1952 and a subsequent edition in 1969; a minor revision of the DSM-II, which removed the homosexuality diagnosis, was published in 1974 (Decker 2013; Greenberg 2013; Shorter 1997). However, virtually no one, certainly not psychiatrists, took these pre-1980 editions of the DSM seriously. The DSM-III, though, was altogether different than these prior versions in terms of its origins and ideological foundations.

As noted above, the 1970s crises in professional psychiatry served as an important impetus for the development of a revised version of the DSM. Robert Spitzer was chosen to lead the process of developing this new diagnostic guide. Spitzer, a psychiatrist who was also trained as a psychoanalyst, did not enjoy the ambiguities of psychotherapy. However, he had a strong interest in psychiatric nosology, a quality that made him a suitable choice to lead the revision process (Decker 2013; Spiegel 2005).

Prior editions of the DSM had drawn from psychoanalytic language and assumptions about mental health conditions. Given the ideological climate, it would have been unwise to simply continue these Freudian underpinnings and make them the basis for the revised DSM. Although there was still a strong faction of psychoanalytic psychiatrists during the mid-1970s, psychoanalysts were rapidly being displaced by biological psychiatrists, who generally thought that Freudian assumptions were useless, unproven, conjectures about mental functioning that kept professional psychiatry from progressing into the new, biological age (Decker 2013; Greenberg 2013; Shorter 1997). Furthermore, the field of clinical psychology had numerous theoretical influences, including humanistic, psychodynamic, and behavioral orientations (Fancher 1995). Psychologists generally received intensive training in one of these orientations, thereby creating separate ideological factions of clinical psychologists. Given this ideological diversity and active contentiousness between rival groups, it would certainly be difficult to select a singular ideology upon which to base the new DSM. In the midst of these challenges, Spitzer made an interesting choice, which would set the course of mental health culture through the present day.

Spitzer decided to revive nineteenth-century Kraepelinian descriptive psychiatry and make it the ideological foundation of the new DSM (Decker 2013; Greenberg 2013; Mayes and Horwitz 2005; Shorter 1997). In other words, disorders would be classified exclusively according to symptoms. Spitzer reasoned that categorizing people by symptoms alone would circumvent the strong ideological differences that had caused the helping professions to become factionalized. Psychoanalysts and biological psychiatrists, for instance, could presumably avoid activating their contentious ideological debates by limiting their conversations to symptoms, which are observable phenomena about which all parties, despite their differences, could potentially agree. Furthermore, if psychiatry were to advance, researchers needed to study homogenous groups. Clustering patients by observable symptoms would, it was hoped, provide a universally agreed upon homogeneity, regardless of the theoretical preferences of researchers.

Given the times, it is easy to understand Spitzer's choice of descriptive psychiatry as the ideological foundation for the new DSM. He presumed that categorizing disorders exclusively by symptoms would be atheoretical, thereby allowing professionals who had different, and actively opposing, theoretical orientations to agree about categories of disorders. Although there are monumental differences between psychoanalytic and biological understanding of the causes of and treatments for depression, for instance, both groups could presumably agree on who was eligible for a diagnosis of depression if observable symptoms were the only criterion to consider. If everyone agreed on the groupings, then researchers could eventually determine the causes of and best treatments for the disorders. Knowledge could presumably advance after Spitzer had undone the psychiatric Tower of Babel and revived a universal, atheoretical linguistic system that all participants in mental health culture could understand and agree upon.

As it turned out, though, it was naive to characterize a descriptive psychiatric approach as unbiased and atheoretical (Greenberg 2013). An exclusive focus on symptoms strongly favors a materialistic, biological approach to mental health care, which regards symptom remission as tantamount to cure. With a descriptive psychiatric approach, the symptoms are the problem; disorders are defined as clusters of symptoms. By extension, then, if a drug, or other intervention, gets rid of the symptoms, the problem, by definition, has been cured. In addition to strongly favoring a biological approach to treatment, this descriptive psychiatric definition of health as the absence of symptoms is not only extraordinarily counterintuitive, but it can arguably create damaging consequences for people who seek help.

For instance, suppose a woman comes to a mental health provider with symptoms of depression, such as sadness, anhedonia, and difficulties sleeping. The reason for the depression, which the descriptive psychiatric vision purposefully ignores, is that the woman feels trapped in a relationship with an abusive husband. However, the psychiatrist, operating from a contemporary symptom-focused ideology, prescribes an antidepressant and the symptoms eventually remit. The woman, now "cured," is able to endure the abuses of her marriage because she is in a drug-induced, semi-anesthetized state. As another example, consider a man who comes to therapy complaining about anxiety. He is stuck in a dissatisfying career and is unsure what to do. He has fears associated with seeking other options, such as additional education, but also fears that he will be stuck in his current career for the remainder of his working life. The man's DSM-oriented psychotherapist views the anxiety as the problem and implements a cognitive-behavioral treatment plan to lessen the anxiety. Once the anxiety is under control, the man no longer meets the criteria for an anxiety disorder and is thereby cured. He continues in his old job, but is now able to cognitively convince himself that it is not so bad after all.

Alternatively, there are arguably cases where focusing on symptom remission and ignoring meaning systems is probably the best treatment option. In the case of a person suffering from schizophrenia who believes that aliens are reading his thoughts, for example, it is arguably better to treat the symptoms than to explore the meaning behind the delusion. However, this equation of symptom remission with cure, as noted above, is arguably not a desirable perspective to adopt with most people who seek help for a mental health complaint. As in formal medicine, sometimes pain is simply pain and the best option is to get rid of it. However, perhaps on most occasions, pain is a sign that something else is wrong, such as when headaches are indicative of a brain tumor. Simply prescribing a pain reliever for the headache would stop the symptom, but it would certainly not cure the problem. In fact, the alleviation of the headache pain would actually serve to hide the problem, make it less detectable, and provide a harmful, false sense of security that everything is okay. Analogously, in the mental health domain, killing the pain messenger can provide a cover under which the underlying problem can hide.

Descriptive psychiatry is not an unbiased, atheoretical ideology, then; it equates symptoms with disorders and, by extension, symptom remission with cure. In addition to problems noted above with the adoption of a symptom-only treatment perspective, the descriptive psychiatric vision can never, within its own ideology, answer vital questions (Frances 2013; Greenberg 2013), such as what constitutes a symptom? Crying, more often than not over a period of two weeks, for example, might be considered a problem that could be symptomatic of a disorder. However, what if the crying is due to the death of a loved one? What about the loss of a job or a divorce? At what point does a behavioral manifestation become a symptom that is part of a larger constellation of problems, which constitutes a disorder? Indeed, what is the test to determine if something is a disorder or, alternatively, should be considered within the realm of normative, or even noble, human functioning?

Without biomarkers (and arguably even with them) the only way to derive answers to these questions is through human judgment in the form of professional consensus or majority vote, as was the case with homosexuality. The categories used in Spitzer's DSM, then, were determined by vote and negotiations with various, opposing professional factions. For instance, the inclusion of axis II, which was used to indicate character disorders in the DSM-III, was a concession to psychoanalytic psychiatrists, who insisted that characterological problems be a part of the new psychiatric nosology (Decker 2013). The resulting DSM-III, then, can be more accurately characterized as a political document than a scientific one. Regardless of the factors that went into creating it, the new DSM, which was published in 1980, was a wild success, and a descriptive, symptom-based approach to mental health care, which purposefully ignored meaning systems, began to overtake mental health culture. All subsequent DSMs, including the current DSM-V, were based on the same descriptive psychiatric ideology that formed the foundation of the DSM-III. Thus, the introduction of the DSM-III was a watershed moment that set the ideological course of mental health culture for the subsequent decades.

The success of the DSM-III was largely due to factors that were active in mental health culture at the time of its introduction (Decker 2013; Murray 2009; Shorter 1997). For instance, insurance companies were turning to a managed care model to control costs. Rather than pay for interminable, exploratory therapies, managed care companies eagerly adopted the DSM-III descriptive diagnostic approach, which defined cure as symptom remission. Symptoms could serve as an objective criterion for judging whether a person continued to require treatment and the insurance money to pay for it. To managed care companies, then, the descriptive psychiatric model was a cost-cutting marvel. The DSM-III was also an ideal fit for the new biological psychiatry. Psychiatric drugs help to alleviate the suffering caused by mental health symptoms. Therefore, a symptom-based ideology automatically favors a biological approach. The pharmaceutical industry seeing the dollar signs on the wall, were highly supportive of the new, symptom-based model and poured billions of dollars into research and advertising, which fortified and elevated the medical model as a defining feature of mental health culture.

During the 1980s, psychiatrists continued their rapid abandonment of psychoanalysis and were well on their way to becoming a profession of prescription writers (Shorter 1997). Talk therapy was largely conducted by psychologists, social workers, and counselors. Wanting a piece of the new psychiatric action, talk therapists gradually embraced the DSM-III and lobbied for the right to bill insurance companies for their services. These lobbying efforts were generally successful, and nonpsychiatric psychotherapists began to label their clients with descriptive, psychiatric diagnoses, write prescriptive treatment plans (i.e., matched psychotherapeutic techniques with specific symptoms), track outcomes based on symptom remission, and play other elements of the insurance reimbursement game. As the game continued, though, it took on a life of its own, and the idealization of symptoms resulted in a trivialization of meaning systems, ironically, even within the talk therapy professions, wherein meaning systems should be the primary focus of concern.

Perhaps feeling threatened by the dominance of the psychiatric medical model, academic psychologists launched an empirically validated treatment (EVT) movement during the early 1990s (Leibert 2012; Marquis and Douhit 2006; Wampold 2001). The proponents of this movement advocated the use of research methods to determine optimal psychological treatments for particular mental health disorders. At the time, psychiatrists were having tremendous professional success by using prescriptive medical treatments for disorders; psychologists reasoned that, with EVTs, they could also use research findings to recommend prescriptive treatments, in the form of psychological interventions for particular disorders. With this EVT research agenda, psychologists adopted a medical paradigm for the talk therapies, a move they hoped would keep their profession relevant in the new age of biological psychiatry.

On the surface, using research to determine the most helpful psychological treatments for particular disorders sounds like a reasonable idea. Upon further examination, however, the EVT movement was fraught with problems. First, generally speaking, popular forms of psychotherapy work about equally well for a variety of mental health problems. Specific techniques probably account for less than 1 percent of the variance in psychotherapy outcomes (Wampold 2001). Therefore, empirical attempts to optimally align particular psychological treatments with various disorders is a strategy that is largely inconsistent with research findings about psychotherapy outcomes.

Second, proponents of the EVT movement decided to model their research after randomized controlled trials (RCT), a methodology used in drug research (Leibert 2012). In RCT methodologies subjects are randomly assigned to different treatment conditions. If significant differences between groups are observed after the treatment is introduced, then these differences are likely caused by the treatment, because randomization ensures that the groups are fairly equivalent with respect to subject characteristics. In other words, if variables are primarily held constant except for the treatment, then the treatment would be the most likely cause of any observed changes. As applied to psychotherapy outcome research, a RCT approach would mean that subjects with a particular disorder would be assigned to various psychotherapy treatment conditions; observed changes in the severity of the disorder could reasonably be attributed to the effect of the treatment.

However, it is difficult, if not impossible, to translate the RCT methodology to psychotherapy outcome research (Leibert 2012; Wampold 2001). Notably, in drug research, all subjects of a group who are assigned to receive a drug will receive precisely the same amount of an equivalent chemical compound. What, though, as in psychotherapy research, if a treatment group is designated to receive humanistic therapy? How can researchers ensure that all subjects in the group receive the same "dose" of the exact same type of humanistic treatment? There are significant variations in the way treatment is conducted, even by practitioners who identify with the same orientation. How, then, can psychotherapy outcome researchers, who aspire to model their studies after RCT methodologies, ensure that treatment groups receive the same doses of identical treatments?

The solution to this dilemma was to use manualized treatments (Wampold 2001). Treatment manuals outline the session by session activities of the therapist. By having therapists in treatment conditions conduct psychotherapy according to guidelines specified in manuals, outcome researchers could have some degree of certainty that subjects in a particular group were receiving near equivalent treatments. Although manualized treatments provided a solution to the problem of implementing RCT methodologies in psychotherapy outcome research, they created other significant problems. Notably, not all treatment orientations can be manualized. Humanistic and psychodynamic practitioners, for instance, follow the lead of the client; it is impossible to plan the course of treatment ahead of time, using a manual, when these therapy orientations are used. However, cognitive-behavioral treatments are generally well suited for manualization. Therefore, RCT methodologies created a strong bias to research cognitive-behavioral treatments and ignore others. The frequently cited finding from this era that cognitive-behavioral treatments are superior to other types of psychotherapy is largely a methodological by-product of the manualization requirement of RCT designs. Because cognitive-behavioral treatments could be manualized, they were the primary treatments studied; it should be no surprise that they kept coming up the winner.

In addition to the problem of keeping the dose of treatment constant across subjects in a particular group, EVT outcome researchers also had to ensure that the subjects in their groups had the same disorder. This is also highly problematic. Unlike medical studies wherein a discrete condition can be identified and verified with biomarkers, psychotherapy outcome studies have to rely on the DSM, or similar diagnostic guide, to verify the existence of a singular, discrete disorder. However, in addition to the facts that psychological problems are complex, never exactly the same in two people, and that people often have several problems at once, not just one, the DSM is a very unreliable guide for rendering diagnosis. Because DSM diagnostics are arrived at using interviews, observation, and clinical judgment, inter-rater agreement about diagnostics is crucial to the integrity of the diagnostic system. If independent raters using a diagnostic system regularly disagree about the diagnosis of the same client, then the diagnostic system is an unreliable guide to disorders because it is dependent on the diverse, subjective judgments of clinicians. In this regard, the inter-rater reliability of DSM diagnostics is generally low (Fancher 1995; Frances 2013; Greenberg 2013; Kirk and Kutchins 1994). Using DSM guidelines, independent raters often come up with different diagnoses for the same clients. Of course, this regular finding calls the integrity of empirical outcome research, including EVT studies, into question, as it is not clear that subjects in a particular diagnostic group of a study are the same with respect to their actual diagnostic status.

The EVT movement eventually gave way to other forms of psychotherapy outcome research that were less rigid about adhering to RCT methodologies (Leibert 2012). However, the medicalized research goal of pairing particular treatments with discrete disorders has remained a strong element of psychotherapy outcome research, despite overwhelming evidence that all orientations work about the same, and that the factors common to all psychotherapies (e.g., development of a strong treatment alliance), not the specific factors of a particular orientation, likely account for client change (Wampold 2001). The continuance of this misguided, medicalized research agenda, however, served to further ensconce the medical model, and the concomitant devaluation of meaning systems, as a core element of mental health culture for talk therapists.

Other factors were also active during the EVT era that contributed to the medicalization of mental health culture. For instance, during the 1990s advertising restrictions for pharmaceutical companies in the United States were lifted (Ventola 2011). Once drugs could be directly marketed to consumers, Americans were regularly treated to television advertisements highlighting cartoon depictions of neurochemical processes paired with images of formerly depressed people happily gardening and enjoying time with their families. A clear, nightly message was beamed into American living rooms: The chemical contents of your brain is what matters, not what is on your mind.

In response to this cultural shift, graduate training programs increasingly required courses in diagnosis, treatment planning, manualized psychotherapies, and even psychopharmacology in their curricula (Hansen 2009). As this mechanistic, medicalized trend in psychotherapy training has increased, the emphasis on meaning systems has decreased. Traditional training in case conceptualization and listening skills have largely been traded for technical topics in educational programs for helping professionals. McWilliams (2005) related an interesting anecdote about her experience as a psychotherapy educator that illustrates this shift to a medicalized culture of helping. In McWilliam's capacity as a consultant, she overheard a psychiatric resident, who had witnessed her intervene with a patient, say that he was going to use one of McWilliam's lines in his future clinical work. This resident had advanced training in diagnostic interviewing. McWilliams, curious to know the line that the resident had found so novel and helpful, asked the resident what he was referring to. The resident reported that it was "can you say more about that?" (142).

I have also noted a strong, medicalized shift in mental health culture in my capacity as a practitioner, supervisor, and trainer. When I attended case conferences during the 1980s, and even the 1990s, the primary topics usually related to meaning systems, such as a client's perspective, psychological conflicts, and the therapeutic relationship. Nowadays, the prominent topics in the case conferences I attend are usually diagnoses, specific techniques that can be used to combat particular symptoms, and psychopharmacology. Again, I am absolutely not taking the position that a medicalized perspective is inherently unhelpful. There are certainly clients who benefit from medicines and specific techniques. However, I maintain, the fundamental concern for talk therapists should be what is on a client's mind, not what is in a client's brain; talk therapy quite obviously involves minds, not brains. Furthermore, therapeutic understanding should usually be prioritized over fixing. And, research evidence strongly demonstrates that the quality of the therapeutic relationship, not the implementation of specific techniques, should be the primary focus of attention for psychotherapists and counselors (Wampold 2001).

In the midst of this giant cultural wave of medicalization, nonmaterial movements, which emphasize meaning systems, have struggled to emerge. However, these movements have not gained enough power and momentum to cause a cultural shift back to the valuation of meaning systems in mental health culture. In addition to the obvious factors that keep the material culture in place, such as the power of the pharmaceutical industry, perhaps there are other, more subtle forces that also prevent the culture from shifting back to nonmaterial, meaning based paradigms. The next section reviews some relatively new meaning-based trends, which have recently sprouted, and the subtle forces that may be preventing them from flowering.

MEANING-BASED TRENDS AND OPPOSING FORCES

During eras when a material view of mental health care is in vogue, nonmaterial perspectives, which value meaning systems, often become underground movements that have little impact on the overall culture. This is arguably the case in contemporary mental health culture. The material, medical model, with its symptom-based definitions of disorders and prescriptive treatments, has become the standard, virtually universal paradigm for both biological and psychotherapeutic helping modalities. Within this monolithically materialist culture, however, the distant rumblings of nonmaterial meaning-based perspectives can still be heard. Some of these rumblings are from perspectives that originated decades ago, which are still being taught in training programs, such as humanistic and psychodynamic approaches. Other contemporary meaning-based paradigms are derivatives of traditional orientations to helping. Strength-based approaches (Jones-Smith 2014) and motivational interviewing (Miller and Rollnick 2012), for example, can be viewed as extensions of humanistic ideals, particularly with regard to the importance of the relationship in helping, the value of client perspectives, a de-emphasis on diagnostics, and a focus on strengths. However, not all contemporary meaning-based systems of helping have been derived from traditional approaches. Some genuinely novel helping orientations have been introduced. Many of these approaches have been inspired by a postmodern epistemology, which has posited radically different conceptualizations of truth and self than the conceptualizations of traditional modernism.

The basic assumptions of postmodernism were outlined in the previous chapter. However, these assumptions are worth reviewing and elaborating in the service of understanding some of the new meaning-based approaches to counseling and psychotherapy. In this regard, postmodernism is the name of a general intellectual movement, which has various sub-movements. For counseling and psychotherapy, the important sub-movements are constructivism and social constructionism (Hansen 2004).

Essentially, constructivism presumes that individuals create realities (Hansen 2004). There is an intuitively sensible element to this proposition. That is, processing of any stimulus that impinges upon the sensory apparatus of an individual occurs within the individual. The sight, taste, and smell of a particular food, for example, may inspire fond memories in one person, be revolting to another, and remind someone else of a particular relationship; same food, different meanings. Sometimes to impress my students with constructivist assumptions, I stand in front of the classroom and ask the group how many classes are taking place in the room at the moment. Students ordinarily reply that there is one class—the class in which everyone is currently participating. Using constructivist assumptions, I respond that there are as many classes taking place as there are students. Each student is processing the incoming information in a different way, depending on their idiosyncratic meaning systems, developmental history, current preoccupations, and other factors.

If constructivism is taken to its logical conclusion, however, it leads to the idea that everyone is trapped within their own experience. This creates a problem called solipsism, which means that people are incapable of escaping their own minds (Hansen 2010b). With this set of assumptions, there would be no way to disprove whether all of reality, your entire life and everything around you, is an illusion. On a psychological level, real-world influences and relationships are always secondary, or even irrelevant, when compared to the processing that occurs within enclosed, separated individual minds. With these ideological roadblocks, it was difficult for constructivism to evolve into a useful psychological explanatory system and inspire novel treatment approaches (Rudes and Guterman 2007).

Social constructionism, alternatively, posits that groups create realities (Gergen 1999; Hansen 2004). To illustrate this point to my students, I invite them to consider the student-professor arrangement. Students have a particular role. They come to class, listen respectfully to the professor, participate, and attempt to acquire knowledge and achieve a good grade. Professors possess specialized knowledge that they formally impart to students through an educational structure, which includes progression through various levels of study, grading of assignments, and the awarding of degrees. These roles and arrangements were not found pristine in nature. They were quite obviously constructed by people, and, I tell my students, we just happen to be participating in this construction and have come to think of it as a reality. I ask students to consider other socially structured roles and arrangements in which they participate and reflexively regard as completely natural and true, such as work, family life, and other communally defined activities. From a social constructionist perspective truth and reality are defined by groups.

Within this social constructionist point of view, selves are also socially constructed. The self, then, is not an individual, internal structure, like a kidney. Rather, selves are located in the social matrices that create and maintain them (Hoffman, Stewart, Warren, and Meek 2015; McNamee 1996). For instance, the same person probably adopts different selves depending on whether the social situation calls on her to be a mother, friend, worker, devout Catholic, or competitive softball player. Again, from the social constructionist perspective, selves are a function of groups, not individuals.

Because I continually present a variety of ideas to my students, they have often sensitized me to the usual objections people sometimes have to certain concepts. The idea that the self is a constructed social phenomenon rather than an internal, individual one often results in fairly intense and excited student reactions, far more than I typically get with other ideas that I present. Perhaps this is because people are generally accustomed to thinking of self as a deeply personal, internal entity. Enlightenment-inspired traditions have created strong cultural messages that it is important to discover your inner self and be true to it. Social constructionism generally turns all of these assumptions on their head.

In this regard, I suspect that most readers probably agree that different selves are activated in different social situations. However, some might object that there is still an underlying, core individual self that is present across all situations. For instance, if a person tends to be honest, or quick-tempered, or self-deprecating, or values human life above all else, then it is likely that these individual self-factors, my students sometimes argue, will be present in all social situations, regardless of the role pressures that are part of a particular social matrix. By extension, they argue, this means that the self is not entirely socially constructed, but is also an internal property of individuals that is active across various groups in which a person participates. Playing devil's advocate, my usual reply to this reasonable objection is that perhaps a person appears to have a relatively consistent, internally-based self merely because they continually participate in the same types of social groups, which create similar patterns of self-expression. For instance, if someone is involved in social milieus wherein they regularly adopt the role of father, husband, and factory worker for a quarter century, it is likely that the person will display a common set of role-determined characteristics that an observer might mistakenly attribute to an internal self. However, if the person suddenly won the lottery, had his arm amputated, or found himself in a foxhole during a war, it is reasonable to think that different varieties of self would emerge as a function of the social demands created by these situations.

Whether one is persuaded by the logic of the social constructionist position, social constructionists have given us novel perspectives on truth and self that are counter to traditional, modernist positions. Indeed, regarding a singular, unified self, Gergen (1995) has suggested that it is adaptive to wear many masks rather than to be "burdened by the code of coherence" (143). This is the exact opposite of traditional assumptions about psychological functioning, which emphasize the importance of discovering one's inner self and being true to it. However, Gergen cogently argued, it is probably more adaptive to be able to fluently adopt different selves for various social demands than it is to insist upon one, unified self that is consistent across all situations. Postmodernism, generally speaking, and social constructionism, in particular, calls into question many modernist psychological assumptions that people tend to take for granted.

New meaning-based ideological trends, such as social constructionism, however, should certainly not be regarded as representative of truth. Indeed, it would be completely contradictory to regard a system of thought that rejects the assumption that people can access the intrinsic nature of reality as being foundationally true (Hansen 2014a). Rather than conveying transcendental truths, new ideologies can jar us out of our old ways of thinking and present novel possibilities, which we would have never considered while operating within the intellectual parameters of our usual assumptions. For example, if considered from an exclusively individualistic perspective, the seemingly odd behavior of a person continually raising her hand is inexplicable. However, when this behavior is viewed through a social lens, the hand raising makes sense as a customary part of the educational social matrix, wherein students raise their hand when they wish to speak. Therefore, there may be strong pragmatic benefits to adopting new ways of conceptualizing behavior and meaning systems. In this regard, social constructionism offers new explanatory structures that make sense of meaning making processes, which may have been inexplicable from an individualistic, modernist perspective (Gergen 1999). Furthermore, the social constructionist undoing of the isolated, individualistic self is arguably liberating. Under the social constructionist ideology, people no longer have a modernist duty to find and be faithful to a coherent, inner self. Rather, they are free to create various selves according to adaptive, relational demands (Gergen 1995).

Postmodern ideas generally, and social constructionist principles specifically, have been translated into new, meaning-based helping orientations, which incorporate assumptions that are counter to the ideological foundations of traditional, modernist approaches. Narrative (White and Epston 1990) and solution-focused orientations to counseling (deShazer 1985), for example, emphasize the creation of new meaning systems, not the discovery of old ones that are supposedly buried deep within the psyche. As an everyday example of how these new meaning-based orientations to helping operate, imagine someone who is continually distressed about traumatic events that occurred in his past. Eventually, he comes to the conclusion that he is grateful for these traumas because he would not have become the strong person he is today if the events had not taken place. This new way of thinking about his past brings him a lasting sense of peace. Operating within traditional, modernist assumptions, an observer might wonder whether his conclusions actually functioned to suppress certain psychological elements of his experience or whether he was deluding himself and avoiding the truth. From a postmodern perspective, however, the truth, and a fixed, inner self, are not tenable constructs. Therefore, within postmodern ideology, the adoption of the new meaning system would be judged exclusively according to whether it served the person well, not by whether it was true (Hansen 2007). If this new perspective provided him with a sustainable sense of peace, then the adoption of this narrative would be considered a successful outcome. Notably, postmodern reconceptualizations of meaning systems have not only resulted in new ways of viewing counseling processes but have also stimulated the creation of novel techniques, such as the miracle question and externalization of symptoms.

As a further illustration of the influence of new ideas about meaning systems on the psychotherapy process, psychoanalytic theory has undergone important evolutions in the past several decades that can, at least partially, be attributed to the influence of postmodern ideas. For example, traditional psychoanalysis emphasized the importance of therapeutic neutrality (Gabbard 2005; Gill 1994). If the therapist remained relatively anonymous and took a neutral stance about the issues that clients discussed, then it was presumed that the meaning systems that emerged during therapy sessions were exclusively a product of client psychology. Within this modernist set of assumptions, if a client became angry with her therapist, and the therapist had maintained a neutral stance throughout the course of treatment, then the anger was presumed to have emanated exclusively from the psyche of the client. In this clinical situation the psychoanalyst might make the transferential suggestion that the client was actually angry with her father, for instance, because modernist psychoanalytic practitioners presumed that the therapist, by virtue of the neutral stance, could not have elicited the anger. Therapeutic neutrality was thought to allow the psychoanalyst to view client psychology in pristine form, uncontaminated by the personality of the therapist. Just as a microbiologist, seeking to learn the truth about a specimen, would ensure that the lens and slide of the microscope were free from contaminants, traditional psychoanalysts aspired to keep the therapeutic relationship free from the contaminating influence of the therapist.

The goal of obtaining the foundational truth about clients becomes untenable, however, within a postmodern ideology. Moreover, a social constructionist perspective severely challenges the idea that the psychological influence of one of the participants in a relational dyad can be entirely subtracted through the supposed use of therapeutic neutrality (Gergen 1999). As an example, an often-cited traditional training dictum in psychoanalytic and even humanistic, educational programs is that a therapist should refrain from passing a box of tissues to a tearful client. The reasoning behind this guidance is that passing the tissue box inevitably sends subtle messages (e.g., that the therapist is intolerant of emotional displays). This communication would necessarily be a departure from therapeutic neutrality and, as such, might unduly influence and derail the pure expression of client psychology. If a client takes away the message that the therapist does not approve of crying, for example, then the client might become hesitant to express emotion. Furthermore, from a traditional psychoanalytic perspective, subtle communications to the client might contaminate the blank, neutral screen of the therapist, thereby compromising the ability of the client to form a pure, developmentally-based transference (Gabbard 2005). Therapists, then, should never toy with the Kleenex box. Do not be fooled by its innocent appearance. The ubiquitous, office tissue container is actually a delicate psychological bomb that might explode if handled improperly. Just leave it alone and pretend that it is not there, even in cases of profuse client sobbing.

I make fun of the Kleenex box rule because, in light of contemporary thinking about meaning systems, it is easy to do so. A central tenet of social constructionism is that realities are social phenomena, constructed by groups of people who negotiate the ideas that they call truth (Gergen 1999). From this perspective, therapists and their clients co-construct the meanings that constitute the realities of the helping encounter (Gill 1994; Hoffman 1998). It is thereby impossible to subtract the psychological influence of one of the participants from the therapeutic dyad. To illustrate this point using the Kleenex box example, suppose a counselor, in an effort to maintain therapeutic neutrality, chose to refrain from passing the tissue box to a distressed client. Would this be a neutral act? Indeed, the client might perceive the counselor's failure to slide the box over as rude or hostile. Alternatively, it might be perceived as the therapist having confidence in the ability of the client to be independent. Inaction is not equivalent to neutrality. Not taking action, remaining stoic or neutral in the face of social situations that usually call for a response, sends a communication; it is not neutral. Either by inaction or action, people who are interpersonally engaged are always sending messages to one another.

In an effort to base their practices on a traditional, scientific paradigm, psychotherapists have wrongly equated inaction with neutrality. In scientific experiments, inaction on the part of investigators can reasonably be equated with neutrality. It is important to note, however, that this presumption of scientific neutrality has been persuasively critiqued (Kuhn 1996). Putting this critique aside for the moment, though, a key component of the scientific paradigm is that investigators can achieve a certain degree of dispassionate neutrality by removing themselves from their experiments. In double-blind designs, for example, neither the investigator nor the administrator of the treatment is aware of which subjects are receiving the treatment and which are exposed to the placebo. This double-blind procedure serves to promote neutrality by preventing investigator bias from contaminating the results. This version of neutrality is at least somewhat defensible in the natural sciences, because the insentient hunks of matter that natural scientists study do not formulate meanings in response to being investigated. However, this scientific paradigm cannot be wholly imported to the interpersonal realm of psychotherapy because both the investigator and the subject of investigation continually construct systems of meaning. Molecules, chemicals, or cells do not have experiential reactions to being investigated; people do.

One would think that the simple idea of mutual interpersonal influence would have been obvious to the originators of traditional systems of psychotherapy. However, during the first half of the twentieth century, theorists were so mesmerized by the scientific paradigm that it seemed like a natural fit for the helping scenario (Hansen 2002). Eventually, though, postmodern ideas, and other factors, jarred psychoanalysts out of their modernist, hypnotic trance and caused them to acknowledge what now seems like common sense: that two people in an interpersonal dyad are always influencing one another, even if one of the parties attempts to refrain from influencing the other. This psychoanalytic insight, which was leveraged by social constructionist ideas, has been called a two-person psychology, as opposed to the one-person psychology of traditional psychoanalysis (Gill 1994). This two-person psychology has pulled the ideological rug out from underneath many foundational psychoanalytic principles, therapeutic neutrality being a prime example. Indeed, the new emphasis on thoroughgoing co-construction has spawned reconceptualizations of old psychoanalytic ideas, such as "cotransference" (Orange 1995, 63) instead of the traditional, singular transference, and intersubjective theorizing (Stolorow, Atwood, and Orange 2002) as a constructionist substitute for a focus on the isolated, subjective universe of the client.

Postmodern ideas have also supported multiculturalism and qualitative research, two monumentally influential movements in contemporary social science and the helping professions (Hansen 2010a). Giving up the idea of transcendent truth is a vital ideological prerequisite to appreciating diverse worldviews (i.e., multiculturalism). Rather than ranking various perspectives according to their relatively proximity to transcendent truth, postmodernism, by abandoning truth, provides an ideological license to appreciate alternative cultural points of view. Likewise, postmodern ideologies have served as an important critique to the assumption that quantitative, scientific methods provide an objective view of the intrinsic nature of reality. This postmodern dethroning of quantitative methodologies has supported the rise of qualitative methods, which cultivate meaning systems in regional environments, where they are constructed and linger in the lived experience of participants.

Therefore, there have clearly been revolutionary changes in the way that meaning systems have been conceptualized in the past few decades. Given these advances, what are the reasons, then, that the historical material/nonmaterial pendulum has not swung back to the nonmaterial side? Why is mental health culture still beholden to a materialistic, medicalized, symptom-based view of human problems and solutions when, if history is the guide, it is long overdue for a nonmaterial, meaning-based correction? In prior eras, the pendulum has swung back and forth with some degree of regularity. Contemporarily, though, it seems stuck in a medicalized red zone, which has virtually no regard for the meanings that animate and give purpose to living. Even with tremendous ideological advancements in the conceptualization of meaning systems, the pendulum has not budged. What is this mysterious, cultural glue that keeps the pendulum fixed to the material side?

As a psychoanalytic thinker, I tend to conceptualize problems in terms of manifest, surface content and underlying, latent motivations. With regard to the relatively obvious factors that prevent mental health culture from returning to meaning-based paradigms, the pharmaceutical industry certainly plays an enormous role (Frances 2013; Murray 2009). Billions of dollars from drug manufacturers have obviously propped up and kept the medical model alive for decades. Pharmaceutical profits depend upon the public perception that problems of living are discrete, diagnosable disorders, which have chemical cures. In addition to this manifest cultural motivator, however, I believe that there are also subtle motivational forces that contribute to the sticky pendulum phenomenon that characterizes contemporary mental health culture.

Before elaborating these latent motivational forces, I want to emphasize that I am not calling for the elimination of material approaches or the medical model. In this regard, nonmaterial, meaning-based approaches have certainly had their cultural excesses. The recovered memory movement of the 1980s is an example of a psychological, meaning-based approach that caused incredible harm (Wright 1994). The mid-century dominance of psychoanalysis also had damaging consequences, such as psychopathological theories of and treatments for homosexuality and epilepsy (Shorter 1997). Furthermore, material, biological interventions are sometimes the only means by which someone can be helped. For good reason, biological interventions are the treatment of choice for persons suffering from schizophrenia, intractable, chronic forms of depression and the disorder that was formerly called manic depression (as distinguished from the severely over-diagnosed bipolar disorder of today).

Again, the larger problem is not a particular helping paradigm. Rather, it is the cultural dominance of either material or nonmaterial approaches during certain eras. When either material or nonmaterial orientations to helping dominate mental health culture, the explanatory power of the dominant model is regularly taken to damaging extremes. Contemporarily, by virtue of its cultural dominance, the material, medical model has gone on a pathologizing binge in an attempt to bring virtually every human ailment under its dominion. I believe that this "medicalization of everyday life" (Szasz 2007) has been an extraordinarily harmful cultural transition, which has suppressed the meaning systems that animate lives and are integral to the helping process. Economic factors have certainly kept the material model dominant. However, there are arguably subtler forces that are also supporting the cultural dominance of the medical model, particularly as this model relates to psychotherapy and counseling.

Indeed, what are the reasons that talk therapists are generally not rallying against the medical model? Conducting relational therapy with clusters of symptoms, instead of human beings, is about the worst fit imaginable. Yet, psychotherapists and counselors continue to endorse the medical model, entrenching themselves further into an impersonal, one dimensional, mechanistic view of human problems and solutions that virtually ignores the depths of meaning from which problems of living arise. Again, one reason for this bizarre cultural turn is undoubtedly economic (Leibert 2012). Third-party payers define practice according to the medical model, so therapists, naturally wanting to get paid, also adopt this model. I have nothing against therapists being reimbursed for their work by insurance companies, and I also earn part of my living through third-party payments. However, the medical insurance-based model, with its descriptive diagnostics and specific techniques for discrete symptoms, has also been widely adopted as a guide for the practice of talk therapy, rather than just being regarded as some bothersome insurance company requirements that actually undermine the practice of psychotherapy and counseling. Why have therapists largely adopted this insurance based, medical model of treatment rather than resisting it?

One explanation might be mass cognitive dissonance. Cognitive dissonance theory essentially posits that it is difficult to hold contradictory beliefs or attitudes (Festinger 1957). For instance, I recently went to a fine restaurant and spent many times more than I usually spend for a meal. Because I paid a high amount, it was difficult for me to come to the conclusion that the meal was not very good. In other words, there was cognitive dissonance between the knowledge that I had spent a large sum of money and my belief that the food was mediocre. To resolve this dissonance, I attempted to convince myself that the food was actually very good. Perhaps there is an analogous process operative in modern counseling and psychotherapy. Contemporary psychotherapists and counselors usually work in an extraordinarily dissonant situation. On the one hand, talk therapists regularly document their work according to third party, medical model demands. However, the important ingredients of effective psychotherapy are the therapeutic relationship and the rich, dynamic, multi-layered meaning systems of clientele, a focus that is the opposite of the medical model. One way to resolve this dissonance is to become supportive of the medical model. Indeed, perhaps cognitive dissonance is operative at a mass, cultural level, not just an individual one, as counselors and psychotherapists resolve the dissonance inherent in their work by convincing themselves that the medical model is actually a reasonable paradigm for relational helping.

Modern talk therapists arguably gain more benefits from endorsing a model that virtually obliterates the meaning systems that should be central to their work than simply a resolution to their dissonance, though. In this regard, human problems often originate within, and are sustained by, complex systems. For example, I have known children in counseling, usually diagnosed with bipolar disorder, ADHD, or oppositional-defiant disorder, who have a history of trauma, abuse, disrupted attachments, and who currently live in poverty and are regularly neglected by addicted parents. There is no money to be made in addressing these larger, systemic issues. Indeed, it is difficult to know what to do about them even if they are acknowledged. However, there is plenty of profit in individualizing these problems by diagnostically endorsing the idea that something is wrong with the child. I am certainly not claiming that therapists are primarily motivated by greed and do not care about the actual problems of their clientele. Most therapists I know are well-intentioned and giving, not greedy. The medical model in which helping professionals participate, however, transforms systemic problems into individual ones that can presumably be addressed by mental health practitioners (Hillman and Ventura 1992). The medical model is appropriate for medical professionals, who treat the body as a unit. If someone has heart disease, the problem lies within their body. However, when this medical model logic is extended to the mental health realm (note even the term "mental health" is individualistic), larger systemic problems are regularly ignored as all problems are diagnostically collapsed into sick individuals. The fact that this individualization of problems is the cultural norm, and that it also makes practitioners who see individual clients money, probably results in a strong, underlying motivation for helping professionals to reflexively keep the model going, without giving much critical thought to their practices.

Indeed, listening to clients can be costly. In this regard, Elkins (2009) posited an interesting hypothesis about the reason for the decline of humanism in psychotherapy and counseling. Rogers (1951), the central proponent of person-centered or humanistic therapy, argued that clients should be considered the experts, not therapists. Counselors provide a supportive, accepting therapeutic environment, which facilitates client growth. However, therapists, according to traditional Rogerian humanism, have no business directing or diagnosing their clients. Clients should be considered the ultimate authorities on their own lives. The idea of client expertise is intuitively appealing, bestows ultimate respect on clients, and even seems downright commonsensical. However, when Rogers proposed his ideas, they were revolutionary and threatened to undermine the power-based infrastructure of mental health culture. Dethroning the expertise of counselors and psychotherapists, not to mention psychiatrists, perhaps threatened to disempower helping professionals. Rather than sacrifice the power, status, and money that comes with expert knowledge, Elkins maintained, mental health professionals instead chose to abandon humanism precisely because of its claim that the client is the expert, not the therapist.

Perhaps Elkin's (2009) interesting hypothesis can be extended beyond humanism to mental health culture generally. Listening to meaning systems automatically empowers clients. If psychotherapists really listen to their clients, take what is on their minds seriously, and delve into deeper layers of subjectivity, then clients are placed in the power position. The validation that comes from supportive listening empowers clients and reduces therapists to the noble but disempowered role of facilitators of client growth. Client meanings, when seriously considered, trump therapeutic expertise. However, if helping professionals assert their supposed expertise by regarding clients as diagnostic entities, mere clusters of symptoms to be eradicated through the use of specific techniques, then helping professionals have the power. Naming some precise, important-sounding diagnostic condition does far more to support the perceived power and authority of a therapist than respectful consideration of idiosyncratic client perspectives. Perhaps, then, on some level, therapists have collectively endorsed the medicalized culture of helping so that they, not their clients, have the power. A necessary casualty of this power play is the meaning systems that animate the lives of their clientele.

Flax (1990) offered a related cultural critique from a feminist perspective. According to Flax, prestige and status in work culture are associated with prototypical masculine ways of being, such as aggressive battling, penetrating problems to find solutions, and competition. Lawyers battling opponents in the courtroom, physicians cutting into bodies to remove tumors, and stock brokers competing to make the best investments are given high status in work culture. Alternatively, passive, feminine relational motifs are devalued in the workplace. Teachers who sensitively respond to the needs of young children have lower status and pay than representatives from occupations that draw from iconic masculine ways of solving problems and managing conflicts. The relational work that women have traditionally done in the home is given low status when it is extended into the workplace. Of course, this emphasis on masculine ideals is clearly a cultural phenomenon, not a representation of the way that work should be regarded, and the opposite type of work culture, wherein feminine ways of being are given the highest status and signs of masculinity are devalued, could easily be imagined. Our current culture simply happens to place a high value on archetypally masculine work roles. Effective psychotherapy and counseling are essentially passive, relational activities wherein the therapist facilitates client growth through attentive, patient listening and responding. As a fundamentally feminine way to make a living, then, being a therapist would have low status in a work culture that values masculine ideals and devalues feminine ones. Therefore, according to Flax, to raise their status, prestige, and income, talk therapists have adopted a masculine model for their work, which emphasizes battling symptoms with particular techniques. This is certainly an intriguing hypothesis and suggests an interesting, underlying motivation for helping professionals to embrace the medical model.

There are a variety of potential underlying reasons, then, that contemporary counselors and psychotherapists have embraced a model that devalues the meaning systems that should be at the center of their work. Perhaps another reason for the mass adoption of the medical model is that it is simply difficult to continually listen to and empathize with people for a living (Hansen 2005). I wish that I remembered the author or source, but, years ago, I read a brief comic strip that nicely illustrated this point. Two therapists at the end of their work day regularly encounter each other in an elevator. In the first few scenes, one of the therapists standing in the elevator looks tired, haggard, and disheveled, while the other appears fresh and energized. After this elevator encounter occurs several times, the tired therapist asks the other one, "How do you manage to look so fresh after listening to clients all day?" The other therapist responds, "Who listens?"

Empathic listening can be extraordinarily draining. Furthermore, clients sometimes talk about aspects of their lives that are unsettling for therapists to hear, such as descriptions of abuse. On an individual level, therapists may respond to difficult material by creating distance from their clients, changing the subject, or avoiding topics that stir uncomfortable feelings (Karon 1992). *Countertransference* is the term Freud (1910/1957) originally used to describe various personal, psychological reactions that the psychoanalyst had about the client. Drawing on the concept of countertransference, it is also reasonable to suppose that the continual drain of close empathic contact may cause helping professionals to reflexively withdraw from the helping encounter. Speculatively, perhaps this countertransferential need to withdraw has been enacted collectively in the form of a mass endorsement of the medical model and suppression of meaning-based approaches to talk therapy (Hansen 2005). Granted, this is a speculative hypothesis. However, given that careful listening is a difficult, draining, and sometimes traumatizing way to make a living, it is not unreasonable to suppose that talk therapists, collectively and unconsciously, have decided to endorse a model that minimizes the significance of attending to meaning systems in the helping process. Thus, for various reasons, counselors and psychotherapists likely contribute to keeping the historical pendulum of mental health culture stuck in the material position.

SUMMARY

For centuries, the helping professions have alternately endorsed material and nonmaterial models of healing. When one of these models was prevalent during a particular era or in a certain region, the other was usually suppressed. Contemporarily, the material, medical model is dominant and meaning based nonmaterial approaches have been relegated to a lowly status. Ironically, counselors and psychotherapists have generally endorsed this dominant medical model, even though the success of their helping endeavors is dependent upon careful listening to the meanings that their clients present.

In the midst of this contemporary, medical model dominance of mental health culture, new meaning-based paradigms have been proposed. Indeed, some of these orientations, such a social constructionism, are revolutionary and challenge the tenets of traditional, modernist approaches to helping. However, even with the introduction of new meaning-based systems of thought, the cultural pendulum has remained stuck in the material, medical model position. I have suggested several factors that have prevented mental health culture from returning to an emphasis on meaning systems, as it has regularly done in the past after a protracted materialistic phase. The primary, obvious reason is the influence of the pharmaceutical industry, which has poured billions of dollars into the highly profitable, material, medical model. However, particularly with regard to psychotherapy and counseling, I have also suggested seamier, relatively hidden factors that keep mental health culture stuck in a materialist mode, such as therapists' need for power and a collective countertransference reaction against the stressors that result from intimate listening.

Chapter Four

Contemporary Culture and Objectification

In the previous chapter, I detailed some of the historical trends and alternations between material and nonmaterial cultures of mental health care. While this gross, aerial view of history is vital to understanding how we arrived at the current culture of objectification, each era, whether material or nonmaterial, had its own unique forces that shaped and maintained the cultural ideals of the time. For example, the strong dominance of psychoanalytic psychiatry during the mid-twentieth century was arguably the central force in forming and maintaining the nonmaterial, psychological culture during that era (Shorter 1997). Likewise, the pharmaceutical industry has clearly played a large role in shaping and maintaining the contemporary culture of objectification (Davies 2013; Frances 2013; Murray 2009). Again, as I stated previously, neither value system, material or nonmaterial, provides a complete picture of mental health problems or the means to provide helpful interventions. However, material and nonmaterial visions of human problems and solutions seldom, if ever, appear to interact harmoniously during a particular era, despite the ideological lip service that is occasionally paid to supposedly integrative conceptualizations, such as the biopsychosocial model.

Why, however, have the material and nonmaterial visions largely failed to operate harmoniously? Logic and evidence clearly point to an integrationist approach, wherein both physical and psychosocial factors are considered an important part of professional helping. In this regard, there must be a force that trumps logic and evidence, a force that is more powerful than reason, one that is able to cause us to regularly ignore common sense and naively forge ahead with singular, dominant visions, which take over a culture and blinds its inhabitants to other possibilities. This force is power.

History teaches us that when people, and the institutions they create, gain power and the benefits associated with it, such as control, status, and profit, they put measures in place to maintain their position, even if the ideologies that undergird their power structures are no longer beneficial, or are even outright harmful, to the people who subscribe to them. In short, when people acquire power, they often use their influence to put measures in place to maintain their power rather than to promote the common good. Even the most cursory view of history verifies this principle. Christian crusaders, in a flagrant violation of the core principles of Christianity, tortured and killed numerous people in an effort to bring them under ideological control; cult leaders isolate, dominate, and take advantage of their followers; throughout their careers, political leaders fail to ideologically evolve and continue to espouse the same rigid, harmful political visions that resulted in their initial political success; cigarette manufacturers long denied that smoking was harmful, despite unequivocal evidence to the contrary. On a smaller scale, consider the administrators at some workplaces who often spend their time generating useless procedures and paperwork to secure their positions. As a postmodern thinker, I am generally opposed to sweeping generalizations about human nature. If I had to endorse one such generalization, though, it would probably be that when people acquire power they use their influence to maintain and strengthen their position, often with little regard for the impact of their ideologies on the well-being of other people.

When either the material or nonmaterial forces of mental health culture become empowered and institutionalized during a particular era, then, the leaders of the dominant movement are unwilling to give up their power; they do what they can to keep their movement alive for the benefits it can provide them, despite the harm their myopic vision might cause the larger culture. In this way, the material and nonmaterial movements in mental health are analogous to the alternation of republican and democratic political movements. When one side is in power, they institutionalize their ideologies and put measures in place to make them difficult to undermine. This has certainly been the case in mental health culture. Nineteenth-century biological psychiatrists did not simply acquiesce to moral treatment methods, for example. It took strong reform movements to unseat their power (Dowbiggin 2011; Shorter 1997; Whitaker 2002). During the 1950s, 1960s, and 1970s, psychoanalytic psychiatrists, as a group, did not readily concede that their biologically-oriented counterparts had some potentially useful ideas. Rather, they became more stubbornly entrenched in their narrow ideological vision (Decker 2013; Shorter 1997). Drawing from my experience of sitting through numerous luncheon presentations sponsored by pharmaceutical salespeople, the research and flashy graphs that are presented never compare drug and psychotherapy treatments. Indeed, even though psychotherapy is definitively known to be very helpful to people who have mental health problems, more so than pharmaceuticals in many cases (Kirsch 2010), I have never heard a drug representative mention psychotherapy as a viable treatment option that may be superior to drugs. During occasions when I have asked about research comparing the drugs the salesperson was promoting to psychotherapy, the representative inevitably responded with superficial courtesy, saying something to the effect that this might be an interesting idea, but that they are unaware of any research in this area. However, their annoyance and embarrassment that I had asked such a question is usually quite evident, despite the thinly veiled, polite, professional response that they struggle to provide.

The general aim of this book is to promote awareness of the factors that contribute to the objectifying culture of psychotherapy and counseling. When one is continually immersed in a social value system, it can be difficult to see outside of it and recognize the absurdity of the practices that are being promoted. Awareness, then, entails a recognition of the power structures that promote objectifying value systems in mental health care, an understanding of the parties that benefit from implementing the cultural party lines, and a logical, evidence-based critique of current counseling and psychotherapy practices. In this regard, if talk therapy had never been invented, and you were charged with creating it, what would you create? Suppose, even though psychotherapy had never been invented, you somehow had access to the research, theories, and insights that had been gained about the helping professions during the past century (via your special ability to access a parallel universe that had invented psychotherapy). What would you create? Would it resemble contemporary counseling and psychotherapy practice? Which aspects of contemporary mental health culture would you retain, and which would you abandon as useless or harmful? Artificially operating outside of the cultural norms can be an antidote to the blindness created by cultural immersion.

When I engage in the thought experiment of creating talk therapy anew, I become sensitized to the absurd and potentially harmful objectification of clients that is culturally prominent in the contemporary practice of counseling and psychotherapy. There is substantial evidence, both from empirical research and everyday commonsense, that the quality of the therapeutic relationship has the strongest association with therapeutic outcomes (Lambert 1992; Wampold 2001). Of course, one does not foster quality relationships by treating other people as if they are broken objects. To illustrate this point, imagine that a friend comes to you upset, explaining that he has had an argument with his spouse. What do you do to make him feel better? Do you tell him that his distress means that he probably has a mental disorder and that you have some techniques that might help him? Your relationship would almost surely suffer from this cold, objectifying, problem-oriented approach. Note that this is precisely the type of help that counselors and psychotherapists are expected to provide in contemporary mental health culture. Therefore, one does not need high level abstract thinking or complex statistical models to see the absurdity of current cultural trends in professional helping; all it takes is brief reflection on experiences of everyday helping.

If the objectification of a person seeking help from a talk therapist is often counter to the task of helping them, why has this insight generally not been incorporated into the contemporary practice of counseling and psychotherapy? What are the ideological structures that create, maintain, and proffer ideologies of objectification and who benefits from their continued existence? To answer these questions, current cultural trends and contemporary iconic institutions of mental health care must be critically examined and critiqued.

ICONS OF CONTEMPORARY MENTAL HEALTH CULTURE

The values of mental health culture often parallel the larger culture. For instance, during the 1960s and 1970s when finding oneself and critical reflection were in vogue, therapeutic systems generally emphasized introspection and insight. Contemporarily, in the age of reality television, social media, and celebrity worship, appearances, quick fixes, and superficial styles of relating are arguably dominant values in the culture. As in previous eras, contemporary mental health culture, with its emphasis on objectifying diagnostics and technical interventions, is reflective of this larger culture (Hansen 2014a). If one were to go back in time and ask clients from forty years ago about their experience of counseling, they would likely describe novel insights, new discoveries related to their inner life, and the evolving nature of the therapeutic relationship. Alternatively, contemporary clients would likely respond to the same inquiry with a description of their diagnosis and the techniques that their therapist is advocating to mitigate their mental disorder. Again, these differences in client descriptions of therapy represent a tremendous cultural shift, which is reflective of the societal values of the respective eras.

It is not as if one type of culture is intrinsically bad and the other is highly desirable. There are certainly benefits to technical interventions, quick pain relief, and purposeful avoidance of the messy subjective factors that can sometimes interfere with effective healing. Likewise, there are advantages to taking time to reflect on life and immersing oneself in the ambiguous realm of meaning systems. When taken too far, each of these value systems can be harmful. The authority and interpretative latitude that was culturally awarded to psychoanalysts in the mid-twentieth century certainly led to harmful consequences, such as the minimization of the importance of biological factors in human problems and the proliferation of the assumption that penis envy was at the foundation of the female psyche (Schwartz 2003; Shorter 1997).

Likewise, the current biological, material culture has arguably been overextended into harmful territory because it eschews the meanings systems that are integral to life and psychological healing.

Given that mental health culture is often reflective of the values of the larger culture, it should be no surprise that contemporary professional helpers generally devalue meaning systems. Indeed, emphases on achievement, resume-building, and competition have arguably taken over contemporary culture. The values of capitalism, when they culturally run amuck, transform people into commodities, items to be bought, sold, and consumed (Michaels 2011). People internalize the values of the larger culture and come to think of themselves as objects in a marketplace instead of as persons with unique perspectives, rich inner lives, and inherent worth (Hansen 2010b; Parker 2007). Appearances, material possessions, immediate gratification, and getting ahead become the aims of living rather than rich relational moments and an appreciation for the fruits of an examined life.

Operating in step with these larger cultural trends, mental health culture has become increasingly objectifying and intolerant of the nuances of subjective life. The biological, descriptive wing of professional psychiatry has gradually become supremely dominant during the past four decades (Davies 2013; Decker 2013; Frances 2013; Greenberg 2013; Luhrmann 2000). To gain money and status, psychotherapists and counselors have followed this psychiatric lead into the realm of objectification, where clients have disorders, not problems of living; therapists develop treatment plans, not therapeutic relationships; and psychological suffering is a sign of pathology that must be eliminated, not the voice of a psychic messenger to be heard and understood (Hansen 2014a). Indeed, the way that a culture regards suffering is arguably one of the latent, subtextual values that animate the larger cultural icons and institutional offshoots.

Contemporarily, the larger culture and the subculture of mental health generally view suffering in a highly negative light (Davies 2012). Pain is not something that people should have to endure. Strong elements of the weight loss and financial services industries, for instance, thrive on promoting the questionable notion that there are quick, painless ways to reach goals that were formerly associated with hard work and sacrifice. In dominant, capitalistic monocultures suffering detracts from one's value as a commodity, and the attitude that quick fixes should be purchasable prevails (Michaels 2011). In parallel fashion, contemporary mental health culture is founded on ideologies that view suffering as an enemy to be immediately anesthetized (Davies 2012). Even grief, a form of suffering considered normative throughout human history, has been redefined as a pathological state in the current version of the Diagnostic and Statistical Manual (American Psychiatric Association 2013).

These forces of objectification in mental health culture, which have largely been adopted by counselors and psychotherapists, have become institutionalized as dominant, unquestionable assumptions about professional helping (Hansen 2014a). As such, these forces continually determine and shape the attitudes and professional identities of the cultural actors. The best defense against this cultural indoctrination into ideologies of objectification is awareness, which is achieved through critical analysis of the icons of contemporary mental health culture that support and maintain this objectifying vision. In this regard, three primary cultural icons, which institutionalize, support, and promote objectification, are diagnosis, biological reductionism, and the medical model for counselors and psychotherapists. Although I have mentioned these topics (particularly diagnosis and the medical model) in previous sections of this book, my aims in this chapter are to reiterate some of the logical critiques of these cultural icons, speculate about the functions they serve in contemporary mental health culture, and offer some alternative conceptualizations that may be useful to practitioners.

Diagnosis

There is nothing inherently wrong with diagnosing a person who is in need of help. The use of some type of nosological shorthand, which captures the primary elements of a problem, can be useful to professionals who help people with problems of living. Indeed, the ability to come to the psychological aid of a client may rely on a type of professional pattern matching, whereby talk therapists recognize the fundamental elements of a problem without having to reconsider the pieces of a puzzle anew with every client they see (Polkinghorne 1992). Notably, however, there are numerous ways that problems of living can be classified. Indeed, some systems of classification are based on inner psychological life (e.g., McWilliams 2011).

As mentioned in the previous chapter, the Diagnostic and Statistical Manual (DSM), since 1980, has relied on a descriptive psychiatric ideology, which purposefully eschews meaning systems and categorizes people according to symptoms alone. I have described the evolution of the DSM and its impact on mental health culture. Alternatively, in the following discussion of diagnosis, I elaborate and expand the critique of the DSM, particularly with regard to the individual, professional, and societal functions that it serves. Looking at the impact of diagnostic culture more microscopically requires revisiting some logical critiques of the DSM, speculating about the underlying reasons for the cultural dominance of this objectifying ideology, and following the financial breadcrumbs through the economic forest to see where they lead. Again, this analysis is designed to promote awareness of elements of mental health culture that are often blindly followed by its professional inhabitants.

Perhaps the most harmful aspect of generating a list of diagnostic labels based on observable symptoms is that people (both clients and therapists) come to believe that the labels represent actual discrete entities. There is no doubt that people suffer psychologically. However, when different varieties of psychological suffering are clustered exclusively according to symptoms, people tend to regard these socially constructed symptom constellations as actual disease entities, which have an independent, ontological existence beyond the label that was assigned to them. In short, created symptom clusters become mistaken for discovered entities.

Throughout human history people have reified socially constructed sets of signs as representative of actual, underlying processes. If one has a nightmare, the crops are dying, and mists can be seen emanating from the local volcano, these seemingly disparate events can be grouped together as signs of an underlying problem, perhaps, for example, that one of the gods is angry. Cultures appoint and give high status to interpretative experts who make sense of and categorize various happenings as indicative of underlying processes. Certainly, there are both evolutionary and existential reasons that people and cultures regularly assign meanings to environmental events. Those who had the ability to read signs that might be indicative of a dangerous threat undoubtedly had a better chance of survival than those who lacked this ability. The reification of an underlying structure of meaning that is detected from signs, then, is a trait that probably has the strong force of natural selection behind it. Likewise, the sheer enormity, randomness, and potential dangerousness of environmental events has undoubtedly caused, and continues to cause, severe existential anxiety. What do the forces of nature indicate? Why do people suffer? What should we do to make our lives better? These existential questions naturally arise when large-brained bipeds congregate in communities and seek solace from the harshness of nature. Indeed, the hunger for answers to these questions virtually defines the factors that distinguish human beings from other animals.

In some ways, science has helped humanity to move beyond culturally appointed experts who interpret the meanings of signs. The scientific method has discovered that epilepsy is a neurological disorder, not an indication of demonic possession. Earthquakes are caused by identifiable seismic irregularities, not angry gods. Life forms, in all of their diversity, were not suddenly created by a supernatural force. Rather, life slowly evolved and diversified through the process of natural selection (Dennett 1995). Scientific investigation has provided objective, evidence-based answers to questions that have haunted humanity for millennia. However, in areas where answers are still not definitive or available, culturally-appointed experts continue to interpret and reify clusters of signs. Mental health professionals are examples of modern, culturally-appointed experts who interpret signs. These professionals use the DSM, which contains reified lists of mental health signs, as their interpretative guide.

Recall that the modern DSM simply consists of lists of symptom clusters (Decker 2013; Greenberg 2013). Psychiatric sleight of hand has contributed to these clusters being reified as freestanding disease entities. People regularly attribute their angry outbursts to "my bipolar disorder," for instance. Of course, bipolar disorder is merely, at least at this point in psychiatric history, a list of symptoms. Attributing the cause of an emotional state to a list of symptoms in the absence of a unifying, underlying process that is responsible for the symptoms is logical gibberish. It is tantamount to claiming that mood fluctuations occur because mood fluctuations occur. This reification of symptom clusters as causal entities is quickly revealed as absurd when it is subjected to logical scrutiny. However, the consumers and professionals who operate in contemporary mental health culture are often blind to the logical errors they commit when clusters of symptoms are reified as explanatory constructs.

For example, I supervised a talk therapist who was trying to help a client who had a propensity to cut herself. During a supervisory session, after this therapist had provided an extensive description of the case and the material that the client had discussed during their prior session, I asked the supervisee to conceptualize the case, specifically with regard to the reasons that the client often cut herself. The supervisee boldly, with a sense of professional authority, said that the cutting was due to borderline personality disorder. People with this affliction, she explained, had a tendency to engage in self-cutting. Following her interesting line of reasoning, I asked the supervisee how she knew that the client had this disorder. She confidently explained that cutting oneself was a hallmark sign of being borderline. The supervisee, by uncritically spouting the ideological values of contemporary mental health culture, had completely missed the logical tautology of her case formulation. That is, the cutting was caused by borderline personality disorder, and the cutting, in turn, served as the evidence that the client had the disorder. Clearly proud of her diagnostic acumen, I tried to sensitively impress upon the supervisee that her formulation said precisely nothing. I took her inability to understand my critique, even though she was very bright, as a sign of her strong indoctrination into contemporary diagnostic mental health culture.

This mass reification of symptom clusters as explanatory constructs has consequences for practitioners and their clients. In the case of my supervisee, it caused her to completely overlook the client meaning systems that were connected with the self-cutting. The unquestioned acceptance of the descriptive psychiatric explanatory systems by talk therapists causes practitioners to miss meaning systems, overlook chances to strengthen therapeutic relationships, and forego opportunities to formulate explanatory narratives that might promote client betterment. Entire client presentations are neatly summarized by a diagnostic label, which is merely a list of symptoms that has no explanatory power or utility to guide the helping encounter for talk therapists.

In the previous chapter, I emphasized the professional benefits that psychotherapists and counselors gained by endorsing this medicalized, symptom-focused view of problems of living. In particular, talk therapists achieved the status of pseudo-medical providers and the financial rewards associated with this status. In addition to these professional benefits, quick diagnostic summaries can foster the illusion that one has understood the fundamental elements of a case and has the ability to master them. Diagnosis erases the complexities, pain, and messy grey ambiguity of human problems. Tying up cases with neat diagnostic bows can provide a false, but reassuring, sense of mastery that defensively keeps psychotherapists and counselors from experiencing the raw, ambiguous elements of professional helping, such as the sense of being lost in the relational darkness of suffering, the gnawing emptiness of not-knowing, and the painful sharpness of poignant existential questions that cut to the heart of what it means to be a person. When given the choice to either generate a diagnosis that casts a client as disordered and the therapist as a removed expert, or, alternatively, to consider a client a potentially knowable fellow human being who is simply carrying a psychic backpack of conflict and pain, just like the therapist, it is not surprising that psychotherapists and counselors have continually fought for the right to act like pseudo-psychiatrists instead of as deeply connected, empathic helpers.

The defensive use of psychiatric diagnostics to avoid facing troubling realities is not only used by therapists and their clients but has arguably been adopted by the larger culture. To illustrate this point, I had the occasion to interview a man who had committed a particularly heinous crime, shortly after an extensive manhunt had resulted in his capture. Having just been jailed a couple of hours before I saw him; he had not yet had the opportunity to speak to his attorney or the press, so he was in a psychologically raw and forthcoming state of mind. Before entering his cell, I prepared myself to make the absolute greatest use of my psychological perspicacity and training during the interview so that I might discern the psychological reasons that a seemingly ordinary man could so coldly and viciously kill a person whom he had presumably loved. We talked for about an hour. I left the interview with no psychological clues about the reasons he had committed the crime. There was nothing remarkable that I could detect about his psychological presentation. He was naturally upset about the events that had transpired, but there were certainly no obvious personality variables that could account for his actions. Indeed, if anything stood out to me, it was his ordinariness.

Over the next few days, numerous psychological pundits, none of whom had met the inmate, appeared in the media to express their opinions about the reasons he had committed the crime. These experts generally agreed that the inmate was afflicted with antisocial personality disorder (American Psychiatric Association 2013, 659). In terms of their reasoning, the pundits had committed the same logical error as my supervisee. Antisocial personality disorder is simply a socially constructed list of symptoms that is not associated with any biomarkers or definitively known underlying causal processes. Therefore, a mere list of symptoms cannot serve as an explanatory construct to account for a symptom, just as classifying a pen as a member of a group called "writing instruments" cannot account for the existence of the pen or the words that have been written with it.

Despite the absurdity of their psychological explanation, the pundits, media interviewers, and the public clearly seemed satisfied with this expert opinion. As I considered these events, I began to hypothesize that there were a variety of collective psychological incentives for experts to publicly appear and offer a definitive reason that a seemingly ordinary person could suddenly commit such a vicious crime. Of course, the experts themselves benefited from the media exposure. It seemed odd to me, though, that none of the interviewers asked these experts seemingly obvious questions. For instance, why did no one spot the fact that this person had antisocial personality disorder before the crime? Other than the crime, how do the experts know that he has this disorder? What about other people who might be afflicted? Will they suddenly commit crimes too? How do we know if people have this disorder? Is there some way to test for it, or is it always just diagnosed after someone behaves in a particular way? If it is only diagnosed after the behaviors that define it, what good is the diagnosis in the first place (and what good are the supposed diagnostic experts)? How can a diagnosis that is merely a collection of symptoms serve as an explanatory construct to account for one of the symptoms that defines the diagnosis in the first place?

Perhaps the questionable assertions of the experts were never challenged because these expert opinions served a soothing function to the public, analogous to witch doctors who might reassuringly announce to their anxious tribe that mysterious, frightening, seemingly random, and potentially deadly natural events are due to completely understandable, spiritual causes. In both cases (psychological experts and witch doctors) the public is reassured that an expert has illuminated the frightening darkness, identified the reasons for horrifyingly inexplicable events, implied that there is some way to predict and control these happenings, brought order to the disconcerting existential ambiguities of life, and offered a sense of mastery over seemingly random occurrences. In the case of the crime, the psychological experts also implied that there was a reassuring answer to questions that must surely have been on the minds, albeit beneath the surface, of some people who became aware of the circumstances of the crime: "Given that I am an ordinary person who sometimes becomes angry, will I ever suddenly snap and become like this criminal? Are the seeds of evil inside of me, waiting to sprout? What about the people around me who seem normal? Will some of them suddenly and unpredictably become dangerous?" By attributing the crime to a discrete disorder, the experts implied that the public should not worry about any of these questions. The criminal was sick with an identifiable, concrete problem. Ordinary people are not afflicted, and it is not contagious. Challenging the experts with probing questions about how they arrived at their conclusions would serve to undo the calming effects of their proclamations, just as questioning the witch doctor would undermine the reassuring function that his role was designed to fulfill.

My work at a psychiatric hospital, particularly on a child and adolescent unit, has also caused me to speculate about the societal needs that are fulfilled by mental health diagnostics. In this regard, it is quite common nowadays, in my experience, for children to be given a diagnosis of bipolar disorder when they are admitted to a psychiatric hospital. I have worked with children, some of whom were only four years old, who, because of their angry outbursts, were diagnosed with this condition and prescribed medications for it. These children almost always had unimaginably horrific histories, which consisted of trauma, neglect, poverty, addicted caretakers, severe abuse, and multiple attachment disruptions. Given these wide-ranging, multifaceted systemic origins, it has always been remarkable to me that, upon crossing the threshold of the psychiatric hospital, the source of any behavioral problem was suddenly positioned within the skull of the child, definitively redefined by experts as a neurochemical disorder that required psychopharmacological treatment.

As in the example of the criminal case noted above, I believe that mental health diagnostics also serve a societal function in the case of psychiatrically hospitalized children (Hansen 2014a). On a smaller scale, the psychiatric diagnosis serves to absolve families of any responsibility for the problems of their children. When a child is given a mental health diagnosis, there is no need for family members to feel guilty, responsible, or to consider changing their behaviors; the brain is to blame. Of course, there are often therapists involved in these cases who urge family members to change their dysfunctional behaviors for the benefit of their child. However, in the face of the powerful psychiatric proclamation that their child has a diagnosable, brain-based problem, and the prescribed medication that symbolically reinforces this narrative, this therapeutic guidance quickly becomes nagging, background noise that is easily brushed aside by the dominant psychiatric perspective.

Beyond the family and hospital milieu, society is also arguably reassured by the psychiatric collapse of difficult systemic problems into discrete, brain-based abnormalities. Poverty, abuse, and trauma are complex and troubling realities for which there is no obvious solution. Mental health diagnostics perhaps serve to reassure the public that they should not worry about these difficult systemic problems. Highly-trained experts have determined that the source of problems is individual brains, not larger societal issues. "Do not worry about the problems in your communities," the mental health experts reassuringly imply. "We have determined that they are not the cause of the suffering and unrest of your children. The problem lies in their brains, and we, who are experts on the brain and its treatment, have everything under control." Perhaps, then, there is an unconscious collective agreement between mental health providers and society. Society awards status and prestige to experts who diagnostically reduce complex systemic problems to individual brains. The payoff for awarding these benefits is that it provides the cultural participants with professionally-sanctioned permission to ignore, dismiss, and forget about the anxiety-arousing social problems that threaten to disturb their consciousness.

In support of this thesis, generations ago it was women who were sometimes psychiatrically diagnosed and hospitalized if they reacted negatively to their oppressive circumstances. Wanting an education, hoping for a life beyond mind-numbingly bland domesticity, and failing to respect the authority of one's husband could result in a diagnosis of "moral insanity" and subsequent psychiatric hospitalization (Masson 1994; Rimke and Hunt 2002). Once women became empowered through liberation movements, however, they could no longer be psychiatrically scapegoated for oppressive, systemic problems. A new, disempowered scapegoat for societal ills had to be found. Children are the new women.

Indeed, a strong theme of the history of mental health diagnostics is the gradual envelopment of problems, which were formerly in the moral and legal realms, into the domain of psychiatry (Hansen 2005). Child molesters have been transformed into pedophiles; drunks now have alcohol abuse disorder; and juvenile offenders have been redefined as persons with oppositional-defiant disorder. From immorality to illness, and from delinquency to disorder, psychiatric expansionism has planted the mental health flag on numerous human problems that were formerly classified in the moral and legal domains (Szasz 2007). Indeed, there was recently a movement to redefine racism as a psychiatric disorder (Guindon, Green, and Hanna 2003). Racism is a moral problem; it seems bizarre to consider it a psychiatric disorder. However, if the advocates of this questionable initiative had achieved their goal, cultural common sense would begin to change. People would start to think of racism as a mental health problem, psychotherapists and counselors would bill insurance companies to help those afflicted with this condition, researchers would use neuroimaging to pinpoint the parts of the brain that are associated with racism, and pharmaceutical companies would market drugs to treat it. Of course, the word racist would have to be changed to something medical sounding to legitimize its status as a psychiatric disorder. Perhaps *racial misattribution syndrome*, with various subtypes (e.g., African-American subtype) and severity ratings, might fit the bill.

In addition to continually acquiring new disorders, diagnostic expansionism operates by lowering the diagnostic thresholds on existing disorders. Frances (2013), the psychiatrist who headed the DSM-IV (American Psychiatric Association 1994) revision, has expressed regret over the DSM-IV diagnostic criteria, which, he argued, created false epidemics of autism, bipolar disorder, and ADHD due to the lowering of diagnostic thresholds. Aside from creating false outbreaks of particular disorders, the lowering of diagnostic thresholds in the service of psychiatric expansionism is also problematic because false diagnostic homogeneities are created.

To illustrate this point using a medical analogy, a migraine headache is diagnostically defined as a particular type of headache that is typically associated with auras and various symptoms at prodrome, attack, and postdrome phases. Suppose, however, that the diagnostic criteria for a diagnosis of migraine headache were widened to include any headache, regardless of whether it had the characteristic features of a migraine. After this definitional change, headaches that are caused by stress, hangovers, injuries, and brain tumors, to name a few examples, would all be grouped within the unitary diagnostic category of migraine headaches, despite the fact that these headaches have different causes and require different treatments. Fortunately, medical conditions often have known origins or unique, highly-defined presentations. These features and known origins serve to curtail the expansion of the diagnostic criteria based on symptoms alone. That is, if similar medical symptoms have different detectable causes, the medical diagnostic groupings will be based on the causes, not gross symptom similarity. Stomach pain, then, is not a unitary diagnosis. There are different medical diagnoses for stomach pain depending on whether the cause is indigestion, ulcers, or appendicitis, for example. In formal medicine, knowing the causes or the stereotypical presentations of disorders anchors diagnostic definitions and prevents them from expanding based on mere symptom similarities alone.

Mental health diagnostics, however, are based exclusively on symptoms. There are no definitive causal markers to anchor the diagnostic categories and prevent them from expanding on the basis of symptoms alone (Frances 2013; Greenberg 2013). This descriptive psychiatric diagnostic orientation, then, sets the stage for diagnostic expansionism and false homogeneities. As an example of false homogeneities, if a person's symptoms matched the criteria, they would be eligible for a diagnosis of major depressive disorder (American Psychiatric Association 2013, 160), regardless of whether their depression had been with them since childhood or had occurred more recently; whether it was characterized by inner feelings of emptiness or by excessive guilt; or whether their sadness was a reaction to a specific event or no identifiable precipitant had occurred. Indeed, with the most recent edition of the DSM (American Psychiatric Association 2013) the bereavement exclusion has been removed, an instance of diagnostic expansionism that means people who are grieving may be eligible for a diagnosis of Major Depressive Disorder.

Simply because two people are sad, losing weight, and having difficulty sleeping does not necessarily mean that their symptoms are caused by the same source and require the same treatment, just as the symptom of stomach pain in different people does not necessarily point to a singular cause and treatment strategy. Without biomarkers, of course, there is no way to tell which symptoms should be grouped together based on cause. However, it seems extraordinarily counterintuitive to put a person who is stricken with grief in the same category as a person who has had deep, dark, unrelenting chronic depression for decades with no identifiable precipitant. In terms of presenting symptoms, these two people may have striking similarities, such as crying, hopelessness, and anhedonia. Again, though, it is an extraordinary violation of psychological common sense to suppose that their problems should be defined by the same category.

Symptom-based diagnostic expansionism and false diagnostic homogeneities are not simply an accidental by-product of descriptive psychiatric ideology. Rather, there are strong professional incentives for widening the diagnostic net to include more people. The pharmaceutical industry, for instance, is a major financial beneficiary of psychiatric expansionism (Davies 2013; Frances 2013; Murray 2009). If an increasing number of people are defined as psychiatrically ill, then medication sales and profits will increase accordingly. Likewise, if a disorder that was formerly reserved for severe problems expands to include less severe problems, or even problems that were formerly considered an ordinary part of life, these false homogeneities can also be exploited for profit by the pharmaceutical industry. In this regard, now that the bereavement exclusion has been removed for Major Depressive Disorder in the latest version of the DSM, I predict that in the coming years the pharmaceutical industry will market antidepressant drugs as a treatment for the newly pathologized problem of grieving a loss.

Mental health practitioners, including psychiatrists, psychotherapists, and counselors, also benefit from diagnostic expansionism. Billing opportunities for mental health professionals are a function of the number of people who are designated as having disorders; additional disordered people translate to increased billing opportunities. Therefore, the mental health incentive structure for industries and practitioners is clear: more disorders equals more money. Symptom-based diagnostics and the lack of anchoring biomarkers, then, have been exploited to expand the diagnostic net, cast it outward, and reel in the financial rewards.

For psychotherapists and counselors, this diagnostic expansionism causes practitioners to dismiss the meaning systems of their clients. Symptom-based diagnostics are like a giant wet blanket that covers and extinguishes the fires of meaning that ignite in the offices of talk therapists. Complex systems of meaning are reduced to clusters of observable symptom; clients who are frequently upset have intermittent explosive disorder (American Psychiatric Association 2013, 466); sad clients are stricken with depression; worried clients have an anxiety disorder. These handy, professional-sounding symptom summaries counter the emergence of meaning. Inquiries into what the anger, sadness, or worry is about; how it is unique to this person; its developmental origins; the inner conflicts it represents; and the cultural factors associated with it are increasingly disregarded as irrelevant distractions in the contemporary culture of mental health, which educates and indoctrinates professionals to define clients exclusively according to their symptomatic presentation.

Furthermore, diagnostic expansionism automatically results in a narrowing of the definitional range of normalcy (Frances 2013). The yin of abnormal is always tied to the yang of normal; as abnormal expands normal shrinks. In this regard, if the ever-expanding DSM is a comprehensive list of mental disorders, then the absence of any DSM disorders must, by logical extension, be the definition of normalcy. What would a person without any DSM disorders be like, though? What image of normal does the DSM vision of abnormal point toward? Using the analogy of *homo economicus*, a term borrowed from the field of economics to describe a fictitious, implausible person whose behavior is exclusively driven by self-interest and cold, rational appraisals of economic incentives (Kickert 1978), I propose the term *homo normalis* (HN) to describe a person who lacks any mental health disorder, as such disorders are currently defined. What would HN, this paragon of normality, be like?

It is difficult to obtain a precise fix on the characteristics of HN because the current DSM criteria are thoroughly peppered with ambiguous qualifiers, such as *inappropriate, marked, severe, excessive, clinically significant, significant impairment, often*, etc. These terms clearly call for subjective clinical interpretation, which makes it difficult to determine the precise points at which the vast grey middle of the human spectrum shades into definite abnormality at one end and unequivocal normalcy at the other. Despite the inherent ambiguity of the DSM criteria, a rough picture of HN can be drawn.

HN would be completely unflappable in the face of life changes. Never falling prey to adjustment disorder (American Psychiatric Association 2013, 286), he would be immune to developing "emotional or behavioral symptoms in response to an identifiable stressor(s)" (286). HN would always follow rules, obey authority, and conform to the expectations of his culture. He would never "actively def[y] or refus[e] to comply with requests from authority figures or with the rules" (462), a possible sign of oppositional-defiant disorder (462). In keeping with his passive, obedient disposition, HN would strictly avoid any symptoms of general personality disorder (646), including making sure that he never displays behavior that "deviates markedly from the expectations of [his] culture" (646). Clearly, HN is not a civil rights leader, agent of social change, or a person who challenges the status quo in any realm.

HN would also be a model of level-headedness and self-control. Indeed, he would have an almost completely dispassionate approach to living. To avoid binge-eating disorder (American Psychiatric Association, 350) he would always refrain from "eating until feeling uncomfortably full" (350). HN would also carefully monitor his coffee and energy drink intake to ensure that he does not fall victim to caffeine intoxication (503) and the "restlessness" and "nervousness" (503) that accompany this state. In keeping with his strong level of self-control, HN's mood would be characterized by rock solid stability. So he does not meet the criteria for major depressive disorder (160), HN would never experience excessive or prolonged sadness, even when grieving. Likewise, HN would always keep his emotional excitability in check to keep from displaying the symptoms of a hypomanic episode (124).

HN would be strictly conventional, even with regard to his subjective experience. Indeed, his strict allegiance to conventionality would cause him to always be on guard to make sure that he is not subject to "inner experience and behavior that deviates markedly from the expectations of [his] culture" (American Psychiatric Association 2013, 646). Related to his conventional nature, HN would never "hold fixed beliefs that are not amenable to change in light of conflicting evidence" (87). Of course, being a strict conformist, HN would define what constitutes "evidence" according to the norms of his culture.

I acknowledge that I have cherry-picked particular phrases from the DSM to construct HN. Also, people absolutely suffer with mental health problems, and, by proposing the concept of HN, I certainly do not intend to trivialize this suffering. With the above caveats in mind, I believe that a particular construct of normality is implicitly suggested by the DSM. Critical examination of the DSM, then, should not only entail a review of the psychopathological states that are listed in the manual, but should also attend to the subtextual definitions of normality that are implied by the absence of these states. From my reading, the flip side of the DSM psychopathological coin points toward a particular ideal of normality, one that is characterized by extreme conventionality, a focus on self-control, severely limited emotional responsiveness, indifference to events that most people would find stressful, hyperrationality, a humorless, grey inner life and, overall, an eerily dispassionate approach to living. HN seems more like a robot than a person.

All mental health practitioners who structure their practices and conceptualizations according to the DSM, then, by definition, are striving to transform their clients into HN. When symptoms are idealized, and meaning systems are viewed as irrelevant distractions, the goal of treatment is to eliminate symptoms as they are currently defined. *Homo normalis* is the ultimate expression of that goal.

The creation of a new version of normality, however, was not part of the original vision of descriptive, symptom-based diagnostics. The idea behind classifying problems of living according to symptoms was to create a diagnostic nosology that would be atheoretical, thereby avoiding the problem of theoretical favoritism (Decker 2013; Greenberg 2013). Participants in mental health culture, regardless of theoretical orientation, could presumably agree about observable symptoms. The ordinarily contentious psychoanalytic lion and behavioral lamb could peaceably co-exist at a conference and discuss cases if they restricted their conversations to the supposedly atheoretical realm of symptom clusters. Like many grand visions, however, descriptive psychiatric diagnostics did not live up to its promises. Indeed, it strongly favored one of the key icons of contemporary mental health culture: biological reductionism.

Biological Reductionism

The symptom based DSM-III (American Psychiatric Association 1980) was introduced at a time when biological psychiatry was beginning its strong ascension in mental health culture. Although there were no known biomarkers for DSM disorders (and, generally speaking, there are still none [Davies 2013]), psychiatrists during the late twentieth century developed drugs that, indeed, helped to alleviate certain mental health symptoms (Greenberg 2010; Shorter 1997). Compounds for symptom clusters associated with depression, anxiety, and schizophrenia were introduced as pharmaceutical companies increasingly turned their attention to the production of highly profitable psychiatric drugs. The supposedly atheoretical DSM-III, with its exclusive focus on symptoms, turned out to be a perfect match for a biological view of mental health problems (Greenberg 2010). Lacking biomarkers, biological sources of mental suffering could not be targeted directly. Therefore, the overall goal of biological psychiatric interventions was to use drugs, or other physical means, to alleviate symptom constellations. The 1980 version of the DSM, and all subsequent editions, consisted simply of menus of symptoms. Far from being atheoretical, then, the DSM-III and biological psychiatry were a match made in heaven. The powerful synergy of the pharmaceutical industry, biological psychiatry, and the symptom based DSM propelled the value system of biological reductionism to a position of strong dominance in mental health culture.

The reduction of mental suffering to biological processes is an incredibly seductive proposition. It is tempting to suppose that psychological turmoil, anxieties, strange ideas, addictions, relational conflicts, and problems of living could all be caused by discrete, malfunctioning bodily processes. In this regard, one of the cruel ironies of mental suffering is its nonmateriality. People generally feel a reassuring sense of mastery when they are able to manipulate a concrete, observable aspect of the physical world. However, guilt, worry, rage, sadness, and regret reside in the intangible realm of the psyche, a dimension where the rules of physical reality do not apply. It is no wonder, then, that, throughout human history, there has always been a strong desire to find ways to transform nonmaterial psychic pain into concrete, manageable, physical processes, which can potentially be measured, controlled, and mastered.

It is perfectly reasonable, though, to presume that certain varieties of psychological suffering are primarily caused by physical processes. Schizophrenia, for instance, is associated with strong, stereotypic symptoms, emerges during a fairly predictable age range, severely impairs functioning, and seems to run in families (Torrey 2013). Although there is certainly a psychological component to schizophrenia, the evidence strongly suggests that there is some kind of biological vulnerability that sets the stage for someone to be afflicted with this problem. I have worked with numerous people diagnosed with schizophrenia. Despite the claims of certain psychotherapists (e.g., Karon and VandenBos 2004) I have never witnessed a substantial alleviation of schizophrenic symptoms that was brought about by psychotherapy alone. However, I have seen medication work wonders. I certainly hope that increasingly effective biological treatments for chronic mental health conditions will continue to be discovered.

Ideally, then, the value system of mental health culture should honor both psychological and biological, nonmaterial and material, ideological approaches to understanding and treating mental health problems. The Cartesian split between mind and body, which has animated Western culture for centuries (Tarnas 1991), is rapidly being abandoned. Mind and body mutually influence one another; to focus exclusively on one or the other ignores this mutual influence and positions inquiry squarely within the Cartesian dualism that we would be better off abandoning. Unfortunately, mental health care, because it is arguably determined more by the power dynamics of its participants than by logic or common sense, has generally, throughout its history, failed to produce a balanced, mind-body culture. During eras when nonmaterial approaches to mental health care dominated (e.g., mid-twentieth century), physical conditions, such as epilepsy, were wrongly attributed to psychological causes. Contemporarily, mental health culture is just as out of whack as it was six decades ago. Only nowadays, biological reductionism is the primary value.

Just as a culture that over-indulges psychological explanatory systems can be shortsighted and cause harm, so can a culture that focuses on biological reductionism. Reducing memories to molecules, or life journies to genes, comes with its own set of problems. The dominance of biological reductionism has produced a mental health culture that is perilously dismissive of the psychological, relational, and cultural dimensions of life.

In this regard, mental suffering can be positioned on a spectrum. On the far left are ordinary problems of living, such as reactions to developmental transitions, grief, and the emotional ups and downs that characterize everyday life. Schizophrenia, manic depression (not the modern, over-diagnosed bipolar disorder), and chronic, debilitating forms of depression and anxiety are on the far right end of the spectrum. Of course, there is a vast area between these endpoints. Generally speaking, it is reasonable to presume that the right side of the spectrum has far stronger biological determinants than the left. In turn, although constitutional factors undoubtedly play a role in virtually every way of being, it would be a mistake to characterize the conditions on the left side of the spectrum as biologically determined. The ideology of biological reductionism and physical treatment is sensible for the right side. However, problems on the far left are best understood as psychological, developmental, or relational phenomena.

Regarding treatment, there is good evidence that psychotherapy should be an important component of treatment for the entire spectrum, even for clients on the far right side who suffer with severe mental health problems. Psychotherapy for schizophrenia, for instance, has been shown to promote social adjustment (Kurtz and Mueser 2008) and reduce rates of re-hospitalization (Bach and Hayes 2002). However, psychotherapy alone is not sufficient for clients with severe conditions. A primary component of treatment for far right side clients should be biological interventions, such as medication. Alternatively, for clients on the left side who have relatively mild problems of living, psychotherapy alone is ordinarily an effective treatment. Medications or other biological interventions are unnecessarily intrusive and extreme for those on the far left side of the spectrum. Regarding the middle part of the spectrum, clinical judgment should be used to determine whether problems call for medication or can be treated with talk therapy alone. Talk therapy is less intrusive and fosters greater independence and psychological growth than medication. Therefore, practitioners should always be cautious about referring middle spectrum clients for biological treatments. However, sometimes medication is a suitable option.

I believe the above spectrum represents a balanced, commonsensical view and is consistent with what is currently known about mental suffering. In short, *a singular ideology or treatment is not appropriate for the entire spectrum*. Ideologically, it is potentially harmful to use biological reductionism to understand people with mild, left-side problems, but biological reductionism is probably the best ideological hope for those on the extreme right side. Likewise, the exclusive use of psychological understandings and treatments is usually insufficient for people with chronic, severe, stereotypical mental health problems.

Throughout history, the entire spectrum of mental health problems has been taken over by the proponents of the culturally dominant ideology. During the mid-century and beyond, severe chronic mental health problems were often understood and treated as psychological phenomena (Shorter 1997). Contemporarily, the mental health spectrum has been hijacked by the ideology and treatment vision of biological reductionism. Treating a person with mild transitional psychological problems, such as worry and sadness about job stress, with biological interventions is an extraordinarily odd, counterintuitive, and harmful component of contemporary mental health culture. However, the treatment of people who have far left side problems with medication is business as usual in modern day mental health care.

Diagnostic expansionism and the false homogeneities that are baked into modern diagnostic categories have been leveraged to justify the provision of intrusive medical treatments for clients who would not even be considered candidates for medication a generation ago. In my experience, if someone goes to a primary care physician or a psychiatrist complaining that they have been sad, worried, and their eating and sleeping patterns have changed over the past few weeks, they will virtually always be given a prescription for psychiatric medication, even if their depression is relatively mild and due to a transitional problem, such as work stress. In addition to the prescription, the person may also told that their problem is due to a neurochemical imbalance. Just as it is inappropriate to use psychological ideologies and treatments alone for someone on the right side, conceptualizing and treating left side problems with biological approaches is also harmful.

When people come to a mental health professional, they not only receive treatment; they also receive an ideological explanatory system that indoctrinates them into thinking about their problem in a particular way (Frank and Frank 1993). When a person is prescribed mental health medication, the usual explanatory system they receive is that their problem is due to a chemical imbalance, even though no causal chemical imbalances for mental health conditions have ever been discovered and academic psychiatrists are rapidly abandoning this theory due to lack of scientific evidence (Davies 2013). Regardless of the evidence, when a person who is held in high professional regard communicates to a suffering client that her or his problems are due to an incurable biological defect, the person coming for help is likely to believe the authority. Therefore, it is important to consider the greater psychological implications of this biological explanatory system. Indeed, the explanatory system that comes with the medication may have a far greater impact on the person than the medication itself.

The primary implication of telling a person that a biological defect is the cause of their problems is that other potential factors are relegated to a minimal or irrelevant status. While the biological defect explanatory system might ultimately turn out to be true for people with severe problems, it is certainly not true for people on the mild side of the spectrum. Ironically, however, people with relatively mild problems may welcome, and even enthusiastically embrace, the idea that they have a biological defect in order to avoid dealing with their psychological and relational difficulties. As an example of this phenomenon, I was counseling a woman who suffered from sadness and worry. Over many sessions, as our relationship developed and her defenses began to remit, she began to discuss her marital problems, which had plagued her for decades. At this point in the treatment, she decided, without telling me, to see a psychiatrist. During the counseling session after her psychiatric visit, she announced that she was quitting counseling. She explained that the psychiatrist had told her that her anxiety and depression were due to a chemical imbalance, and he had prescribed medication for her disorders. Relieved that her problems were biological, and not due to her marital unhappiness, she stopped coming to see me. It was easy for me to empathize with her decision.

In counseling, I was offering her the opportunity for psychological growth. However, to get to this destination, she had to face the hurt and anger she had been pushing aside for decades. In my judgment, her symptoms were easily understandable on a psychological level and were not severe enough to warrant medication. Furthermore, I thought that she could achieve some resolution to her longstanding problems if she was willing to endure the emotional pain that would come from finally facing them. I certainly respect the choice of wanting to numb pain rather than experience it for the sake of growth. However, she was not given this choice. She was told by a representative from a profession that is usually considered the highest authority in mental health culture that her problems are due to a chemical imbalance.

Another problem with the ideology of biological reductionism, then, is that it often encourages people to anesthetize their psychological pain rather than to experience and grow from it (Davies 2012). Again, for severe problems, medical relief from mental suffering is often the best option. However, as the ideology of biological reductionism has increasingly spread throughout the left side of the spectrum, people with relatively mild problems are forfeiting opportunities to gain lasting psychological resolutions to their emotional difficulties by anesthetizing their pain with relatively intrusive treatments (i.e., medication), rather than by directly addressing their problems via less intrusive methods (i.e., talk therapy), which foster growth, mastery, and independence.

Regarding independence, an important component of the ideology of biological reductionism, at least in its current, widely-promoted chemical imbalance form, is that mental health problems are permanent conditions that can only be managed, never cured. While this may turn out to be true for people afflicted with severe problems, it is a dangerous message for those who have relatively mild problems. Sadness and worry that are due to life stressors, for instance, can ordinarily be addressed and resolved effectively with talk therapy. When people are prescribed drugs for relatively mild problems, they receive, either explicitly or implicitly, the message that their problem emanates from an irreparably defective, biological source. This message can be the worst side effect of the medication.

In this regard, Frances (2013) made the interesting point that the relatively low side effects of modern psychiatric medications often results in people wrongly coming to believe that their psychological problems emanate from a biological source. To illustrate this point, suppose a person is prescribed medication to treat mild depression, which had been caused by life stressors. The depression may naturally remit when the impact of the stressors has passed. However, if the person had been taking medication to supposedly treat the depression, he or she may misattribute the remission of the symptoms to the effectiveness of the medication instead of to the resolution or passing of the stressors. Because of the low side effects of the medication, the person might understandably reason that the safest bet is to continue to take the medication, which has few, if any, aversive consequences, rather than to discontinue the medication and risk the return of the highly aversive depressive state.

The situation of people with relatively mild problems becoming psychologically dependent on psychiatric medications (and concomitantly believing that they have a biological defect) is particularly troubling considering the evidence regarding medication effectiveness. Indeed, there is good evidence that antidepressant medication may be no more effective than a placebo for mild and moderate depression (Kirsch 2010). Psychotherapy and counseling, however, have proven effectiveness for many types of mental health difficulties, including depression (Wampold 2001).

There are multiple potentially harmful consequences, then, of using biological reductionism as an explanatory model to account for mild psychological problems. The underlying logical justification for broadly applying this model to the ever-expanding universe of mental health disorders is that human beings are ultimately reducible to biological processes. After all, without the brain, there would be no consciousness. Therefore, this questionable reasoning goes, we should stop ineffectively tinkering with the intangible smoke of the mind and directly address the tangible fire of the brain. Contemporary mental health culture, with its prominent value of biological reductionism, is arguably suffused with this reductionist reasoning. Is this reasoning sound and sensible, though?

This reductionist logic is dependent on the underlying assumption that breaking humans down into increasingly smaller, tangible bits, will bring us ever closer to the essential foundations that define and determine humankind;

our souls will eventually be discovered if we just keep increasing the magnification on the microscope. Does moving from gross sections of the brain, to neurons, to genes, and perhaps then to molecules, atoms, and subatomic particles bring us steadily closer to knowing who we are, what makes us tick, and, ultimately, how to end our suffering? Again, the current trajectory of contemporary inquiry into mental health problems strongly implies this underlying rationale. Is this a reasonable way to consider human nature, though? I do not think that it is.

To illustrate my critique of the reductionist assumptions that form the ideological foundation of contemporary mental health culture, consider text on a computer screen. It is certainly true that if the guts of a computer were destroyed, no text would appear on the screen. This does not mean, however, that the real, essential computer, the area that should be of primary concern, and the place where all of our focus should be, is the microprocessor or hard drive. As a writer, my goals would never be met if my attention were devoted to these mechanical and electronic innards. However, for someone who is involved in the manufacture or repair of computers, the internal parts should be their area of focus. For a physicist who studies electromagnetism, a small component of the processes within the microprocessor might be the appropriate area of study. Alternatively, a sociologist, who is interested in the impact of technology on society, would study computers at a macro level. Note that computers, like people, can be considered on many levels, from a unit of inquiry that consists of hundreds of thousands of computers down to the subatomic level that operates within microprocessors. Which of these levels, though, represents the true, foundational essence of computers? At which level should all of our focus be directed?

An obvious and logical answer to these questions is that we should not think of computers as having true, foundational essences. Different individuals and communities perceive computers in various, legitimate ways. People who interact with computers, such as physicists, writers, sociologists, and manufacturers should focus on the level that advances their purposes. There is no transcendentally correct level or way of perceiving computers.

Analogous to computers, there is no transcendentally correct way to understand human beings. As a counselor, I attempt to understand the thoughts, feelings, experiences, and conflicts of my clients. It would be bizarre, inappropriate, and unhelpful for me to spend the counseling hour talking about sociological or molecular issues, for example. For other professionals, however, these areas of concern would be appropriate for their realm of inquiry. The idea that the mind is ultimately reducible to the brain, then, is illogical and misguided. The mind and brain are simply different domains of concern for different types of professionals. One is not intrinsically better, truer, or more foundational than the other.

The flashing lights of neuroimaging machines have hypnotized the participants of mental health culture into believing that the brain is the foundation of human nature. Incidentally, simply because different mental health conditions differentially light up various parts of the brain, it does not prove that the brain is the cause of these conditions (Fancher 1995). As an alternative explanation, perhaps experiencing the condition causes the brain to respond in a particular manner, not the other way around. Depending on whether one is worrying, arguing, exercising, or meditating, the brain would likely appear differently in a neuroimaging machine. In these examples, the state of mind causes the brain changes. In similar fashion, perhaps the states of mind brought about by having certain mental health conditions causes particular areas of the brain to light up. Instead of the brain changes causing the experience, perhaps the experience causes the brain changes.

Again, I sincerely hope that neuroimaging and other biological investigations eventually uncover physical causes that are behind severe, stereotypic mental health conditions so that better treatment options can be developed. My critique, then, is not of biological reductionism per se. Rather, I am critiquing the cultural dominance of biological reductionism as a central explanatory system for the entire spectrum of mental health problems. Biological explanations are probably the best hope for helping people with severe problems. However, attentiveness to relationships, meaning systems, conflicts, emotions, and other products of the mind have proven effectiveness with numerous problems in the mental health realm. Different professionals should rely on different systems of thought. There is no singular, intrinsically correct ideology that is suitable for all clients or helping professionals.

However, talk therapists have been increasingly participating in the ideology of biological reductionism. Psychologists are currently fighting to gain rights to prescribe psychiatric drugs (Fox et al. 2009), a professional agenda that is absurd on multiple levels. Psychotherapists and counselors are embracing neuroscience as an explanatory system (e.g., Luke 2016). Contemporarily, talk therapists are often considered part of a larger, medical team that is headed by a physician. What people refer to as interdisciplinary collaboration nowadays used to be called breaches of confidentiality. There is ordinarily no reason for psychotherapists or counselors to communicate with a physician about a case, any more than there would be reason for a therapist to share case information with a client's accountant, dentist, or personal trainer. Contemporary mental health culture blurs the differences between mind and brain professionals, lumping them all together in the same biological, reductionist category.

The primary danger of talk therapists embracing biological reductionism is that client meaning systems are inevitably devalued. Psychotherapists and counselors cannot simultaneously place a high value on the importance of client meaning systems while also believing that a biological defect is responsible for their clients' problems. Clients, in turn, cannot be expected to actualize their lives, explore the meanings that have caused their conflicts, struggle with the pain that is a usual part of psychological growth, or strive to overcome their difficulties if they are told, either subtly or directly, by their therapists that their problems are caused by incurable biological defects. Mind professionals and body professionals are both needed in mental health culture. However, with the dominance of biological reductionism, contemporary mental health culture has become mindless; the mind is being lost to the brain.

Psychiatric diagnostics and biological reductionism, then, are dominant value systems in contemporary mental health culture. When these values are adopted by talk therapists, the meaning systems of clients are inevitably devalued, a consequence that is undesirable for numerous reasons specified above. Furthermore, adoption of diagnostics and biological reductionism results in a particular mode of practice for counselors and psychotherapists: the medical model.

Medical Model for Counselors and Psychotherapists

The primacy of diagnostics and biological reductionism in contemporary mental health culture has created a particular vision of practice for all mental health professionals, including counselors and psychotherapists. This vision is that client complaints represent particular, diagnosable problems, and that diagnoses should determine the type of treatment that clients receive (Elkins 2009; Wampold 2001). This medical model chain of events in practice operates as follows: a) a client has a presenting complaint; b) the professional diagnoses the complaint; and c) the professional selects the best, specific treatment to address the diagnosis. Although I discussed the impact of the medical model on meaning systems in a previous chapter, in the following section I position the logical critiques of this model within the dynamics of contemporary mental health culture. Furthermore, I offer an empirically-supported, meaning-based alternative to the medical model, which can be used to guide the work of counselors and psychotherapists.

It is perfectly reasonable for nonmental health physicians to use the medical model to guide their work. A broken leg requires a different type of treatment than kidney failure. Aligning particular treatments with specific conditions is simply good practice in the realm of formal medicine. Indeed, the medical model is also a defensible model of practice for biological psychiatrists, albeit probably not to the same degree as nonpsychiatric physicians. Mental health diagnoses, unlike many medical diagnoses, are simply collections of symptoms, which are generally not associated with underlying, causal processes. However, particular psychopharmaceutical treatments are sometimes helpful in ameliorating certain clusters of symptoms. Therefore, generally speaking, it is not unreasonable for biological psychiatrists to use the medical model as a rough framework for their practices.

What about counselors and psychotherapists, though? Implementation of the medical model for talk therapists means that particular psychotherapeutic techniques (analogous to drugs in medicine) should be optimally aligned with particular diagnostic conditions. A person with Major Depressive Disorder, for example, might be prescribed cognitive behavioral therapy. However, is the medical model (i.e., the prescriptive matching of techniques with diagnoses) an effective framework for talk therapists? Generally speaking, it is not. Meta-analysis of psychotherapy outcome studies have consistently demonstrated that the quality of the therapeutic relationship is the within treatment variable that has the highest association with outcomes (Lambert 1992). Specific techniques likely account for less than 1 percent of the variance in psychotherapy outcomes (Wampold 2001). The prescription of psychotherapeutic techniques for particular diagnostic conditions, then, is, generally speaking, a relatively ineffective paradigm for talk therapy practice.

The common factors approach is a viable, evidence-based alternative to the medical model of specific techniques for particular conditions approach (Laska, Gurman, and Wampold 2014). Because outcome differences between specific treatments are usually negligible across various diagnostic conditions, it is reasonable to presume that the nonspecific factors common to all treatment approaches are primarily responsible for outcomes, not the specific techniques associated with particular theoretical orientations. These common factors include, but are not limited to, a healing setting, a caring therapist in whom the client can confide, a culturally congruent explanation for the problem, the establishment and maintenance of a treatment alliance, and the arousal of hope in the client (Laska, Gurman, and Wampold 2014; Frank and Frank 1993; Wampold 2001). Although specific treatments have proven effectiveness for certain conditions, these cases are the exception, not the rule. For instance, when clients suffer from a phobic anxiety, exposure to the feared object or situation has proven to be an effective part of an overall treatment strategy (Laska, Gurman, and Wampold 2014). However, despite the superior effectiveness of specific factors with a small minority of particular conditions, the overall evidence is that the common factors of treatment are largely responsible for client change.

Ironically, despite its relative ineffectiveness, the medical model has overtaken psychotherapy practice and research agendas in the talk therapies (Elkins 2009). The prestige, status, and reimbursement associated with the medical model has resulted in the widespread use of this model by talk therapists, despite the fact that it is an exceedingly poor fit. The continued use of the medical model has also been fueled by psychotherapy outcome research, which usually operates within the medical model framework. Indeed, within the culture of academic research "exploration of scientific factors other than treatment methods have been discouraged or labeled as 'unscientific'" (Laska, Gurman, and Wampold 2014, 467). With the strong dominance of the medical model in mental health culture and academia, it is no wonder that this paradigm has been adopted en masse by counselors and psychotherapists.

In addition to the general lack of empirical support for the use of the medical model by talk therapists, there are logical problems with the application of this model to the work of counselors and psychotherapists. To illustrate a primary problem, medical treatments are generally effective cross-culturally, but, in contrast, the effectiveness of psychotherapy methods are a function of client meaning systems (Frank and Frank 1993). For example, antibiotics have been found to be effective for treating infections. These drugs generally work regardless of culture or time of human history when they are employed because the laws that govern the human body are relatively invariant. Although the cultures, values, and beliefs of an African tribal person and a typical American are strikingly different, proven medical treatments would likely have very similar levels of effectiveness if both of these individuals had the same physical disorder.

In contrast to medical treatments, however, the effectiveness of psychotherapeutic methods is highly dependent on the meaning systems of the client (Frank and Frank 1993). Cognitive-behavioral techniques, for instance, would almost certainly be ineffective for a tribal person who believes that healers must have a connection to the spiritual world in order to be helpful. Likewise, many treatments that are effective at alleviating psychological suffering in other cultures would likely fail if used with American clients.

Even within cultures there can be great variation in the structures of meaning that people regard as helpful. For example, I have had initial meetings with prospective clients who subsequently decided that they would not be able to work with me because I do not counsel from a biblical, Christian perspective. These clients probably made the right choice. If a religious meaning system is vital to their worldview, they would likely be better off seeing a professional who shares their perspective rather than someone who operates from a secularist position.

If researchers find that a specific psychotherapeutic technique is helpful for treating a particular psychological disorder, then, this finding must necessarily have very limited generalizability. Again, this is in contrast to formal medicine, wherein a finding about a treatment for a bodily problem would almost certainly have great generalizability, across cultures, regions, and eras, because the essential properties of human bodies are relatively invariant. Research findings about psychotherapy cannot possibly be universally applicable because, unlike formal medicine, effectiveness in the talk therapies is dependent upon the cultural and individual meaning systems of the people who come for help (Frank and Frank 1993). Simply because psychotherapy outcome researchers use the broad paradigm of the medical model to frame their investigative efforts, it does not mean that findings from psychotherapy research have the same degree of generalizability as findings from formal medical research, just as wearing borrowed clothing does not mean that a person acquires the characteristics of the original owner.

When the medical model is adopted by psychotherapy researchers, however, an implicit, unwarranted assumption that findings are highly generalizable, just as in formal medical research, also tends to be erroneously adopted. In this regard, I have never seen anything like the following reasonable disclaimer in the limitations section of a psychotherapy outcome research article: "Although we, the researchers, found significant results when method x was used to treat condition y, it should be remembered that the effectiveness of psychotherapeutic methods is highly dependent on the beliefs and values of the participants. The method that was found to work in this study may not work in a different era, region, or culture. Therefore, the generalizability of these findings is likely limited to people who have the same worldview as the participants."

Unlike medical disorders, mental suffering cannot be physically or conceptually separated from the sufferer (Luhrmann 2000). Emotional problems are always inseparably tied to people and their meaning systems. To illustrate this point, a cancerous tumor is an identifiable abnormality that is physically distinct from nonpathological tissue. It is reasonable, therefore, for physicians and medical outcome researchers to treat and study cancer as a relatively freestanding entity, which is ontologically distinct from the people who suffer from it. In contrast, however, it is unreasonable for talk therapists to make the claim that they treat depression, for example. Depression is an inseparable part of psychological and social processes. Psychological distress is not a bounded, pathological entity with a demarcated, ontological status that distinguishes it from other aspects of a person; it cannot be isolated and treated as a freestanding pathological chunk like a tumor.

Given the above distinctions between medical and psychological varieties of suffering, it is, indeed, reasonable for medical professionals to claim that they treat disorders. However, it is unreasonable for talk therapists to make the same claim. Counselors and psychotherapists help people who experience psychological suffering; it is a logical error to claim that they treat person-removed disorders. Likewise, it is logically erroneous and misleading to frame psychotherapy outcome research in terms of treatments and disorders. Instead, outcome research in the talk therapies should be conceptualized as investigations regarding the impact of psychotherapeutic interventions on the psychological suffering of subjects who have particular historical, cultural, and individual structures of meaning.

The adoption of the medical model by researchers and practitioners in the talk therapy professions has blurred the distinctions between the use the medical model in formal medicine versus the use of this model in the domain of counseling and psychotherapy. The use of the same overarching paradigm in different fields does not mean that the paradigm has the same meaning, value, or implications for the different fields. The medical model has radically different implications for the talk therapies than it does for formal medicine. Because of the strong professional benefits associated with posing as quasi-physicians, however, the illogical and harmful elements of the use of the medical model by counselors and psychotherapists have been dialogically suppressed in contemporary mental health culture; rather than explore and become aware of the implications of this model, cultural participants have generally decided that it is better to keep quiet and reap the benefits.

As noted above, the common factors approach is a logical alternative to the use of the medical model in counseling and psychotherapy. The conclusion that the common factors of various therapeutic approaches, not specific techniques, are responsible for treatment effectiveness is based on the consistent findings that: a) psychotherapy is helpful; and b) generally speaking, all treatment methods work about equally well (Wampold 2001). Therefore, it is reasonable to presume that the nontechnical, relational factors, which are present in all types of psychotherapy, are the key ingredients that make talk therapy effective. However, like all psychotherapy outcome research, the common factors conclusion is based on studies that investigated subjects who had particular meaning systems. Perhaps, then, common factors are only effective for the types of subjects who participated in the psychotherapy outcome studies that informed the common factors conclusion. Maybe the same factors would not be effective with subjects from different cultures, for instance. Therefore, it is potentially useful to conduct a cross-cultural analysis to determine if there are factors that are common to all healing arrangements, regardless of culture.

Frank and Frank (1993) have taken the common factors finding to the next level by examining healing across various cultures to determine whether the healing paradigm has cross-cultural common denominators. Their book, *Persuasion and Healing*, is a fascinating overview of healing in various cultural contexts, such as cults, non-industrialized societies, the Western World, and religious forms of healing. From their analysis, the authors, indeed, concluded that there is a relatively universal framework for healing, which has tremendous implications for understanding the work of counselors and psychotherapists. Specifically, like other forms of healing, all talk therapies have four elements: a) "An emotionally charged, confiding relationship with a helping person" (40); b) "A healing setting" (41); c) "A rationale, conceptual scheme, or myth that provides a plausible explanation for the patient's symptoms and prescribes a ritual or procedure for resolving them"

(42); and d) "A ritual or procedure that requires the active participation of both patient and therapist and that is believed by both to be the means of restoring the patient's health" (43).

As applied to counseling and psychotherapy, Frank and Frank's (1993) model suggests that a person who is suffering comes to see a talk therapist because the therapist is designated as a healer in the society in which he or she operates. The client and therapist form a healing bond around an explanatory system (i.e., psychodynamic, cognitive-behavioral, etc.), which is consistent with the client's worldview and provides an alternative way of conceptualizing the client's suffering. Certain rituals, which emanate from the explanatory system, are prescribed (e.g., cognitive homework, free association, etc.). These rituals inspire hope and fortify the bond between the therapist and client. The client, having been indoctrinated into the explanatory system by the therapist, believes that the therapist has correctly identified the reasons for the problem and that the rituals will result in healing.

Note that in Frank and Frank's (1993) model the contextual factors of the therapeutic relationship are responsible for healing (Wampold 2001). The counselor or psychotherapist must offer an explanation for the client's suffering. However, the healing explanatory system does not have to be true (whatever that would mean) or scientifically validated. The primary criterion for effectiveness is that the explanatory system must be plausible to the client. Therefore, according to this model of healing, the reason that extant systems of psychotherapy are effective is not because they are accurately reflective of human nature. Rather, they are effective because these systems of thought are consistent with the worldview of many of the Western clients who seek help during contemporary times.

For example, clients are often persuaded by cognitive-behavioral therapists that dysfunctional patterns of thinking are responsible for their suffering. This cognitive narrative is a persuasive, compelling, and culturally acceptable storyline in contemporary Western society. Along with this explanatory system, certain rituals, which are consistent with the cognitive storyline, such as cognitive reframing, are also prescribed. These rituals help to solidify the explanatory system and the treatment alliance. Again, it is not the relative truth or falsity of the explanatory system that matters; rather, it is the potential of the system to persuade clients to view their suffering through a new, hopeful lens.

Indeed, drawing from Frank and Frank's (1993) insights, I strongly suspect that the healing claims of certain fringe movements are at least somewhat accurate. Scientologists, for example, undergo a process of auditing (Wright 2013). The trained auditor connects the client to an e-meter, which records the client's physiological changes in reaction to particular, probing questions, which are asked by the auditor. By reading the e-meter responses, auditors claim to be able to spot and eliminate engrams, or negative influences, which, according to the doctrines of Scientology, are responsible for client suffering. Eventually, when the troubling engrams have been eliminated, the client can graduate to a state of becoming *clear*. Despite the commonplace objections to Scientology, note that this Scientology paradigm has all of the healing properties that are specified by Frank and Frank. Specifically, a healer who is regarded as an expert (at least within the subculture of Scientology) administers a treatment. The healer offers an explanatory system and associated rituals to the client. Of course, if one does not believe the postulates of Scientology, the method would not work, just as if one does not believe the postulates of cognitive-behaviorism, this system would not work either. Again, though, the truth (whatever that would mean) of the explanatory system is not the relevant factor responsible for the healing effect. Rather, it is whether the client endorses the system as offering hope for the alleviation of her or his suffering. When viewed from an objective distance, it is arguably equally plausible to blame suffering on thoughts or engrams. However, the key discrimination between these two explanations with regard to healing potential is that most people do not find the engram explanation plausible, while the dysfunctional thought explanation has become so culturally prominent that many people consider it a compelling, persuasive narrative.

As further support for Frank and Frank's (1993) hypotheses, the explanatory systems of various cultures clearly promote healing within their respective cultures. For instance Torrey (1972), an anthropologist who became a psychiatrist, described his experiences learning about the healing practices of witch doctors. He observed that witch doctors, who were given the designation and associated status of a healer in their tribe, named a tribal person's problem, raised a sufferer's expectations that recovery was possible, offered a spiritual explanation for problems, and prescribed rituals to appease the spirits that the sufferers had offended. Torrey's observation about the healing process and the effectiveness of witchdoctors led him to conclude that "I, as a psychiatrist, was using the same mechanisms for curing my patients as they were" (70). Counselors and psychotherapists are witch doctors of the West.

Frank and Frank's (1993) hypothesis about the factors responsible for healing has been called the *contextual model* (Wampold 2001). In my estimation, the contextual model is the best overarching conceptual paradigm for understanding the healing process in the talk therapies. In short, counselors and psychotherapists are societally designated experts who offer hope to sufferers in the form of persuasive explanatory systems and associated rituals. Healing is a by-product of client indoctrination into an alternative narrative, which accounts for suffering and inspires hope. Indeed, not only is the logical and cross-cultural evidence supportive of the contextual model, this model also has strong empirical support. Meta-analysis of psychotherapy outcome studies clearly indicates that the contextual model is vastly superior to the medical model in its ability to account for psychotherapy outcomes (Wampold 2001).

For purposes of this discussion, however, it is particularly important to note two differences between the medical and contextual models. First, the medical model of counseling and psychotherapy trivializes meaning systems. The contextual model, in contrast, highlights meaning systems (in the form of culturally congruent explanatory narratives) as the key ingredient of the healing process. Second, specific techniques are an important component of the healing paradigm in both the medical and contextual models. In the medical model, however, techniques are viewed as discrete interventions, analogous to drugs, which directly cause the healing effect. The empirical evidence is largely unsupportive of this view (Wampold 2001). In the contextual model, alternatively, specific techniques are important because they are part of the larger context of the healing arrangement, not because of their influence as isolated bits. Techniques solidify the explanatory narrative; provide clients with concrete actions to perform, which inspire hope and a sense of mastery over their troubles; and strengthen the bond between counselor and client through the shared performance of rituals. Techniques only acquire meaning and efficacy as a function of the larger context of meaning that animates the healing encounter.

In summary, the medical model is an extraordinarily poor fit for the work of talk therapists. However, this model has been adopted en masse by counselors and psychotherapists because of the status, prestige, and reimbursement that it offers. Not only does the medical model lack empirical support as a paradigm for talk therapists, this model, by design, obscures the meaning systems that are integral to the work of counselors and psychotherapists. As compared to specific techniques, common factors of therapy orientations are far superior in accounting for psychotherapy outcomes. The contextual model takes the common factors paradigm to the next level by specifying the factors that are integral to the healing paradigm across cultures. I have argued that the contextual model, which places the highest value on meaning systems, currently offers the best proposal for understanding the ingredients that make talk therapy effective.

SUMMARY

Three of the primary icons of contemporary mental health culture are: a) diagnosis; b) biological reductionism; and c) the medical model. Although arguably appropriate for investigating and treating severe problems, such as schizophrenia, these iconic values have overtaken the entire spectrum of mental health conditions. Talk therapists, ironically, have embraced these iconic values, even though there is no empirical justification for them to do so, and these cultural icons severely devalue the meaning systems that are integral to the work of counselors and psychotherapists. Societal values and associated professional incentives, however, have created a mental health culture wherein talk therapists regularly formulate symptom based diagnoses and medicalized treatment plans, which specify the use of certain techniques for particular symptoms. With this thoroughly medicalized approach to helping, the vital meaning systems that animate the lives of clients are often trivialized.

Logic and evidence, I have argued, naturally lead to the conclusion that talk therapists should not use the medical model as a paradigm to guide their work. The common factors of psychotherapy orientations, not specific techniques, are the most important within treatment determinants of outcomes in counseling and psychotherapy. As an extension of the common factors model, the contextual model offers an empirically supported, overarching paradigm for understanding and guiding the work of talk therapists. Notably, the contextual model places the highest value on the meaning systems of the participants in the helping encounter.

The fact that counselors and psychotherapists have seemingly acquiesced to the icons of contemporary mental health culture leads to some interesting questions about the educational preparation and training of talk therapists. For instance, should education simply train counselors and psychotherapists to professionally operate in whatever culture happens to be present at the time of their training, or should education be directed to critical thinking about the helping process? Indeed, what is the role of education in a relational profession? Is education even needed for this type of work? What should be the goals of education and training for talk therapists? These questions, and others, are examined in the next chapter.

Chapter Five

Training for Talk Therapists

The idealization of descriptive diagnostics, biological reductionism, and the medical model in contemporary mental health culture implies that training to become a counselor or psychotherapist should be a highly technical process. After all, knowing the details of a thousand-page diagnostic manual, the neurological correlates of mental health conditions, and the precise psychotherapeutic techniques that should be prescribed to treat particular presenting complaints would seem to require years of extensive, specialized training. In contrast to this view of training for talk therapists, Rogers (1957), in his seminal article on the necessary and sufficient conditions of counseling, opined that "intellectual training and the acquiring of information has, I believe, many valuable results—but becoming a therapist is not one of those results" (101). Indeed, Rogers went so far as to deny that any "special intellectual professional knowledge . . . is required of the therapist" (101). Therefore, the strong emphasis on advanced training implied by contemporary mental health culture is radically at odds with the view of one of the most influential and insightful theorists in the history of the helping professions, who relegated education to a minimal, even unnecessary, status. Which vision is correct, though? Perhaps Rogers' nearly six-decades-old opinion is out of date and not in keeping with the current research. On the other hand, maybe the iconic values of contemporary mental health culture have obscured foundational truths about counseling and psychotherapy that were clearly apparent to certain mid-century theorists. Fortunately, numerous research studies have provided some answers about whether training is an important prerequisite for becoming an effective talk therapist.

The general strategy that researchers have used to determine the value of training and education is to compare the therapeutic outcomes of professional therapists and laypeople. If outcomes are significantly better for professional therapists, then training and education is clearly valuable. Alternatively, if paraprofessionals achieve the same outcomes as professionals, the role of education and training in the talk therapy professions is questionable and perhaps even a waste of time. This is a tricky topic to research. There are numerous methodological challenges and potential confounding variables to consider. Furthermore, there are no universally agreed-upon criteria for defining and selecting trained professionals or paraprofessionals. Even with these challenges, however, multiple studies have compared the client outcomes of professionally trained therapists with paraprofessionals. The general finding of these studies, with some minor exceptions, is that there are no significant differences in the client outcomes of paraprofessionals and trained professional therapists (Atkins and Christensen 2001; Berman and Norton 1985; Hattie, Sharpley, and Rogers 1984; Strupp and Hadley 1979). Indeed, some researchers have even concluded that the outcomes of paraprofessionals were superior (Durlak 1979). It appears that Rogers may have been correct.

As an interesting example of this research, college professors who were rated by their students as having high relational ability achieved therapeutic outcomes that were equivalent to experienced psychotherapists (Strupp and Hadley 1979). The conclusion of a single study might rightly be regarded with skepticism, of course. A review or meta-analysis of multiple studies comparing professionals and paraprofessionals with regard to outcomes would be more compelling. Fortunately, a number of these reviews and meta-analyses have been conducted. For instance, Durlak (1979), after reviewing the extant research, arrived at the provocative conclusion that the outcomes of paraprofessionals were actually superior to the outcomes of professionals. Subsequent researchers who summarized the findings in this area have generally found that there are little, if any, differences between the outcomes of paraprofessionals and professionals. For instance, after an extensive review, which eliminated some of the methodologically problematic studies that Durlak used to draw his conclusion, Berman and Norton (1985) concluded that "professional and paraprofessional therapists were generally equal in effectiveness" (401) and that "current research evidence does not indicate that paraprofessionals are more effective, but neither does it reveal any substantial superiority for the professionally trained therapist" (401). Other researchers, using meta-analysis of studies comparing professionals to paraprofessionals, concluded that "paraprofessionals are at least as effective, and in many instances more effective, than professional counselors" (Hattie, Sharpley, and Rogers 1984, 540). The weight of the research evidence, then, severely challenges the common assumption that training and education are important prerequisites for becoming an effective talk therapist.

Of course, it is easy to understand the reasons that a high level of training has been required for counselors and psychotherapists. Generally speaking, professionals acquire status, prestige, and financial incentives when they are associated with advanced, technical training. The mid-century psychoanalysts who dominated mental health culture and whose judgments were held in high regard for decades, for instance, were required to undergo extensive training to become full-fledged psychoanalysts. After four years of college, aspiring psychoanalysts were required to complete medical school, a psychiatric residency, and then enroll in psychoanalytic training for a half-dozen years or so. Given the high level of status and expertise associated with this level of training, the idea that a friendly bartender might be just as helpful to clients as a certified psychoanalyst would have been a heretical idea at the time. However, given the evidence, it may very well have been true.

In this regard, consider a thought experiment regarding education and training. Imagine that a group of ten adults are selected because they are warm, caring, and have the ability to develop close relationships with a variety of people. None of these adults have any training or education in the helping professions, but they have all agreed to undergo a one-year training program to become a talk therapist. The year-long program emphasizes professional ethics, the application of relational skills to helping clients, and the practicalities of working as a therapist. After they have completed the program, they all go to work at a clinic where ten practitioners who have completed conventional training to become a talk therapist also practice. Clients who call the clinic are randomly assigned to a therapist, so the odds of getting a briefly- versus conventionally-trained therapist are even. Clients who are assigned to the briefly-trained therapists are never made aware that their therapist was trained in an unconventional manner. Clients are simply told that their therapist is highly trained, regardless of the type of therapist to whom the client is assigned. Suppose that client outcomes are tracked over a two-year period. Would there be a significant difference between the outcomes of the briefly trained versus conventionally trained therapists?

Of course, the above experiment cannot actually be conducted because it would violate legal and ethical standards. However, it is interesting to conduct the experiment in the realm of thought. My prediction is that the outcomes of the two groups of therapists would not be significantly different. Of course, I do not know whether I am correct, but I believe that the evidence from the paraprofessional research, and the fact that the common, relational factors of therapy have the highest within-treatment association with outcomes (Wampold 2001), supports my conclusion. In fact, given the evidence, I think that the burden of proof should be on those who predict that the conventionally-trained therapists would have significantly better outcomes.

The idea that training might be of little importance to therapeutic outcomes can be a difficult conclusion to accept. After all, aspiring counselors and psychotherapists devote years of their lives, significant financial resources, and sacrifice time that could have been spent on relationships and other meaningful elements of life to be hazed into the helping professions. Extensive years of training, of course, can be considered worthwhile, regardless of whether it contributes to superior outcomes. The only route to practice as a counselor or psychotherapist is to jump through the legally-mandated educational and training hoops. The goal of having a fulfilling career, then, may absolutely be worth the sacrifices. Simply because one is required to follow a certain path to become a helping professional, however, does not necessarily mean that following that path will make one a better practitioner.

The above discussion suggests some interesting questions. Should education and training be required to become a talk therapist? What course of study would optimize outcomes for the future clients of trainees? Ideally, which elements of the current requirements to become a therapist should be retained and which are unnecessary or even harmful? In short, if the entire system of training therapists were suddenly eradicated and had to be rebuilt from the ground up; if all of the politics, legalities, third-party requirements, professional disputes, and medical model nonsense that have contributed to training programs were suddenly a non-issue; and the primary consideration in the design of training programs was the outcomes of the future clients of trainees, what type of training should aspiring therapists be required to undergo, given what is currently known about client outcomes?

TRAINING FOR TALK THERAPISTS

Over the years, I have heard students complain that much of what they are required to learn in graduate school has little applicability to their future work as counselors. I have also heard faculty respond to these complaints with a variety of justifications to support the current type of educational experiences that budding therapists are required to undergo. Given the fairly consistent research finding that client outcomes of trained professionals are generally not significantly different from the outcomes of paraprofessionals (e.g., Hattie, Sharpley, and Rogers 1984), I find it easy to sympathize with student concerns that the content of many of their courses is often irrelevant to their future professional lives. Indeed, in my role as a professor, when I have been engaged in teaching students about a statistical procedure, an obscure theorist, or some esoteric intellectual point, the experiential flow of my teaching has often been interrupted by moments of unexpected, reflective clarity when I am suddenly struck by the feeling that none of what I am saying matters and that there is no defensible reason my students should have to endure it. These moments pass, I cash my university paychecks, and the wheels of educational culture continue to turn. However, rather than dismiss these interruptive experiences, try to forget about them for the sake of justifying my job, or defensively rationalize the reasons that my intuitions are wrong, I would like to amplify and examine these moments. In fact, if you, the reader, are involved in training or educating future therapists, my guess is that you have some familiarity with the experiences I have described.

As a way of organizing the following discussion about training, I ask a series of questions and suggest possible answers. The questions are: a) Should specialized education and training be required to become a talk therapist? b) What should the goals of education and training be? c) Who should be trained to become a talk therapist? and d) Should post-graduate educational experiences and supervision be mandated? Note that I have not organized the questions according to particular professional groups, such as counselors or psychologists. This is because my questions are about training talk therapists generally, not about training someone in the specialized knowledge of a particular field, such as social work. From my experience as a practitioner for over twenty-five years, talk therapists from the social work, counseling, and psychology professions have far more commonalities than differences. Perhaps in other types of workplaces differences between these professional groups are more apparent. However, at the various clinics and counseling centers where I have worked, I have seldom been able to detect any consistent differences between therapists from various professions. My observations have been confirmed by research, which has found that the academic degree of practitioners is unrelated to therapeutic outcomes (Wampold and Brown 2005).

My answers to the questions about training talk therapists are informed by the regular research finding that the common, not specific, factors of therapy are largely responsible for outcomes (Wampold 2001). The contextual model (Frank and Frank 1993), described in the previous chapter, is also used to frame my responses to questions about training. In my estimation, the contextual model, which is highly supported by outcome research (Wampold 2001), is the best overall paradigm for conceptualizing the factors that make psychotherapy effective. Naturally, my responses to the questions are also based on my years of experience as an educator, supervisor, and practitioner. The answers are not intended to be final proclamations about training to become a therapist. Rather, they simply represent my current thinking about these matters.

Should Specialized Education and Training Be Required To Become a Talk Therapist?

This question naturally arises from the general finding that trained therapists are generally no more effective than untrained ones (e.g., Hattie, Sharpley, and Rogers 1984). Why should therapists be required to endure the long, laborious sacrifices of extensive education and training if it does not seem to make a difference in client outcomes? Even in light of these findings about outcomes, I think that there are at least three vital reasons that talk therapists should be required to undergo specialized training.

First, therapists are regularly involved in situations where safety and lives are at stake. To my knowledge, none of the studies that have compared trained therapists and paraprofessionals regarding outcomes have addressed the specialized issue of suicidal clients, for example. Sitting across from someone who has expressed a plan to kill him or herself imminently can be a highly disconcerting experience, even for therapists who have been trained to handle these situations. In this regard, allowing untrained therapists to manage suicidal clients could be disastrous.

In addition to suicidal clients, there are a variety of other potentially dangerous situations that arise with a disturbing degree of regularity in the practices of therapists. Clients who are potentially homicidal or psychiatrically impaired to the point where they cannot care for themselves, for example, are instances of potentially dangerous situations that require specialized training to navigate. Therapists, as a function of their work, also become aware of instances of child abuse and neglect. Managing this information and making proper determinations about it require a degree of expertise that laypeople usually do not have. Therefore, the first, and arguably most important, reason talk therapists should be required to undergo specialized training is that therapists must have the skills to effectively manage situations where someone is at risk. Broad studies about client outcomes tend to blur over this specialized issue of client safety.

Second, although talk therapy is fundamentally a relationship, it is a particular type of relationship that, in order to be effective, must be guided by certain parameters and ethical standards. For instance, it is generally not a good idea to go out to lunch with clients, lend them money, or give them directives about how they should live their lives. The average layperson may not have any awareness of these issues and might suppose that it is perfectly acceptable for a client and therapist to have a relationship outside of therapy, for instance. I suspect that the paraprofessionals who were used in outcome research studies were given overviews about basic boundary and ethical issues before they were allowed to practice. I would not want someone to function as a therapist if they did not have at least a fundamental understanding of these areas.

Third, drawing from the contextual model, knowing that one's therapist has been trained inspires hope and optimism in clients (Frank and Frank 1993; Wampold 2001). Although I do not know of any methodologically sound studies that have isolated the variable of the impact of client perception of therapist training on outcomes, it seems commonsensical to conclude that therapists who tell their clients that they have absolutely no training would not achieve the same level of client outcomes as therapists who provide evidence to their clients that they are highly trained, even if actual level of therapist training is held constant. In our culture, degrees on the office wall inspire hope that one is seeing a specialist who knows how to help; just as in other cultures a display of shrunken heads might inspire confidence that a witch doctor has the requisite skills to alleviate the suffering of tribal members (Torrey 1972). The activation of hope in clients is an important component of the change process. In many of the paraprofessional studies, it is often unclear whether client subjects were explicitly told, or were able to discern, whether their assigned therapists had been trained. Training may be valuable, then, simply because clients believe that it is.

There are at least three important reasons, therefore, that it is necessary for talk therapists to undergo specialized training, despite the findings of outcome studies that suggest there is no difference between paraprofessionals and trained therapists. Broad outcome studies comparing professionals to paraprofessionals tend to obscure issues related to client safety, boundaries and ethics, and the hope clients derive from the perception that their therapist is a trained helper. I suspect that the paraprofessionals in many of these studies were given some initial guidance about potentially dangerous situations and the basic relational boundaries of therapeutic practice. Otherwise, it would have been difficult, if not impossible, for them to safely and convincingly function as therapists. Furthermore, many of the subject clients who were assigned to see paraprofessionals in outcome studies likely did not know that their therapist had no training in the field. Disclosing this information to subjects in advance would have risked confounding the outcome comparison conclusion with the variable of client perception of therapist training. Therefore, it is unwarranted to interpret the findings of studies comparing paraprofessionals to professionals as evidence that talk therapists should not be required to undergo any training.

There are additional reasons, other than the ones discussed above, that aspiring therapists should be required to have a particular type of education and training to become practitioners. Although not as vital as client safety, boundaries and ethics, and the instillation of hope in clients, these additional reasons are arguably important. However, I have reserved the above first section for vital reasons for therapist training. Less vital, but important reasons are discussed in the following section.

What Should the Goals of Education and Training Be?

The primary goal of education and training should be to prepare students to function as effective talk therapists. At a bare minimum, trainees should learn the basic skills discussed in the previous section. However, it is also beneficial for students to: a) acquire supervised experience in the role of a talk therapist; b) develop an appreciation for meaning systems and human differences; c) become familiar with the common factors approach to helping; and d) learn at least one orientation to helping fairly well. While these experiences may not be as crucial as managing dangerous situations and having knowledge about ethics and boundaries, I believe that they contribute to optimal functioning as a practitioner.

Supervised experience as a practitioner is, for good reasons, a standard component of training in many fields. One generally cannot become a physician, teacher, or even a business professional without completing some type of supervised fieldwork experience as part of the educational curriculum. In the talk therapy professions, supervised practice experiences may be particularly important because they bring the abstract ideas and principles of counseling and psychotherapy to life in the context of the helping encounter. One can know what to do on paper with a suicidal client, but it is an altogether different experience to properly provide live, in-the-moment care.

Practicing therapists make their living by forming helping relationships with people who have various backgrounds, perspectives, and worldviews. It is particularly important, then, for counselors and psychotherapists to have an appreciation for diverse ways of being. Other professionals see diverse clientele, but it is not as vital for an accountant, for instance, to have an appreciation of meaning systems as it is for counselors and psychotherapists to have this appreciation. Most professionals advise people on discrete areas of their lives, such as finances, physical health, or legal matters. Therefore, the relationship that the professional establishes with the client is often secondary to the technical guidance that the professional is able to provide. The service that talk therapists provide, alternatively, is highly dependent on the establishment of a strong helping relationship (Wampold 2001). To be effective, talk therapists must strive to empathically see the world through the eyes of their clients. To accomplish these relational goals, talk therapists should have an appreciation for the perspectives of diverse types of clientele. Therefore, educational and training experiences that foster this type of appreciation, such as case conceptualization, empathy training, and multicultural understandings, are important elements of training for aspiring therapists to undergo.

The last two components of therapist training mentioned above are related to the actual work of counseling. Talk therapists should be trained in the common factors of therapy; training in specific, isolated techniques should be deemphasized (Stein and Lambert 1995). The outcome research strongly suggests that relational factors, which are common to all therapeutic systems, are primarily responsible for outcomes, not isolated techniques (Wampold 2001). Therefore, training to become a talk therapist should emphasize the establishment and maintenance of a treatment alliance, empathic listening skills, nonjudgmental tolerance for diverse ways of being, and other relational factors that are common to various schools of thought (Stein and Lambert 1995). These factors should not be taught in isolated, technical ways, such as instructing therapists on the precise body language they should adopt or the exact wording of empathic responses. Rather, budding therapists should be trained to express the common factors in whatever manner is genuine and conducive to their personality and relational style. A good therapeutic relationship should feel genuine to both parties. Experiences of genuineness can be difficult, or impossible, to bring about if a therapist is preoccupied with rigidly following training edicts about the supposedly correct ways to execute therapeutic microskills.

Although the common factors of therapy are almost surely the most beneficial ingredient in the helping encounter, there is strong empirical (Wampold 2001) and cultural anthropological evidence (Frank and Frank 1993) that it is also important for therapists to know at least one theory and its associated techniques fairly well. Recall that the contextual model, which was derived from Frank and Frank's (1993) cross-cultural study of the healing process, posits that a vital part of helping is that the healer presents the sufferer with an alternative explanatory system and associated rituals. For therapists, these explanatory systems are theories, and the rituals are the techniques derived from the theories (Hansen 2006). For instance, a client who feels hopelessly depressed might be reassured, and greatly helped, by a therapist who offers a cognitive explanation, and associated techniques, for the depression. Techniques are useful when they are implemented in the context of a larger explanatory system, but far less helpful when they are presented as isolated bits (Wampold 2001). Because the popular orientations to therapy all work about equally well, students should be instructed to select a favored theory, which they could envision themselves implementing in a genuine, relational way. Also, students should be clearly told the reasons that they have been instructed to learn a particular therapeutic approach in depth. Again, these reasons are that: a) the empirically-based contextual model suggests that an integral part of the healing process is that the healer offers the sufferer an alternative explanatory system, which promotes hope in the sufferer that there is a way out of their pain (Frank and Frank 1993); and b) all current, popular approaches to therapy work about equally well (Wampold 2001). In my experience, students are often told to select a theory, but are frequently mystified about the reasons that they should learn a particular theory well or why they, as novices, should be allowed to make the selection.

In summary, there are six vital educational objectives for programs that train talk therapists to adopt. Trainees should: a) learn how to manage potentially dangerous situations; b) become knowledgable about professional ethics and boundaries; c) acquire supervised experience in functioning as a talk therapist; d) develop an appreciation for diverse meaning systems; e) receive training in the common factors of therapeutic systems; and f) develop theoretical and practical mastery of a particular therapeutic system. There are, of course, many reasonable ways that these objectives can be translated into an educational curriculum. However, it is important for the educational experience of talk therapists to be reflective of the factors that form the basis for effective helping relationships, such as genuineness, warmth, sincere curiosity, acceptance of various perspectives, flexibility, nondefensive openness to challenges, maintenance of appropriate boundaries, and tolerance for ambiguity. Talk therapists in training may learn more from the relational style of their teachers than they do from the content of their courses. Therefore, although it is important to incorporate the above six objectives into training programs, they should not be communicated to trainees in a rigid, uncompromising manner or by faculty who believe that they are enlightened experts who have graciously deigned to share their nondebatable truths with the students who have been fortunate enough to learn from them.

Notably, the educational objectives and model of training proposed above is at least somewhat at odds with the traditional values of the academy. The time-honored view of the university is that faculty researchers make new discoveries, these discoveries are disseminated to practitioners, and professional services continually improve because they are driven by the latest findings in the field (Polkinghorne 1992). This top-down, modernist model of education is probably a good fit for the field of medicine, for example. I certainly hope that my physician is aware of the latest research findings related to my physical health issues. However, in contrast to my physician, I hope that my therapist is paying more attention to me than to academic research. Talk therapists primarily learn their craft from clinical experience, not by keeping up with the latest research, which is often not applicable to the day-to-day work of trying to help diverse individuals.

The general goal of quantitative research is to discover enduring, universal laws of nature (Hansen 2012). Research chemists, for example, endeavor to come to know the principles that govern chemical compounds. Likewise, the broad goal of quantitative research in the social sciences is to uncover universal truths that dictate human behavior. Social science researchers have certainly made important contributions to the understanding of people. However, people differ from objects in that every person is unique, and people are determined by the meaning systems they create and adopt, not just by the laws of nature. Therefore, quantitative research in the social sciences is often of limited value to practicing therapists who are challenged to help one unique client after another, each of whom is driven by highly idiosyncratic systems of meaning. Unlike physicians, who usefully draw from universal physical principles about relatively invariant bodies, modernist inspired quantitative research may be of little value to talk therapists because the object of their work is highly variant human minds, which continually create their own principles. The traditional, top-down modernist structure of university education, then, is arguably not optimal for training and disseminating information to talk therapist trainees. Therapists generally increase their effectiveness by gaining experience in helping diverse clientele, not by knowing research findings (Polkinghorne 1992).

The discussion about training talk therapists could conceivably end at this point. I have argued that there are six essential categories that should guide the education of talk therapists, and that the epistemological structure of the traditional university is almost certainly not an ideal model for training students to effectively intervene in the lives of diverse clientele. However, I believe there is an additional issue that warrants further investigation. This issue derives from the following questions: What should the goal of education for talk therapists be? Should it simply be to train students to meet the demands of working life, or should it also be to instill critical thinking?

Training to become an auto mechanic, for instance, should probably just be focused on preparing trainees to repair cars. However, unlike training to practice a trade, talk therapists should arguably receive additional educational preparation aimed at helping them to become good professional citizens who are able to evaluate information, challenge the status quo, and bring about changes in their field. If a new model car comes out, mechanics should simply learn how to repair it. However, if a new therapeutic system starts to take over mental health culture, should therapists simply learn that system, regardless of whether it makes sense or has proven to help clients? If managed care companies suddenly demanded that practitioners stand on their heads while conducting therapy, should training programs teach students head standing techniques to prepare them for the world of work?

Mental health care generally, and talk therapy in particular, is driven by economic and professional factors that often have little to do with helping clients. Phrenology, eugenics, the denial of childhood sexual abuse, the spread of psychoanalysis into realms where it was not helpful, and the repressed memory movement, to name a few examples, were harmful trends and ideas that eventually lost their dominance because of critical thinkers who opposed the cultural status quo. Practicing therapists, then, should not be trained to simply do what they are told. Ideally, they should be trained to critically evaluate information in order to make determinations about what is best for their clients. History teaches us that professional helpers have regularly been encouraged to intervene in unhelpful, or outright harmful, ways (Masson 1988). Therefore, training students to think critically should ideally be a part of the education of talk therapists.

Like the fundamental principles of training, I believe that there are a variety of ways to incorporate critical thinking into training programs. Students should be able to critically evaluate research findings, know about the history (particularly the history of unhelpful and damaging ideological fads) of the helping professions, and be exposed to critiques of contemporary practices. Unfortunately, contemporary training programs for talk therapists are increasingly becoming like trade schools, which prepare students for the practicalities of their working lives but do not teach them to critically evaluate information. Additional critiques of contemporary education to become a talk therapists are elaborated in a subsequent section.

Who Should Be Trained to Become a Talk Therapist?

Talk therapists receive the foundation of their training in university graduate programs. The traditional requirements to be admitted to a program of study at a university is that prospective students must have a strong aptitude for academic achievement, as evidenced by grade point average, standardized test scores, and other criteria. If there are limited slots available, students with the best grades and highest scores are often the ones who are admitted.

This method of selecting students is probably suitable for disciplines that are purely academic or research-oriented. However, it is almost certainly not the best method for screening people to enter a relational profession, particularly given the evidence that the person of the therapist accounts for a significant proportion of the variance in outcomes (Wampold and Brown 2005). Most people can easily recall meeting someone who is academically brilliant, but relationally challenged. Programs that train therapists, then, should arguably establish relational pre-screening processes that inform admission decisions.

Indeed, I am not certain that an undergraduate education should be a prerequisite for admission to training programs for talk therapists. Paramedics, nurses, firefighters, and certain professionals who operate in the substance abuse community seem to regularly perform their vital, often complex, human service duties well without having a background in literature, philosophy, algebra, foreign languages or other course content that is ordinarily a part of undergraduate curricula. Are there good reasons that the professionals noted above are generally not required to have a college degree to practice, but talk therapists must have an undergraduate and graduate education before they are permitted to enter the workforce? This question becomes particularly challenging when the regular research finding that the outcomes of paraprofessionals are generally no different from professional therapists is considered (Hattie, Sharpley, and Rogers 1984). In contrast to this finding, I am quite certain that a comparison of professional versus paraprofessional nurses, for example, would reveal that professional nurses are significantly more effective than paraprofessionals. I doubt that this type of study would ever be conducted, however, because it would place lives at risk. In this regard, it is perhaps ironic that talk therapy professionals have a much higher educational requirement for entry into their professions than other human service professionals whose work clearly requires advanced training.

A college education, of course, is probably an important preparation for critical thinking. Although I view critical thinking as a desirable skill for talk therapists to possess, it is not essential to their work. Training in the six vital areas noted above probably do not require a college education as a prerequisite, particularly given the relatively consistent equivalency finding between paraprofessionals and trained therapists. Even though a formal college education may not be an important prerequisite for training, perhaps prospective trainees should acquire a certain amount of life experience before they are allowed to enter training programs. It is difficult to empathize with a variety of client problems when one has never had an intimate, long-term relationship, extended contact with children, experiences associated with living independently, and exposure to perspectives and worldviews that are different from one's own. Therefore, perhaps a minimum age of entry (28?) might be a better general screening criterion for talk therapy training programs than a college degree.

I recognize that it is controversial to suggest that a minimum age requirement might serve as a substitute for a college education in screening applicants for admission to talk therapy training programs. Keep in mind, however, that I am not proposing these requirements as a route to becoming a full-fledged social worker, psychologist, or counselor. There are many advanced, scholarly elements to each of these professions and it is reasonable to require a college education, and other academic standards, for applicants to be admitted into these professional courses of study, which have traditionally served as the training grounds for talk therapists. To clarify my suggestions, I am proposing that it is probably not necessary for talk therapists to identify with one of the traditional helping professions in order to be effective. If old training standards were suddenly abolished and had to be built up anew, I cannot think of any reasons that the traditional model of training talk therapists (i.e., three separate professions that require advanced graduate training) would be an obviously superior choice to other alternatives that could be implemented. As one alternative to the current model of training, I could certainly envision a two-year educational program, which would not require a college degree for entrance, but would provide intensive training in the six vital areas noted above, as an adequate program for training talk therapists. This program would not be designed to produce social workers, counselors, or psychologists, of course; it would only graduate trained talk therapists who do not have any affiliation with the traditional professions. I believe that if only mature, relationally talented people were admitted to such a program, regardless of whether they had a college education, the program would graduate competent and effective practitioners.

It may seem like a radical idea to disconnect the training of talk therapists from graduate programs in social work, counseling, and psychology. Consider, however, that these professions were not originally founded to train talk therapists. Social work was traditionally devoted to helping the poor and disenfranchised; the counseling profession had its origins in career and school guidance; the traditional focus of psychology was on testing and research. Talk therapy was only gradually added as a component to these professions after they had already been in existence for over half a century. Talk therapy became linked to psychology, social work, and counseling for historical, cultural, professional, and economic reasons; this linkage was arguably not logical or obvious. To illustrate this point, consider that, in the mid-twentieth century, the idea that talk therapists must be trained as medical doctors was a culturally commonsensical assumption. During this era, only psychiatrists were allowed to practice and many would have been shocked by the suggestion that medical school training should not be required to become a talk therapist. Perhaps the current assumption that talk therapists should be required to undergo training as a psychologist, counselor, or social worker is also the result of entrenched, cultural beliefs rather than rational appraisals of the evidence.

Should Post-Graduate Educational Experiences and Supervision be Mandated?

I preface my response to this question with two important caveats: a) I believe that talk therapists should continue their education throughout their careers and regularly consult with experienced colleagues; and b) I reflexively react with outrage at the thought of professional mandates. Perhaps my strong reaction against mandates is partially due to my personality style or the fact that I have been operating within the protective bubble of academic freedom for a couple of decades. Regardless of the source of my strong feelings against professional mandates, the reader should be aware that my biases influence my position on these matters. Again, my objection is to mandates, not postgraduate learning experiences, which I strongly support.

For multiple reasons, I am opposed to mandatory, post-graduate continuing education for talk therapists. First, there is no evidence that mandatory continuing education requirements have any impact on client outcomes. Without this evidence, there is no justification for the mandates. Second, therapists generally become increasingly effective as practitioners by helping clients, not by being exposed to information (Polkinghorne 1992). Mandatory continuing education might be a reasonable policy for professionals who need to know the latest research findings to be optimally effective as practitioners (e.g., physicians). However, there is no evidence that regular exposure to information results in improved effectiveness for talk therapists. Third, when mandates are in place, accrediting bodies are charged with deciding which continuing education experiences are approved. In my experience, accreditors in the talk therapy professions generally approve topics that are consistent with the cultural status quo (such as medical model topics) and seldom approve topics that are critical of or counter to the values of contemporary mental health culture. Mandatory continuing education, then, often serves to uncritically support and promote conventional ideologies and practices, regardless of whether these ideologies and practices make sense, are supported by research, or are helpful or harmful to clients. Professional progress in the realm of talk therapy has virtually always been the result of challenges to conventional practices, not uncritical support of them. Fourth, related to the third point, professionals should be free to make their own decisions about the types of postgraduate educational experiences that they would like to pursue based on what they find useful, interesting, or growth enhancing. I am appalled that various groups of bureaucrats deem their judgments about postgraduate educational experiences to be inherently superior to the judgments of individual therapists. In the eyes of these bureaucrats, talk therapists must be like children who cannot be trusted to independently choose educational experiences that enhance their work. If left to their own devices, talk therapists might read a useful book, talk to a colleague about a case, write a professional article, or seek their own therapy. Instead, because of the supposedly superior judgment of the bureaucrats, talk therapists must sacrifice the time that they could have devoted to meaningful, self-directed educational pursuits to attend administratively approved seminars about the latest DSM disorder, treatment fad, or other topic, which may be completely counter to the attendee's professional values and irrelevant to the type of work that they do. Here is the bottom line: Who should decide what counts as continuing education for talk therapists? Individual therapists or bureaucrats?

Instead of mandates, I believe that a strong ethic of lifelong learning should be instilled in trainees during their educational programs. I have presented my position on mandatory continuing education on a number of occasions to people who disagree with me (and who even charge that I am somehow undermining the talk therapy professions or demeaning the value of education by being opposed to mandatory continuing education requirements), so I am familiar with the usual counterargument, which goes something like the following: Even if an ethic of self-directed, career-long continuing education is promoted in training, not all students will internalize this ethic and participate in continuing education activities after they graduate. Therefore, it would be better to mandate continuing education to ensure that all talk therapists are engaged in continuing education throughout their careers.

This counterargument is not persuasive to me. The four objections enumerated above far outweigh any benefits that might be gained from mandating continuing education requirements. Furthermore, if professionals are inherently unmotivated to acquire new information, forcing them to sit through seminars will not suddenly change their attitude and magically transform them into people who place a high value on learning. Rather, they will resent the obligation, zone out during the informational presentations, and sign up for seminars that cost them the least amount of time and money to attend, regardless of content. Proponents of mandatory continuing education confuse seminar attendance with learning; the two are not the same. There will always be people in the talk therapy professions (indeed, in all professions) who place little value on lifelong learning, despite the best efforts of teachers to promote ongoing education as an integral part of professional life. This subset of people cannot be forced to learn new information. The best educators can do is to admit applicants who place a high value on education into their programs and attempt to instill an ethic of lifelong learning in their students. Mandating that someone must care about something that they care little about is not an effective strategy in any realm, including education.

I am opposed to mandatory supervision for many of the same reasons that I am opposed to mandatory continuing education. There is no compelling evidence that mandatory postgraduate supervision is necessary or contributes to effectiveness (Watkins 2011). As part of their educational experience, students should be continually reminded that consultation with senior colleagues is often useful and necessary. However, graduates should be left to decide when they need help, who has the expertise to provide it, and the form that the help should take. I am not as strongly opposed to mandatory postgraduate supervision as I am to mandatory continuing education. As noted in a previous section, I recognize that supervised experience is a vital part of training to become a talk therapist. However, after the commencement ceremony has passed, I would prefer that full-fledged talk therapists be given the freedom to make their own decisions about the type of consultations they find useful, rather than having the number of sessions, duration of supervision, and professional affiliation of the supervisor mandated by a third party. Given my emphasis on meaning systems, and the ways that dominant cultures of objectification often suppress and trivialize these systems, it would be inconsistent, and perhaps outright hypocritical, of me to take the position that the values and meaning systems of talk therapists regarding their postgraduate education and supervision should be decided and mandated by institutional monoliths, which disregard, suppress, belittle, and ignore the values of individual talk therapists.

In summary, I believe that training for talk therapists is necessary, despite the equivalency findings from the research comparing outcomes between paraprofessionals and professionals. Vital aspects of education to become a talk therapist include training in potentially dangerous situations, ethics, and appropriate therapeutic boundaries. Training should also promote supervised experience, an appreciation for diverse ways of being, a common factors approach, and relative mastery of at least one system of therapy. As a bonus, it is also beneficial to foster an attitude of critical thinking in trainees. Applicants should be chosen for training programs primarily on the basis of their relational, rather than academic, talents. It might be useful to substitute a minimum age requirement for applicants instead of the usual requirement of an undergraduate degree. Last, postgraduate continuing education and supervision should not be mandated.

Readers may disagree with my recommendations about training. Indeed, I will probably disagree with some of them as my position evolves. The point of the above exercise, however, is not to decide upon the final principles that should guide the training of talk therapists. Rather, a thought experiment, which abolishes all current training requirements and challenges the experimenter to recreate these requirements anew based on research, their experience, and commonsense, is designed to promote critical thinking about training and artificially strip away the layers of professional politics that have contaminated the educational process. As an educator, this experiment has also helped me to put my teaching in perspective, focus on the important elements of my role as a trainer, and adopt an attitude of humility about my work. All, in my estimation, are good experimental side effects.

Note that a focus on meaning systems and relationships is a theme of my recommendations. A common factors approach, mastery of a particular therapeutic system and associated rituals, appreciation for diverse ways of being, respect for the preferences of individual therapists, and other training recommendations noted above give the highest priority to meaning systems and relationships. Furthermore, for many of my recommendations, this priority has strong research support. However, what is the current state of education and training for talk therapists? Is a high value placed on meaning systems and relationships? These questions are investigated in the following section.

CURRENT STATE OF EDUCATION AND TRAINING FOR TALK THERAPISTS

As noted in the previous chapter, mental health culture has fallen under the spell of objectification via the idealization of symptom-based diagnostics, biological reductionism, and the medical model, which has been adopted as a treatment paradigm for all practitioners, including talk therapists. I have argued that ideologies of objectification are an extraordinarily poor fit for professionals whose work depends upon an appreciation of meaning systems and the establishment of intimate helping relationships with diverse clientele. Therefore, there is arguably a strong contradiction between the values of contemporary mental health culture and the type of education that trainees should undergo to become optimally effective practitioners. Whether or not one agrees with the specific training recommendations I outlined in the previous section, the evidence strongly points to the conclusion that an appreciation for meaning systems and therapeutic relationships should be central, unifying themes in the preparation of budding therapists.

However, training programs to become a talk therapist have gradually incorporated the technical, objectifying values of contemporary mental health culture in their curricula. As a counselor educator, I am most familiar with the curricular standards of the Council for Accreditation of Counseling and Related Educational Programs (CACREP), which is the primary accrediting body for counseling programs. As an example from the most recent CACREP standards (Council for Accreditation of Counseling and Related Educational Programs 2009), students must have training in the "current edition of the Diagnostic and Statistical Manual of Mental Disorders" (21) and "treatment planning" (20), even though there is no evidence that symptom based diagnostics and the formulation of plans to reduce specific symptoms have anything to do with effective talk therapy. Consider other CACREP requirements, such as the mandate that students must be familiar with "psychopharmacological medications" (20) and "the relationship among brain anatomy, function, biochemistry, and learning and behavior" (60). These skills take years of extensive training to master and are clearly in the domain of other professions, such as psychiatry and neurology. However, these requirements are typical curricular standards in the training programs of all talk therapists, not just counselors. Why should talk therapists, who do not prescribe drugs or use bodily interventions, be required to learn about medications and the brain, particularly when clients can be referred to professionals who are experts in these areas?

The usual counterargument I receive when I voice this opinion is that medication side effects and the brain can have an impact on psychological well-being and behavior. Therefore, talk therapists should be required to be trained in these areas. I have two responses to this counterargument. First, highly-trained medical experts, not representatives from a nonmedical field whose graduates have virtually no training in these areas, should provide guidance to people with medication or neurological issues. Rather than learning a few scattered bits about medical issues, talk therapists should focus on topics in their own domain and refer clients to appropriate specialists in other fields. A little knowledge can be dangerous. Second, there are numerous factors that have an impact on psychological well-being and behavior. Financial stressors, for example, can have a significant effect on mental health. Indeed, "economic problems" (32) were one of the diagnosable Axis IV psychosocial problems in the previous edition of the DSM (American Psychiatric Association 2000). Should training in personal finances be required for counselors and psychotherapists, then? What about nutrition? Poor nutrition, unhealthy blood sugar levels, and food allergies can contribute to mental health problems. Therefore, according to the logic of those who advocate for medical training in talk therapy curricula, counselors and psychotherapists should receive academic instruction in nutrition and dietary topics. What about exercise? A proper exercise regime can have a remarkable impact on mental health. Should courses in exercise physiology, then, be a required part of the curricula of educational programs for talk therapists? It is easy to think of many additional specialty areas that have an impact on mental health. Should talk therapists receive training in all of these areas?

Here is a novel idea: Instead of training talk therapists to be pseudo physicians, accountants, nutritionists, or personal trainers, why not simply encourage them to make referrals whenever they suspect that clients might benefit from consulting a specialist? In this way, counselors and psychotherapists can focus on the specialty of talk therapy without having to dilute their training with topics from other fields. Of course, I am not suggesting that all mention of the DSM or medications, for instance, be banished from the training programs of talk therapists. These topics might reasonably come up in discussions. However, deliberately focusing education on topics from other fields and requiring courses in symptom based diagnostics or psychopharmacology, for instance, detracts from, dilutes, and outright contradicts, a focus on meaning systems and relationships.

Note, however, that courses on nutrition or exercise physiology have not found their way into the curricula of talk therapy programs, despite the fact that these topics have significant implications for mental health. Medical, psychiatric topics, such as the DSM and psychopharmacology, however, have increasingly become formal parts of training programs for counselors and psychotherapists. Why have medical topics been favored, though, above other domains of study that are tied to mental health issues? To draw from an example used above, it would be just as reasonable to offer courses on personal financial issues to talk therapists as it would be to offer courses on psychopharmacology. Poverty, debt, and other financial difficulties can be enormous stressors, which fuel depression, anxiety, and relationship problems. If talk therapists were trained to spot underlying financial issues it would arguably be just as useful, if not more so, than an ability to spot medication problems. Indeed, most nonmedical talk therapists cannot legally prescribe medications, but they could conceivably provide some direct guidance on optimal ways to manage debt, for instance, if training about financial issues were included as a formal part of their educational curricula. This direct financial guidance would undoubtedly help to alleviate depression, anxiety, and relational conflicts in many clientele. Indeed, personal financial guidance, an area in which talk therapists could actively intervene if given some training, would arguably be far more useful than training in medications, an area in which most nonmedical talk therapists are not licensed to practice.

The purpose of the above discussion was not to argue that training in personal finances should be a part of the curricula of talk therapists. Rather, my point was to demonstrate that the deeply entrenched cultural assumption that talk therapy has a natural connection to psychiatry and medicine is completely arbitrary and logically unsupportable. A connection between talk therapy and the field of medicine is no more sensible than a connection between talk therapy and personal finance. The former connection only seems more natural and justifiable because of cultural conditioning. Before moving on to the implications of this conclusion for the training of talk therapists, it is important to address counterarguments, which are often used to justify the idea that talk therapy and medicine should be considered close disciplinary cousins.

First, some might argue, talk therapy can have a positive impact on physical health and even alleviate the symptoms of medical problems. This is undoubtedly true. If someone is experiencing ulcers due to stress and anxiety, counseling or psychotherapy may reduce, or even eliminate, these physical symptoms by addressing mental health issues. From this fact, however, it does not follow that talk therapy should be regarded as having close conceptual ties to medicine. Realtors regularly alleviate the stress and accompanying physical symptoms of their clients by helping them sell their homes. Likewise, lawyers cure ulcers, headaches, insomnia, and other physical manifestations of stress, by helping their clients overcome legal problems. Simply because the interventions of a particular profession have a desirable impact on bodily processes, it does not mean that the profession should be regarded as having a special conceptual connection to medicine, unless, of course, virtually every human service endeavor is categorized as a quasi-medical activity, a conceptual move that would be absurd and too all-encompassing to be useful (Hansen 2005). The talk therapy professions have no greater kinship with medicine than realty, law, accounting, cosmetology, or any other human services profession that has a trickle down impact on bodily processes.

Second, it is also true that counseling and psychotherapy can result in tangible, brain-based changes that are observable with neuroimaging machines (Linden 2006). This fact might initially appear to be persuasive evidence that talk therapy should be regarded as having a close connection to medicine until it is recalled that virtually any activity results in brain changes, because the brain is a highly dynamic and responsive organ. Jogging, meditating, arguing, eating sushi, and any other activity likely lights up various areas of the brain. Indeed, there is good evidence from neuroimaging studies that learning "sculpts brain structure" (Zatorre, Fields, and Johansen-Berg 2012, 528). Should educators be considered medical professionals, then? If changes to the brain are the criterion for categorizing a profession as being related to medicine, then virtually every profession has a close kinship with medicine. Talk therapists have no special claim on medical territory.

My aim has been to logically debunk the culturally entrenched, but logically unsupportable, claim that talk therapy is a medical activity and the related agenda to formally include medical, psychiatric topics in the curricula of programs that train counselors and psychotherapists. Cultural common sense is sometimes nonsensical; the medicalization of the talk therapy professions is a case in point.

The logical gibberish of those who propound the idea that helping someone with conversational methods has some professional equivalency with medicine has been used to leverage the talk therapy professions to higher levels of status, prestige, and financial compensation. Indeed, these professional benefits are the pellets that reinforce proponents of the medical model to keep hammering away at the bar of medicalization (Hansen 2014a). Consider that it is far more prestigious in contemporary culture to claim that therapists diagnose and treat major depressive disorder with prescriptive, psychotherapeutic methods than it is to claim that therapists develop helping relationships with clients to aid them in overcoming their sadness (Hansen 2014b). It is outright bizarre to frame the act of two people talking as a medical activity. Creating an alignment with medicine and describing work in technical medical language are excellent marketing strategies, though. The problem is that the talk therapy professions have bought their own marketing.

If talk therapy has no natural connection with medicine, then formal inclusion of medical topics, such as symptom-based diagnostics and psychopharmacology, in the curricula of training programs is highly questionable. Some might argue that training should prepare students for the realities of working life; if the DSM is used in practice, it should be formally taught in training programs. This issue of what to include in talk therapy training curricula suggests some interesting questions: What is the purpose of education? Should training to become a talk therapist highlight preparation to function as a practitioner in the working world, or should the emphasis of training be on the principles that make therapy effective, with proportionally less attention to job requirements that have little to do with effective helping? My opinion on these matters is that courses on medicalized topics that are unrelated to effective helping should not be a required part of training programs, regardless of current workplace requirements (Hansen 2003).

Students often take their coursework very seriously. Imagine that a student has a morning class on the principles of effective counseling. After learning about the importance of maintaining a nonjudgmental attitude toward clients, the therapeutic relationship, empathic responsiveness, and respect for diverse ways of being, the student attends her afternoon class on the DSM. In this course she is taught that symptoms, not meaning systems, are of primary importance. Furthermore, she is taught to regard certain categories of people as disordered, a message that is diametrically opposed to the lesson she learned about appreciating diversity in her morning class. This cycle of teaching the student opposite values about the helping process is continually repeated throughout the semester and, in various forms, throughout the student's educational experience. The student values her courses, tries to learn as much as she can from them, and idealizes what her professors tell her.

What is the end product of this type of educational experience? It is often graduates who are very confused about the central principles of effective talk therapy. Some graduates are relatively ineffective therapists, but take great professional pride in their knowledge of the DSM and ability to generate precise, symptom-oriented treatment plans. Others implement the effective principles of therapy, but suffer from low professional self-esteem because they have not incorporated a medicalized, diagnostic focus into their practices. In my experience, few students who graduate from programs that require them to take courses that are derived from the opposing value systems of relational helping and the medical model emerge with a solid, confident grasp of the principles that are important to being an effective talk therapist. Indeed, this is the result that should be expected.

I appreciate, however, that training should prepare students for the workforce. However, so that students do not confuse the important elements of effective therapeutic practice with knowledge that is merely useful to get paid, bright curricular lines should be drawn between these topics of study. One way to draw these lines is to prevent medical model subject matter from becoming required, freestanding courses in training curricula. Students can learn about the DSM, treatment planning, the side effects of various medications, and related topics from seminars, field placement experiences, and discussions in existing courses. Having required courses on medical model topics in curricula symbolically sends students the erroneous message that the material presented in the course is vitally important to helping clients.

SUMMARY AND CONCLUSIONS

Picture a university specific factors psychotherapy outcome researcher who comes home after a day of work, which consisted of conducting investigations aimed at discovering the optimal alignments between particular technical treatments and diagnostic entities. Upon walking in the door, she discovers that her partner is sad and tearful, obviously upset about the events of his day. At this point, does the specific factors researcher offer him the latest, psychotherapeutic techniques for the treatment of depression? In response to his sadness, does she tell him to try the methods that she has been investigating? Responding to his pain in this manner would almost surely be unhelpful and alienating. Rather, because she would like to help him, she decides not to judge or diagnose his feelings, but, instead, to listen warmly and try to understand and appreciate his perspective. They talk for about an hour, and he feels much better as a result. The following morning, she goes to work again, where she tries to discover specific techniques for the alleviation of depression.

Assuming that many proponents of the medical model for talk therapy have good relationships in their personal lives, why have they failed to integrate the lessons they have learned from these relationships into their conceptualizations about talk therapy? To me, it is stunningly obvious that an appreciation for meaning systems and helping relationships should be the foundation of the talk therapy enterprise. I am not sure how someone can completely ignore the consistent evidence from meta-analysis of psychotherapy outcome studies (Wampold 2001), multicultural investigations of healing (Frank and Frank 1993; Torrey 1972), and an overwhelming amount of commonsensical knowledge about helping relationships, which they have acquired over the course of their lives, and boldly propound a medicalized vision of talk therapy. Widespread, conventional assumptions and cultural incentives often create huge blind spots; perhaps this is what has happened in contemporary mental health culture.

Despite research and commonsense, the medical model vision has contaminated training programs for talk therapists. Training has generally followed the culture, not the evidence. In this chapter, I have argued that talk therapists should undergo training, despite the equivalency findings from the comparative paraprofessional outcome research. I have shared my thoughts about the fundamental factors that should be included in training curricula. To formulate these recommendations, I have tried to follow the evidence, my experience as an educator and practitioner, and common relational sense about helping others. I do not intend for these recommendations to be final proclamations about the type of training that talk therapists should undergo. Reasonable people might come to different conclusions. However, I think useful discussions about training can be facilitated if people are willing to question convention and draw from the factors that have proven to be the key elements of relational helping.

In this regard, an appreciation for meaning systems and helping relationships should be at the center of training for talk therapists. Currently, however, with the encroachment of the medical model into training programs, students often learn ideologies of objectification rather than appreciation for diverse systems of meaning. This is a troubling trend, particularly because educational structures tend to culturally calcify, hardening around the factors that perpetuate the status quo (Davies 2009; Fancher 1995; Kirsner 2000). Questioning convention and challenging entrenched, institutional structures and ideologies often leads to progress in many realms, including the training of talk therapists.

Conclusion

Summary and Further Reflections

The continual generation of meaning is a hallmark characteristic of human beings. People live their lives according to the meanings they endorse and create. Some of these meanings greatly enrich life and cause tremendous joy, while others can be sources of pain and suffering.

Viewing people as objects, devoid of meaning systems, is arguably a workable perspective for professions that intervene exclusively in the physical realm, such as medicine. Physical bodies are subject to laws of nature, which are relatively invariant across individuals and cultures. A body temperature of 104 degrees Fahrenheit is an indication that a person is sick, regardless of individual meaning systems, cultural beliefs, or historical era. Human psychology and behavior, however, do not play by the universal laws rulebook. People often abide by the meanings they endorse and create, regardless of natural principles.

For example, humans, lower animals, and nonsentient life forms are driven to ingest nutrients to survive. This seemingly universal principle makes the behavior of most organisms fairly predictable; they will strive to acquire nutrients. The meanings people create can render this natural principle irrelevant, though, which makes human beings far less predictable than other organisms. People may go on hunger strikes for a cause or starve themselves to death for fear of becoming obese. As another example, the principle that organisms strive to avoid pain probably applies universally to life forms capable of experiencing pain, except, of course, to human beings, whose meaning systems sometimes cause them to seek pain, as in the cases of religious self-flagellation, masochism, or self-cutting.

The meaning systems people create regularly override natural laws. Therefore, understanding people, why they do what they do, and how to help them with their psychological suffering necessarily entails delving into their unique meaning systems. That being said, there are varieties of psychological suffering, such as schizophrenia, that almost certainly have a strong constitutional component. Mental health inquiry and practice, then, can be placed on a spectrum. On the far left side are problems of living that are primarily a product of relational and psychological conflicts. The right side of the spectrum contains varieties of psychological suffering that probably have a strong constitutional element, such as schizophrenia and chronic, intractable forms of depression. It is not unreasonable to develop understandings and interventions for the right side that are medical and objectifying. If bodily processes play a strong role in schizophrenia, for instance, widespread suffering might be alleviated if the material elements of this disorder were understood and effective treatments could be developed as a result. Of course, it would also be useful to understand the meaning systems of people afflicted with schizophrenia. However, psychological interventions might reasonably play a secondary role to physical interventions for people who are stricken with severe, stereotypic mental health conditions in which material, bodily factors play a primary role.

Alternatively, in order to provide meaningful, lasting help for people on the left side of the spectrum, it is vitally important to understand and appreciate the idiosyncratic systems of meaning they endorse and construct. In contrast to the right side, personal conflicts, relational difficulties, and developmental experiences are the main determinants of suffering for people on the left side of the spectrum; constitutional, bodily concerns are, at most, secondary. An appreciation for meaning systems is not only vital because they are often the primary determinants of psychological suffering, but also because one of the best ways to develop a relationship with someone is to show an interest in their unique perspectives. The quality of the therapeutic relationship is the within-treatment factor that has the highest association with outcomes (Wampold 2001). Therefore, appreciation for the meaning systems of clientele should be the highest priority for counselors and psychotherapists.

Notably, objectification and appreciation for meaning systems are essentially incompatible orientations. Objectifying orientations presume that problems are the result of a deviation or deficiency; suffering is a sign that something has deviated from normal functioning and needs to be corrected (e.g., broken leg, cognitive distortion). An appreciation for meaning systems, alternatively, presumes that a person's psychological suffering is, at some level, a reasonable response to the way she or he makes sense of world; the person is potentially understandable, not broken. From a perspective that honors meaning systems, psychological suffering is alleviated through the establishment of a relationship, which focuses on progressive understanding, insight, and intimate therapeutic connections. It is difficult, or arguably impossible, to adopt a view of a person as psychologically ill or disordered while also maintaining a high regard for the meanings that the person endorses and constructs. If a client is regarded as disordered, her or his meaning systems will be discounted as the product of a malfunctioning mind. Alternatively, if a client's meaning systems are respected, honored, and understood, it is difficult to conceptualize the client as deficient, ill, or disordered.

Although they are fundamentally incompatible orientations to coming to know a person, both perspectives, objectifying and meaning-based, have a place in the treatment of psychological suffering because, as mentioned above, some problems likely have a strong constitutional element while others primarily arise from meaning systems. History unfortunately demonstrates, however, that one perspective or the other regularly overtakes the entire spectrum of mental health problems during different eras. In the mid-twentieth century, psychoanalytic explanations for psychological suffering were extended into realms where they were mostly unhelpful, and even outright harmful, such as the treatment of schizophrenia (Shorter 1997). In contemporary mental health culture, ideologies of objectification have taken over the culture and have hijacked the entire spectrum of psychological suffering. Psychotherapists and counselors, who should be focused on the meaning systems of their clientele, regularly engage in descriptive diagnostics, symptom-based treatment planning, prescriptive psychotherapeutic treatments, and other objectifying practices, which are not only counter to the empirical evidence about the important elements of talk therapy but also completely defy time-honored, commonsensical notions about relational helping. Such is the power of culture norms; they can be so looming, omnipresent, and powerful that, like gravity, they become invisible forces, determining the actions of the cultural inhabitants beneath the threshold of their awareness. My primary goal in writing this book has been to promote awareness of the central role that meaning systems should play in counseling and psychotherapy, despite contemporary cultural norms and the economic benefits associated with the "medicalization of everyday life" (Szasz 2007).

Indeed, it should be obvious that objectification cannot contribute to psychological understandings of clients, just as chemistry or biology cannot contribute to literary understandings of Shakespearean characters. In this regard, counseling and psychotherapy should be regarded as having a much closer kinship to the humanities than to science (Hansen 2012). The broad goal of science is to discover the intrinsic nature of reality. Scientific investigations gradually eliminate various perspectives to uncover singular truths about the way the universe operates. For instance, if a researcher were attempting to discover the cause of a disease, he might initially entertain multiple hypotheses and gradually eliminate the erroneous ones through progressive experimentation, thereby honing in on the true cause of the disease.

In contrast to a scientific orientation, with its focus on singularity, a humanities perspective attempts to complicate, enrich, and dimensionalize, not simplify. Philosophy, English literature, and historical studies make their advances by continually generating novel perspectives, not by attempting to discover the singular, natural truth about the subject of study. The humanities embrace meaning systems, revel in the ambiguity of multiple truths, and cultivate differences and unusual perspectives.

A scientific orientation to counseling and psychotherapy is, by definition, inhospitable to the cultivation of meaning systems. Approaching clientele with an epistemology of singular truth necessarily forecloses on opportunities to explore the meanings that have sustained problems and also inhibits opportunities to create new ones. Scientific investigation should always be a core source of information about counseling and psychotherapy. It is tremendously valuable to know, for instance, the factors that make counseling and psychotherapy effective. Science is a valuable source of this type of information. Thus, my position is that science should have a particular type of relationship with the talk therapy professions, not that it should be banished from them.

To illustrate the type of relationship I believe science should have with counseling and psychotherapy, consider the work of professional historians. Those who are engaged in advancing understandings of history may use scientific methods to determine the age of historical documents, for example. However, progress in the academic study of history depends on the generation of new perspectives on historical events. Consider music as another example. Science may contribute to the design of superior violins or aid in determining the optimal acoustical structure of a music hall, but music, itself, advances by the generation of new sounds, not by the discovery of singular, correct ones. Like the arts and humanities, science should play a supportive, not lead, role in counseling and psychotherapy. Despite the evidence that therapists should approach their work with a focus on cultivating meanings, a perspective of scientific singularity has come to dominate talk therapy in contemporary mental health culture. Counselors and psychotherapists often approach their clients as if they were disordered organisms in need of repair, rather than as people to be understood. A humanities style appreciation for meaning systems should be at the fore of the talk therapy professions.

Some might argue that devaluing the role of a scientific perspective in counseling and psychotherapy risks losing some of the respectability that talk therapists have gained by being associated with science. Perhaps they would be correct. However, it is important to remember that respectability is a cultural phenomenon, not something that is found in nature. There is nothing intrinsically superior about a scientific perspective over a humanities one.

Each approach to inquiry has its place. Indeed, philosophers of science have compellingly challenged the myth that science should be regarded as an epistemologically superior way to understand the world.

Kuhn (1996), for instance, argued that science is a communal activity. Scientists solve puzzles that are important to communities of scientists. Because the vision of a particular scientific community necessarily limits the questions that are allowed to be asked and the acceptable answers, science can never achieve a pristine, objective view of the supposed intrinsic nature of reality. The scientific method has resulted in tremendous advances to humanity (e.g., eradication of diseases). However, scientific investigations arise out of communal meaning constructions, a fact that makes it unreasonable to conceptualize scientific findings as pristine recordings of nature's truths, which are untainted by human interests. Because the scientific method cannot be regarded as a privileged means to access the intrinsic nature of reality, there is no reason to epistemologically privilege it above a humanities perspective; they are simply different ways of making sense of the world (Rorty 1999).

Kuhn's (1996) conceptualization of science is broad and encompasses any discipline that engages in scientific inquiry. Holt (1978), operating within the bounds of the helping professions, provided a compelling defense of "clinical judgement" (38) against those who have argued that counseling and psychology should be structured by the supposedly superior methods of science. The fundamental source of information in the helping professions, according to Holt, is "verbal meanings" (41). Scientists draw conclusions from numbers; therapists draw conclusions from client verbalizations. Those who have promoted a scientific view of the helping professions have argued that scientific inferences from numbers result in more objective, reality-based information than conclusions drawn from the fuzzy, subjective process of inferring meanings from words.

Holt (1978), in response to this argument, claimed that, by engaging in the analysis of verbal meanings, helping professionals are operating within a tradition that long predates science. Historians, literary critics, anthropologists, and lawyers, for instance, all rely on the analysis of verbal meanings. Furthermore, these disciplines use established inferential methods. A historian may draw conclusions about a particular era, for instance, by analyzing recurrent themes in a historical document from that era. Analogously, talk therapists may learn about their clients by discerning thematic patterns that constitute a therapy session. In both cases, the professional uses a particular method (i.e., internal, thematic analysis) to draw conclusions from verbal/textual data. Holt cited multiple established methods of inference that are used by professions that rely on the analysis of words. Talk therapists, therefore, do not use questionable new methods for inferring information. Rather, therapists, by analyzing verbal meanings, draw from well-established methods, which have been used successfully by many disciplines throughout history, long before the scientific method was introduced.

After positioning the helping professions as part of a longstanding tradition that has well-defined methods for drawing conclusions, Holt (1978) takes on the challenge that science should be regarded as superior to methods that analyze verbal meanings because science is objective, while other methods of inquiry have a subjective, interpretative element. In this regard, one of Holt's most important points is that scientists only draw their conclusions by interpreting the meaning of quantitative data; data never speaks for itself. Scientists interpret the meaning of numbers that are derived from their experiments, just as clinicians interpret the meaning of verbal data that emerges during therapeutic hours. Both approaches to inquiry, science and analysis of verbal meanings, are reliant on human interpretation of raw data to draw conclusions. Therefore, it is inaccurate to frame science as objective, and thereby superior, to methods of inquiry that depend on subjective interpretation; all methods of inquiry, including science, depend on human judgments about the meaning of the raw data.

To further level the ground between science and analysis of verbal meanings, Holt (1978) challenged the argument that science should be regarded as superior to analyses of verbal meanings because science relies on the criterion of prediction to verify its claims, while clinical judgement relies on the supposedly inferior criterion of internal consistency. To illustrate the criterion of prediction, a scientist may claim that mixing two chemicals will produce a particular result. If this result occurs, then the claim is verified. Alternatively, if the result is different from the prediction, then the claim is regarded as erroneous. Therefore, the verification or falsification of scientific claims depends on whether the claims result in accurate predictions.

In the analysis of verbal meanings, however, internal consistency is used to verify claims. For example, a client may talk about a half dozen different topics during a session. These topics may seem disconnected. However, upon analysis, a clinician might detect a theme among these various topics, such as a client's concern about abandonment. The claim that the client is concerned about abandonment, then, is verified by the fact that the various elements of the session are unified by a principle that makes the session internally consistent. In short, when patterns are discovered in clinical material, or, as another example, when an historian discerns unifying themes in various documents, these internal consistencies can be used to verify claims about the meanings of sessions or documents.

Holt (1978) challenged the argument that prediction is inherently superior to internal consistency for verifying claims and the corollary conclusion that the scientific method is epistemologically superior to analyses of verbal meanings. The structure of internal consistency, Holt argued, is logically equivalent to prediction. To illustrate Holt's point, consider the above example of a clinician who has found a consistent theme of concerns about abandonment in a client's verbal material. This theme was detected by a series of mini predictions. The clinician might have entertained a number of hypotheses about the meaning of the first topic that the client discussed. These hypotheses would have led to predictions about what the client might discuss next. When the client discussed the next topic, some of the clinician's hypotheses may have been supported, while others may have proved erroneous. Through the verification and falsification of these predictions, the clinician would progressively narrow down and discern the central themes that make the session internally consistent. Internal consistency, then, consists, of a series of mini-predictions; its logical structure is equivalent to prediction. Therefore, the argument that prediction is a superior criterion for verifying claims than internal consistency, and the corollary argument that science is epistemologically superior to analyses of verbal meanings, are completely unfounded.

Indeed, Holt (1978) argued that the greatest scientists have relied heavily on internal consistency to make scientific inferences. To illustrate this point, imagine that a series of scientific findings about a phenomenon has accumulated. To most scientists, these findings appear disconnected. However, a particularly bright scientist might discern a thread that runs through these findings, thereby demonstrating an internal consistency that others had missed. The detection of these consistencies has often led to tremendous advances in scientific research and theorizing. The discernment of internal consistencies, then, is not only a method used by professionals who analyze verbal texts. The greatest advances in science have arguably occurred when internal consistencies have been detected among a set of findings that were formerly considered unrelated.

The strong implication of these critiques is that the cultural enthronement of science is unwarranted. The scientific method has certainly led to tremendous advances in the quality of human life. However, as a human activity, science can never provide a "view from nowhere" (Nagel 1986, 70). Scientific conclusions are always born out of human interests and should, therefore, not be conceptualized as direct, unclouded routes to the eternal laws of nature. Like other approaches to inquiry, science is useful for some endeavors and useless for others. Science provides useful information about counseling and psychotherapy, but generally does not contribute to the fundamental task of talk therapy, which is to form therapeutic connections with diverse clientele through an appreciation of meaning systems. Talk therapy is a relational art that should be informed by science, not determined by it.

The central issue that animates many of the concerns I have raised in this book, though, is arguably psychological suffering. It is ironic that the mental health professions have been devoted to the alleviation of psychological suffering for over a century, but there have been few philosophical discussions about suffering. What is psychological suffering? What does it mean? What should we do about it? Although these questions have been addressed within the confines of particular theoretical orientations, they have generally not been discussed as broad philosophical issues that are at the heart of the helping encounter. I believe that extended discussions about suffering can help anchor the helping professions, so that their course is not determined by the cultural winds. In this regard, Davies (2012), in his brilliant book, *The Importance of Suffering: The Value and Meaning of Emotional Discontent*, offered some intriguing insights about psychological suffering.

According to Davies (2012), psychological suffering can be productive because it may alert attention to an issue that is unresolved. Listening to the message of suffering, rather than trying to silence it, can cause us to examine and usefully confront our problems. Happiness is "reached by understanding what our suffering is trying to teach us, and by putting those teachings into effect" (9). Currently, however, a negative vision of suffering is predominant and "anesthetic regimes" (71), which benefit financially from providing distractions from, exploiting, and normalizing our suffering have become strong forces in the market and culture. Consumption of products are marketed as a means to happiness; drugs that numb suffering are bestsellers in the pharmaceutical industry; and various types of superficial distractions and opportunities to escape the discomforts of living have flooded the marketplace. When productive suffering is anesthetized, it may stunt psychological growth, increase psychological distress, or simply pass the suffering onto others.

Culture shapes our view of suffering. In this regard, it is ironic that multicultural studies are usually devoted to the study of other cultures, not to a critique of our own. It is vital to continually examine and critique the values and norms of the culture in which we operate. The intersection of meaning systems and mental health culture has tremendous implications for the way clients are regarded and the type of help they receive. Our experience, the meanings we create and endorse, animate our lives. Honoring these meanings should be the highest priority for counselors and psychotherapists.

References

American Psychiatric Association. 1980. *Diagnostic and statistical manual of mental disorders* (3rd ed.). Washington, DC: Author.

———. 1994). *Diagnostic and statistical manual of mental disorders* (4th ed. Washington, DC: Author.

———. 2000. *Diagnostic and statistical manual of mental disorders* (4th ed., text rev.). Washington, DC: Author.

———. 2013. *Diagnostic and statistical manual of mental disorders* (5th ed.). Washington, DC: Author.

Anderson, W. 1990. *Reality isn't what it used to be: Theatrical politics, ready-to-wear religion, global myths, primitive chic, and other wonders of the postmodern world.* San Francisco: Harper & Row.

Arlow, J., and C. Brenner. 1964. *Psychoanalytic concepts and the structural theory.* New York: International Universities Press.

Atkins, D. C., and A. Christensen. 2001. Is professional training worth the bother? A review of the impact of psychotherapy training on client outcome. *Australian Psychologist, 36,* 122–30.

Bach, P., and S. C. Hayes. 2002. The use of acceptance and commitment therapy to prevent the rehospitalization of psychotic patients: A randomized controlled trial. *Journal of Consulting and Clinical Psychology, 70,* 1129–39.

Berman, J. S., and N. C. Norton. 1985. Does professional training make a therapist more effective? *Psychological Bulletin, 98,* 401–7.

Beutler, L. E., and T. M. Harwood. 2000. *Prescriptive psychotherapy.* New York: Oxford University Press.

Brenner, C. 1973. *An elementary textbook of psychoanalysis.* New York: International Universities Press.

Comas-Diaz, L. 2015. Humanism and multiculturalism: An evolutionary alliance. In K. J. Schneider, J. F. Pierson, & J. F. T. Bugental (Eds.), *The handbook of humanistic psychology: Theory, research, and practice* (2nd ed.), (pp. 386–94). Thousand Oaks, CA: Sage.

Council for Accreditation of Counseling & Related Educational Programs. 2009. 2009 CACREP Standards. Retrieved from http://www.cacrep.org/wp-content/uploads/2013/12/2009-Standards.pdf.

Davidson, L. 2000. Philosophical foundations of humanistic psychology, *Humanistic Psychologist, 28,* 7–31.

Davies, J. 2009. *The making of psychotherapists: An anthropological analysis.* London: Karnac Books.

———. 2012. *The importance of suffering: The value and meaning of emotional discontent.* New York: Routledge.
———. 2013. *Cracked: Why psychiatry is doing more harm than good.* London: Icon Books.
Dawkins, R. 1976. *The selfish gene.* New York: Oxford University Press.
DeCarvalho, R. 1990. A history of the "third force" in psychology. *Journal of Humanistic Psychology, 30,* 22–44.
Decker, H. 2013. *The making of the DSM-III: A diagnostic manual's conquest of American psychiatry.* New York: Oxford University Press.
Dennett, D. 1995. *Darwin's dangerous idea: Evolution and the meanings of life.* New York: Simon & Schuster.
DeRobertis, E. M. 2015. Toward a humanistic-multicultural model of development. In K. J. Schneider, J. F. Pierson, and J. F. T. Bugental (Eds.), *The handbook of humanistic psychology: Theory, research, and practice* (2nd ed.), (pp. 227–42). Thousand Oaks, CA: Sage.
Derrida, J. 1995. The play of substitution. In W. Anderson (Ed.), *The truth about the truth: Deconfusing and re-constructing the postmodern world,* (pp. 86–95). New York: G.P. Putnam's Sons.
Descartes, R. 1988. *Descartes: Selected philosophical writings.* New York: Cambridge University Press.
deShazer, S. 1985. *Keys to solution in brief therapy.* New York: W.W. Norton.
Dowbiggin, I. 2011. *The quest for mental health: A tale of science, medicine, scandal, sorrow, and mass society.* New York: Cambridge University Press.
Durlak, J. A. 1979. Comparative effectiveness of paraprofessional and professional helpers. *Psychological Bulletin, 86,* 80–92.
El-Hai, J. 2005. *The lobotomist: A maverick medical genius and his tragic quest to rid the world of mental illness.* Hoboken, NJ: Wiley & Sons.
Elkins, D. 2009. *Humanistic psychology: A clinical manifesto; a critique of clinical psychology and the need for progressive alternatives.* Colorado Springs: University of the Rockies Press.
Ellis, A., and R. Grieger. 1977. *Handbook of rational-emotive therapy.* New York: Springer.
Erikson, E. 1950. *Childhood and society.* New York: Norton.
Eysenck, H. J. 1952. The effects of psychotherapy: An evaluation. *Journal of Consulting Psychology, 16,* 319–24.
Fancher, R. 1995. *Cultures of healing: Correcting the image of American mental health care.* New York: Freeman.
Festinger, L. 1957. *A theory of cognitive dissonance.* Stanford, CA: Stanford University Press.
Flax, J. 1990. *Thinking fragments: Psychoanalysis, feminism, and postmodernism in the contemporary West.* Berkeley: University of California Press.
Foucault, M. 1965. *Madness and civilization; a history of insanity in the age of reason.* New York: Pantheon.
———. 1980. C. Gordon (Ed.), *Power/Knowledge; selected interviews and other writings 1972–1977* (C. Gordon, L. Marshall, J. Mepham, & K. Soper, Trans.). New York: Pantheon.
Fox, R. E, P. H. DeLeon, R. Newman, et al. 2009. Prescriptive authority and psychology: A status report. *American Psychologist, 64,* 257–68.
Frances, A. 2013. *Saving normal: An insider's revolt against out-of-control psychiatric diagnosis, DSM-5, big pharma, and the medicalization of ordinary life.* New York: HarperCollins.
Frank, J. D., and J. B. Frank. 1993. Persuasion and healing (3rd ed.). Baltimore: Johns Hopkins University Press.
Frankl, V. 1963. *Man's search for meaning; an introduction to logotherapy.* New York: Simon & Schuster.
Frederickson, J. 1999. *Psychodynamic psychotherapy: Learning to listen from multiple perspectives.* Philadelphia: Brunner/Mazel.
Fredrickson, R. 1992. *Repressed memories: A journey to recovery from sexual abuse.* New York: Fireside.
Freud, S. 1953a. The interpretation of dreams. In J. Strachey (Ed. & Trans.), *The standard edition of the complete psychological works of Sigmund Freud* (Vols. 4–5). London: Hogarth Press (Original work published 1900).

———. 1953b. Three essays on the theory of sexuality. In J. Strachey (Ed. and Trans.), *The standard edition of the complete psychological works of Sigmund Freud* (Vol. 7, pp. 125–245). London: Hogarth Press (Original work published 1905).

———. 1955. Analysis of a phobia in a five-year-old boy. In J. Strachey (Ed. and Trans.), *The standard edition of the complete psychological works of Sigmund Freud* (Vol. 10, pp. 1–149). London: Hogarth Press (Original work published 1909).

———. 1957. Future prospects of psychoanalytic therapy. In J. Strachey (Ed. and Trans.), *The standard edition of the complete psychological works of Sigmund Freud* (Vol. 11, pp. 141–51). London: Hogarth Press (Original work published 1910).

———. 1959. The question of lay analysis. In J. Strachey (Ed. & Trans.), *The standard edition of the complete psychological works of Sigmund Freud* (Vol. 20, pp. 177–258). London: Hogarth Press (Original work published 1926).

———. 1961. The ego and the id. In J. Strachey (Ed. and Trans.), *The standard edition of the complete psychological works of Sigmund Freud* (Vol. 19, pp. 1–66). London: Hogarth Press (Original work published 1923).

———. 1963. Introductory lectures on psychoanalysis. In J. Strachey (Ed. & Trans.), *The standard edition of the complete psychological works of Sigmund Freud* (Vols. 15–16). London: Hogarth Press (Original work published 1916).

Gabbard, G. 2005. *Psychodynamic psychiatry in clinical practice* (4th ed.). Arlington, VA: American Psychiatric Publishing.

———. 2010. *Long-term psychodynamic psychotherapy: A basic text*. (2nd ed.). Washington, DC: American Psychiatric Publishing.

Gay, P. 1988. *Freud: A life for our time*. New York: W.W. Norton.

Gergen, K. 1995. The healthy, happy human being wears many masks. In W. Anderson (Ed.), *The truth about the truth: De-confusing and re-constructing the postmodern world*, (pp. 136–50). New York: G.P. Putnam's Sons.

———. 1999. *An invitation to social construction*. Thousand Oaks, CA: Sage.

Gevitz, N. 2004. *The DOs: Osteopathic medicine in America* (2nd ed.). Baltimore: The Johns Hopkins University Press.

Gill, M. 1994. *Psychoanalysis in transition: A personal view*. Hillsdale, NJ: Analytic Press.

Greenberg, G. 2010. *Manufacturing depression: The secret history of a modern disease*. New York: Simon & Schuster.

———. 2013. *The book of woe: The DSM and the unmaking of psychiatry*. New York: Blue Rider Press.

Groth-Marnat, G. 2009. *Handbook of psychological assessment* (5th ed.). New York: Wiley & Sons.

Guindon, M., A. Green, and F. Hanna. 2003. Intolerance and psychopathology: Toward a general diagnosis for racism, sexism, and homophobia. *American Journal of Orthopsychiatry, 73,* 167–76.

Hansen, J. T. 2000. Psychoanalysis and humanism: A review and critical examination of integrationist efforts with some proposed resolutions. *Journal of Counseling & Development, 78,* 21–28. doi:10.1002/j.1556-6676.2000.tb02556.x.

———. 2002. Postmodern implications for theoretical integration of counseling orientations. *Journal of Counseling & Development, 80,* 315–21. doi:10.1002/j.1556-6678.2002.tb00196.x.

———. 2003. *Including diagnostic training in counseling curricula: Implications for professional identity development.* Counselor Education and Supervision, 43, 96–107. doi:10.1002/j.1556-6978.2003.tb01834.x.

———. 2004. Thoughts on knowing: Epistemic implications of counseling practice. *Journal of Counseling & Development, 82,* 131–38. doi:10.1002/j.1556-6678.2004.tb00294.x.

———. 2005. The devaluation of inner subjective experiences by the counseling profession: A plea to reclaim the essence of the profession. *Journal of Counseling & Development, 83,* 406–15. doi:10.1002/j.1556-6678.2005.tb00362.x.

———. 2006a. Counseling theories within a postmodernist epistemology: New roles for theories in counseling practice. *Journal of Counseling & Development, 84,* 291–97. doi:10.1002/j.1556-6678.2006.tb00408.x.

———. 2006b. Is the best practices movement consistent with the values of the counseling profession? A critical analysis of best practices ideology. *Counseling and Values, 50*, 154–60. doi:10.1002/j.2161-007X.2006.tb00051.x.

———. 2007. Counseling without truth: Toward a neopragmatic foundation for counseling practice. *Journal of Counseling & Development, 85*, 423–30. doi:10.1002/j.1556-6678.2007.tb00610.x.

———. 2008. Neopragmatic thought and counseling values: Reconsidering the role of values in counseling from an alternative epistemological foundation. *Counseling and Values, 52*, 100–112. doi:10.1002/j.2161-007X.2008.tb00094.x.

———. 2009. On displaced humanists: Counselor education and the meaning-reduction pendulum. *Journal of Humanistic Counseling, Education and Development*, 48, 65–76. doi:10.1002/j.2161-1939.2009.tb00068.x.

———. 2010a. Consequences of the postmodernist vision: Diversity as the guiding value for the counseling profession. *Journal of Counseling & Development, 88*, 101–7. doi:10.1002/j.1556-6678.2010.tb00156.x.

———. 2010b. Ideas on the margins: Professional counseling and ideological insularity. *International Journal for the Advancement of Counselling, 32*, 214–24. doi:10.1007/s10447-010-9102-4.

———. 2010c. Inner subjective experiences and social constructionism: A response to Rudes and Guterman (2007). *Journal of Counseling & Development, 88*, 210–13. doi:10.1002/j.1556-6678.2010.tb00011.x.

———. 2012. Extending the humanistic vision: Toward a humanities foundation for the counseling profession. *Journal of Humanistic Counseling, 51*, 133–44. doi:10.1002/j.2161-1939.2012.00011.x.

———. 2014a. *Philosophical issues in counseling and psychotherapy: Encounters with four questions about knowing, effectiveness, and truth.* Lanham, MD: Rowman & Littlefield.

———. 2014b. Talking about counseling: A plea to return to humanistic language. *Journal of Humanistic Counseling, 53*, 22–33. doi:10.1002/j.2161-1939.2014.00047.x.

Hansen, J. T., M. Speciale, and M. Lemberger. 2014. Humanism: The foundation and future of professional counseling. *Journal of Humanistic Counseling, 53*, 170–90. doi:10.1002/j.2161-1939.2014.00055.x.

Harris, S. 2005. *The end of faith*. New York: W.W. Norton & Company.

Hattie, J. A., C. F. Sharpley, and H. J. Rogers. 1984. Comparative effectiveness of professional and paraprofessional helpers. *Psychological Bulletin, 95*, 534–41.

Held, B. 1995. *Back to reality: A critique of postmodern theory in psychotherapy.* New York: W.W. Norton.

Hicks, S. 2004. *Explaining postmodernism: Skepticism and socialism from Rousseau to Foucault.* Milwaukee, WI: Scholargy Publishing.

Hillman, J., and M. Ventura. 1992. *We've had a hundred years of psychotherapy and the world's getting worse.* New York: HarperCollins.

Hoffman, I. 1998. *Ritual and spontaneity in the psychoanalytic process: A dialectical-constructivist view.* Hillsdale, NJ: Analytic Press.

Hoffman, L., H. Cleare-Hoffman, and T. Jackson. 2015. Humanistic psychology and multiculturalism: History, current status, and advancements. In K. J. Schneider, J. F. Pierson, and J. F. T. Bugental (Eds.), *The handbook of humanistic psychology: Theory, research, and practice* (2nd ed.), (pp. 41–55). Thousand Oaks, CA: Sage.

Hoffman, L., S. Stewart, D. M. Warren, and L. Meek. 2015. Toward a sustainable myth of self: An existential response to the postmodern condition. In K.J. Schneider, J.F. Pierson, & J.F.T. Bugental (Eds.), *The handbook of humanistic psychology: Theory, research, and practice* (2nd ed.), (pp. 105–33). Thousand Oaks, CA: Sage.

Hollander, R. 1981. Moral treatment and the therapeutic community. *Psychiatric Quarterly, 53*, 132–38.

Holt, R. R. 1978. Clinical judgment as disciplined inquiry. In *Methods in clinical psychology. Volume 2: Prediction and research* (pp. 38–54). New York: Plenum Press.

Jacoby, R. 1983. *The repression of psychoanalysis: Otto Fenichel and the political Freudians.* Chicago: University of Chicago Press.

James, W. 1995. *Pragmatism*. New York: Dover Publications.
Janov, A. 1970. *The primal scream; Primal therapy: The cure for neurosis.* New York: Putnam.
Jones, M. 1953. *The therapeutic community*. New York: Basic Books.
Jones-Smith, E. 2014. *Strengths-based therapy: Connecting theory, practice, and skills*. Thousand Oaks, CA: Sage.
Karon, B. 1992. The fear of understanding schizophrenia. *Psychoanalytic Psychology, 9,* 191–211.
Karon, B. P., and G. R. VandenBos. 2004. *Psychotherapy of schizophrenia: The treatment of choice*. Lanham, MD: Rowman & Littlefield.
Kernberg, O. 1976. *Object relations theory and clinical psychoanalysis*. Northvale, NJ: Jason Aronson.
Kesey, K. 1962. *One flew over the cuckoo's nest.* New York: Penguin Books.
Kickert, W. J. M. 1978. *Fuzzy theories on decision making: A critical review*. Hingham, MA: Kluwer Boston.
Kirk, S., and H. Kutchins. 1994. The myth of reliability of DSM. *Journal of Mind and Behavior, 15,* 71–86.
Kirsch, I. 2010. *The emperor's new drugs: Exploding the antidepressant myth.* New York: Basic Books.
Kirsner, D. 2009. *Unfree associations: Inside psychoanalytic institutes*. Lanham, MD: Jason Aronson.
Kohut, H. 1971. *The analysis of the self.* New York: International Universities Press.
Kuhn, T. 1996. *The structure of scientific revolutions* (3rd ed.). Chicago: University of Chicago Press.
Kurtz, M. W., and K. T. Mueser. 2008. A meta-analysis of controlled research on social skills training for schizophrenia. *Journal of Consulting and Clinical Psychology, 76*, 491–504.
Laing, R. D. 1969. *The divided self: An existential study in sanity and madness.* New York: Penguin Books.
Lambert, M. J. 1992. Psychotherapy outcome research: Implications for integrative and eclectic therapists. In J. C. Norcross and M. R. Goldfried (Eds.), *Handbook of psychotherapy integration* (pp. 91–129). New York: Basic Books.
Laska, K. M., A. S. Gurman, and B. E. Wampold. 2014. Expanding the lens of evidence-based practice in psychotherapy: A common factors perspective. *Psychotherapy, 51*, 467–81.
Leibert, T. W. 2012. Response to Hansen: Economic pressures, not science, undermine humanistic counseling. *Journal of Humanistic Counseling, 51*, 206–16.
Lemberger, M. 2012. A reply to Hansen's cultural humanism. *Journal of Humanistic Counseling, 51*, 180–83.
Lidz, T. 1973. *The origin & treatment of schizophrenic disorders*. New York: Basic Books.
Linden, D. E. J. 2006. How psychotherapy changes the brain: The contribution of functional neuroimaging. *Molecular Psychiatry, 11*, 528–38. doi:10.1038/sj.mp.4001816.
Loftus, E. F., and J. E. Pickrell. 1995. The formation of false memories. *Psychiatric Annals, 25,* 720–25.
Luhrmann, T. M. 2000. *Of two minds: An anthropologist looks at American psychiatry*. New York: Vintage Books.
Luke, C. 2016. *Neuroscience for counselors and therapists: Integrating the sciences of mind and brain.* Los Angeles, CA: Sage.
Mahoney, M. 1991. *Human change processes: The scientific foundations of psychotherapy.* New York: Basic Books.
Makari, G. 2008. *Revolution in mind: The creation of psychoanalysis*. New York: HarperCollins.
Marquis, A., and K. Douthit. 2006. The hegemony of "empirically supported treatment": Validating or violating? *Constructivism in the Human Sciences, 11,* 108–41.
Maslow, A. 1968. *Toward a psychology of being* (2nd ed.). New York: Van Nostrand Reinhold.
Masson, J. M. 1984. *The assault on truth: Freud's suppression of the seduction theory.* New York: Farrar, Straus, & Giroux.
———. 1994. *Against therapy.* Monroe, ME: Common Courage Press.

Matson, F. 1971. Humanistic theory: The third revolution in psychology. *The Humanist, 12*, 7–11.

May, R. 1979. *Psychology and the human dilemma.* New York: W.W. Norton & Company.

May, R., E. Angel, and H. Ellenberger (Eds.). 1958. *Existence: A new dimension in psychology and psychiatry.* New York: Basic Books.

Mayes, R., and A. V. Horwitz. 2005. DSM-III and the revolution in the classification of mental illness. *Journal of the History of the Behavioral Sciences, 41*, 249–67. doi:10.1002/jhbx.20103.

McHenry, B., A. Sikorski, and J. McHenry. 2013. *A counselor's introduction to neuroscience.* New York: Routledge.

McNamee, S. 1996. Psychotherapy as a social construction. In H. Rosen and K. Kuchlwein (Eds.), *Constructing realities: Meaning-making perspectives for psychotherapists*, (pp. 115–37). San Francisco, CA: Josey-Bass.

McWilliams, N. 1999. *Psychoanalytic case formulation.* New York: Guilford.

———. 2004. *Psychoanalytic psychotherapy: A practitioner's guide.* New York: Guilford.

———. 2005. Preserving our humanity as therapists. *Psychotherapy: Theory, Research, Practice, Training, 42*, 139–51.

———. 2011. *Psychoanalytic diagnosis: Understanding personality structure in the clinical process* (2nd ed.). New York: Guilford Press.

Menand, L. 2001. *The metaphysical club: A story of ideas in America.* New York: Farrar, Straus, & Giroux.

Michaels, F. S. 2011. *Monoculture: How one story is changing everything.* Canada: Red Clover Press.

Miller, W. R., and S. Rollnick. 2012. *Motivational interviewing: Helping people change* (3rd ed.). New York: Guilford Press.

Muran, J. 2001. An introduction: Contemporary constructions and contexts. In J. Muran (Ed.), *Self-relations in the psychotherapy process*, (pp. 3–44) Washington, DC: American Psychological Association.

Murray, T. 2009. The loss of client agency into the psychopharmaceutical-industrial complex. *Journal of Mental Health Counseling, 31*, 283–308.

Nagel, T. 1986. *The view from nowhere.* New York: Oxford University Press.

Orange, D. M. 1995. *Emotional understanding: Studies in psychoanalytic epistemology.* New York: Guilford Press.

Parker, I. 2007. *Revolution in psychology: Alienation to emancipation.* Ann Arbor, MI: Pluto Press.

Perkins, R., and F. Jackson. 1997. *Cosmic suicide: The tragedy and transcendence of heaven's gate.* Dallas: Pentaradial Press.

Perls, F. 1969. *Gestalt therapy verbatim.* Lafayette, CA: Real People Press.

Pine, F. 1990. *Drive, ego, object, and self; a synthesis for clinical work.* New York: Basic Books.

Plato. 1968. *The republic of Plato* (A. Bloom, Trans.). New York: Basic Books.

Polkinghorne, D. 1992. Postmodern epistemology of practice. In S. Kvale (Ed.), *Psychology and postmodernism* (pp. 146–65). Thousand Oaks, CA: Sage.

Porter, R. 2002. *Madness: A brief history.* New York: Oxford University Press.

Raskin, J. D., and M. C. Gayle. 2015. DSM-5: Do psychologists really want an alternative? *Journal of Humanistic Psychology.* Advance online publication. doi:10.1177/0022167815577897.

Ray, D. 2009. *The God virus: How religion infects our lives and culture.* Bonner Springs, KS: IPC Press.

Rimke, H., and A. Hunt. 2002. From sinners to degenerates: The medicalization of morality in the 19th century. *History of the Human Sciences, 15*, 59–88.

Rogers, C. R. 1951. *Client-centered therapy.* Boston, MA: Houghton Mifflin.

———. 1957. The necessary and sufficient conditions of therapeutic personality change. *Journal of Consulting Psychology, 21*, 95–103.

———. 1980. *A way of being.* New York: Houghton Mifflin.

Rorty, R. 1979. *Philosophy and the mirror of nature.* Princeton, NJ: Princeton University Press.

———. 1998. *Truth and progress; philosophical papers, volume 3.* New York: Cambridge University Press.

———. 1999. *Philosophy and social hope.* New York: Penguin Books.

———. 2000. Universality and truth. In R. Brandom (Ed.), *Rorty and his critics* (pp. 1–30). Malden, MA: Blackwell.

Rosen, H. 1996. Meaning-making narratives: Foundations for constructivist and social constructionist psychotherapies. In H. Rosen and K. Kuehlwein (Eds.), *Constructing realities: Meaning-making perspectives for psychotherapists* (pp. 3–51). San Francisco: Jossey-Bass.

Rosenau, P. 1992. *Post-modernism and the social sciences: Insights, inroads, and intrusions.* Princeton, NJ: Princeton University Press.

Rosenhan, D. 1973. On being sane in insane places. *Science, 179,* 250–58.

Rudes, J., and J. T. Guterman. 2007.The value of social constructionism for the counseling profession: A reply to Hansen. *Journal of Counseling & Development, 85,* 387–92.

Rukeyser, M. 1968. *The speed of darkness.* New York: Random House.

Schmitt, F. 1995. *Truth: A primer.* Boulder, CO: Westview Press.

Schwartz, J. 2003. *Cassandra's daughter: A history of psychoanalysis.* London: Karnac Books.

Seligman, M. 1995. The effectiveness of psychotherapy: The consumer reports study. *American Psychologist, 50,* 965–74.

Sexton, T. 1997. Constructivist thinking within the history of ideas: The challenge of a new paradigm. In T. Sexton and B. Griffin (Eds.), *Constructivist thinking in counseling practice, research, and training* (pp. 3–18). New York: Teachers College Press.

Shorter, E. 1992. *From paralysis to fatigue: A history of psychosomatic illness in the modern era.* New York: Free Press.

———. 1997. *A history of psychiatry; from the era of the asylum to the age of Prozac.* New York: Wiley & Sons.

Skinner, B. 1974. *About behaviorism.* New York: Knopf.

Spence, D. 1982. *Narrative truth and historical truth: Meaning and interpretation in psychoanalysis.* New York: W.W. Norton & Company.

Stein, D. M., and M. J. Lambert. 1995. Graduate training in psychotherapy: Are therapy outcomes enhanced? *Journal of Consulting and Clinical Psychology, 63,* 182–96.

Stolorow, R., G. Atwood, and D. Orange. 2002. *Worlds of experience: Interweaving philosophical and clinical dimensions in psychoanalysis.* New York: Basic Books.

Stompe T., G. Ortwein-Swoboda, K. Ritter, et al. 2002. Are we witnessing the disappearance of catatonic schizophrenia? *Comprehensive Psychiatry, 43,* 167–74.

Strupp, H. H., and S. W. Hadley. 1979. Specific vs. nonspecific factors in psychotherapy: A controlled study of outcome. *Archives of General Psychiatry, 36,* 1125–36.

Sue, D. W., P. Arredondo, and R. J. McDavis. 1992. Multicultural counseling competencies and standards: A call to the profession. *Journal of Counseling & Development, 70,* 477–86.

Szasz, T. 1961. *The myth of mental illness.* New York: Harper.

———. 2007. *The medicalization of everyday life.* Syracuse: Syracuse University Press.

Spiegel, A. 2005, January 3. The dictionary of disorder: How one man revolutionized psychiatry. *New Yorker,* 56–63.

Tarnas, R. 1991. *The passion of the Western mind: Understanding the ideas that have shaped our world view.* New York: Harmony.

Titchener, E. B. 1921. Wilhelm Wundt. *The American Journal of Psychology, 32,* 161–78.

Torrey, E. F. 1972. What Western psychotherapists can learn from witchdoctors. *American Journal of Orthopsychiatry, 42,* 69–76.

———. 2013. *Surviving schizophrenia: A family manual* (6th ed.). New York: Harper Perennial.

Ventola, C. L. 2011. Direct-to-consumer pharmaceutical advertising: Therapeutic or toxic? *Pharmacy and Therapeutics, 36,* 669–84.

Wampold, B. E. 2001. *The great psychotherapy debate: Models, methods, and findings.* Mahwah, NJ: Lawrence Erlbaum.

Wampold, B. E., and G. S. Brown. 2005. Estimating variability in outcomes attributable to therapists: A naturalistic study of outcomes in managed care. *Journal of Consulting and Clinical Psychology, 73,* 914–23. doi:10.1037/0022-006X.73.5.914.

Watkins, C. E. 2011. Does psychotherapy supervision contribute to patient outcomes? Considering thirty years of research. *The Clinical Supervisor, 30*, 235–56.

Watson, J. 1919. *Psychology from the standpoint of a behaviorist.* Philadelphia: Lippincott. doi:10.1037/10016-000.

Watters, E. 2010. *Crazy like us: The globalization of the American psyche*. New York: Free Press.

Whitaker, R. 2002. *Mad in America: Bad science, bad medicine, and the enduring mistreatment of the mentally ill*. Cambridge, MA: Perseus.

———. 2010. *Anatomy of an epidemic: Magic bullets, psychiatric drugs, and the astonishing rise of mental illness in America*. New York: Broadway Paperbacks.

White, M., and D. Epston. 1990. *Narrative means to therapeutic ends.* New York: W. W. Norton & Co.

Whitehead, A. N. 1979. *Process and reality: An essay in cosmology*. New York: Free Press.

Wolpe, J. 1958. *Psychotherapy by reciprocal inhibition.* Stanford, CA: Stanford University Press.

Wright, L. 1994. *Remembering Satan*. New York: Vintage Books.

———. 2013. *Going clear: Scientology, Hollywood, & the prison of belief.* New York: Vintage Books.

Yalom, I. 1980. *Existential psychotherapy.* New York: Basic Books.

Zatorre, R. J, R. D. Fields, and H. Johansen-Berg. 2012. Plasticity in gray and white: neuroimaging changes in brain structure during learning. *Nature Neuroscience 15*, 528–36.

Index

About the Author

James T. Hansen is a professor at Oakland University in the Department of Counseling. His primary scholarly interests are philosophical and theoretical issues in counseling and critical examination of contemporary mental health culture. Dr. Hansen has published about fifty refereed articles in leading counseling journals. He is the author of an award-winning book on philosophical issues in counseling and coeditor of an award-winning book on humanism. Dr. Hansen has more than twenty-five years of experience as a practitioner, supervisor, and consultant.

www.ingramcontent.com/pod-product-compliance
Lightning Source LLC
LaVergne TN
LVHW090402210926
848480LV00002B/424
9781498516327